IMAGES
of America

FARRELL'S ICE CREAM PARLOUR

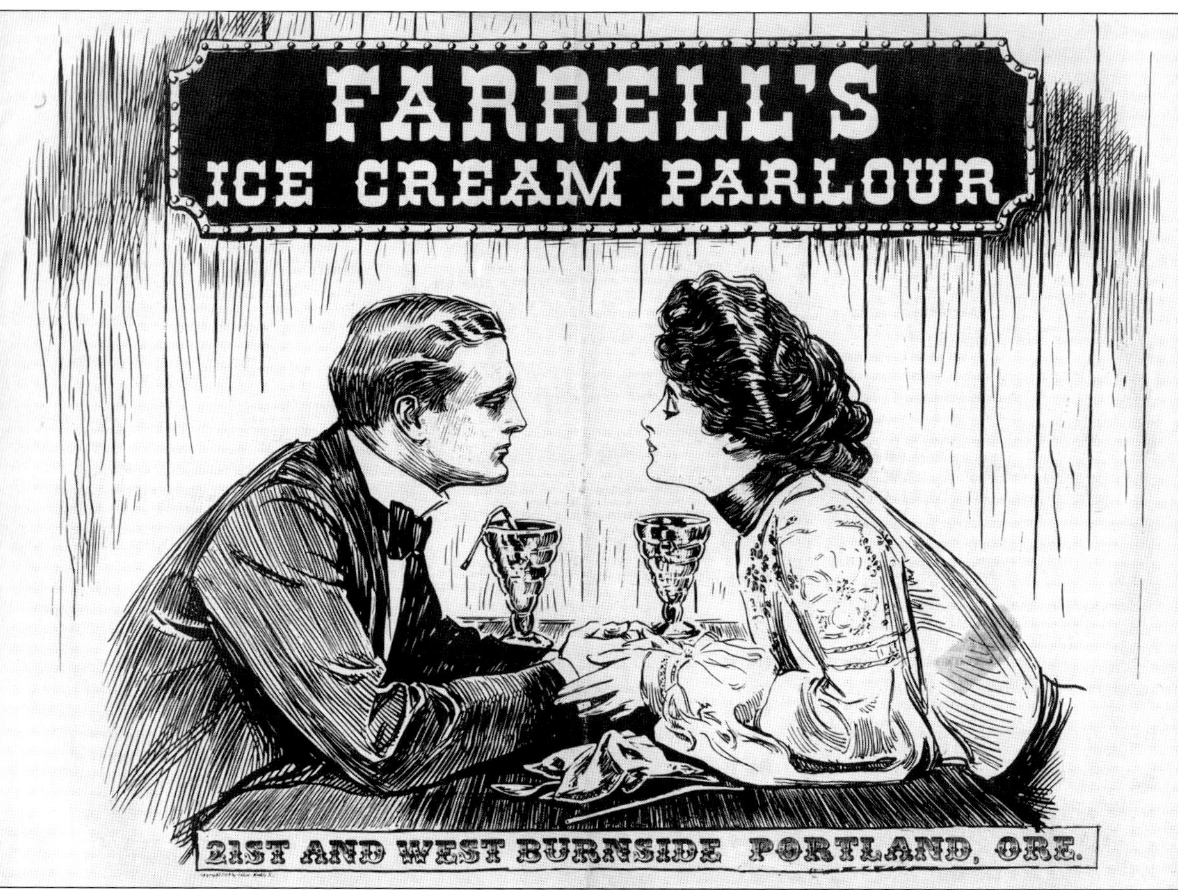

This is the cover page of the first Farrell's Ice Cream Parlour menu from 1963. Cofounder Robert Farrell saw this pen-and-ink drawing by artist Charles Dana Gibson hanging on the wall of his uncle's tavern and believed it represented a simpler time in America. The Gibson Girl is recognized as an iconic personification of the late 19th century and early 20th century. Farrell had already decided to use a 1905 theme for the first Farrell's Ice Cream Parlour, and with a change to include two ice cream sodas and remove the chess board, the Gibson drawing of the couple went on to become identified with Farrell's. (Author's collection.)

On the Cover: Taken September 13, 1969, the Rivergate Jazz Band entertains the crowd in front of the original location of Farrell's Ice Cream Parlour on the sixth anniversary of its opening. Founded in Portland, Oregon, Farrell's grew to a chain with nearly 130 locations across America. (Author's collection.)

IMAGES
of America

FARRELL'S ICE CREAM PARLOUR

Patrick J. Baker

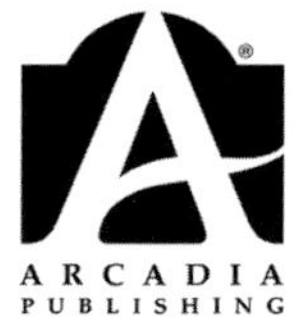

ISBN 978-1-4671-6110-7

Published by Arcadia Publishing
Charleston, South Carolina

Printed in the United States of America

Library of Congress Control Number: 2023949611

For all general information, please contact Arcadia Publishing:
Telephone 843-853-2070
Fax 843-853-0044
E-mail sales@arcadiapublishing.com

Visit us on the Internet at www.arcadiapublishing.com

To my wife Julie, who has encouraged my love of Farrell's for more than 35 years

Contents

ACKNOWLEDGMENTS

This book would not have been possible without the contribution of Farrell's Ice Cream Parlours cofounders Robert E. Farrell and Kenneth E. McCarthy. Their friendship and willingness to share the history of their partnership gave me a better understanding of how Farrell's began and grew. And they showed how Farrell's became the beloved chain it was. All the photographs used in this book were produced for Farrell and McCarthy for promotional purposes and are the property of the author.

I am grateful for the support of Bob Farrell's family, including his wife, Mona Farrell, and their three daughters, Kathy Farrell, Kristie Booster, and Colleen Smith.

I also wish to thank Michael Fleming and Paul Kramer, formerly of Parlour Enterprises, Inc., for reviving Farrell's in 2003 and inviting me to become an investor in the new chain.

My brother Roger Baker contributed greatly with his detailed knowledge of Farrell's history. Having managed multiple locations over the years in three states, he is one of the most knowledgeable experts on Farrell's.

Finally, my wife, Julie Baker, deserves more thanks than anyone else for encouraging me to follow my dream of investing in Farrell's and writing this book about the history of Farrell's. To be fair, we did a lot of research by visiting as many classic ice cream parlors as possible over the last several decades. And that research will continue.

Introduction

"In 1891 there were more soda fountains than bars in New York City." These are the opening words in a beautiful red-and-white franchising brochure published in 1966 telling the story of Farrell's Ice Cream Parlour Restaurants. It tells how two friends rolled back the years to the days of player pianos, barbershop quartets, and the delightfully odoriferous old-time ice cream parlor, with its marble-topped tables, Tiffany lamps, red-flocked wallpaper, and bentwood chairs.

In 1963, Robert E. Farrell and Kenneth E. McCarthy, believing there was a need for an old-fashioned, nonalcoholic family restaurant, opened the first Farrell's at 103 Northwest Twenty-first Avenue in Portland, Oregon. The idea took hold, and Farrell's was a success. Before the strain of running a growing ice cream empire took its toll on their partnership, Farrell and McCarthy opened four locations in Portland and began expanding the chain across the country.

While Farrell's grew into a beloved national chain, it started with one location in Portland, Oregon's Northwest District. Success was not guaranteed, but that did not stop Bob Farrell and Ken McCarthy from working 100-hour weeks to establish their first location.

Two years after opening their first location, the partners franchised the concept to Salem, Oregon, and Belleview, Washington. The Salem location, opened in November 1965, was owned by Harold and Shirley Holland and was troubled from the very beginning. The shopping center the Salem Farrell's opened in was picketed by union members, as the developer used nonunion contractors. Other businesses located in the shopping center were targeted as part of the picketing. Having never achieved profitability, the Salem location closed five years after it opened.

The Belleview location, opened in June 1966, was encouraged by Bob Farrell before the first Farrell's was opened. While the first Farrell's location was under construction in 1963, Farrell met with Jack Fecker and Joe Rutten, two experienced restaurant operators who owned Elroy's Ice Cream Parlour in Seattle. Elroy's had a turn-of-the-century theme like Farrell's and was in a part of Seattle known for its nightclubs but had never made a profit. Fecker believed there was more profit to be made from the sale of ice cream than beer, so he and his partner decided to go all in with the Farrell's concept. After the success of their first Farrell's location in Belleview, they went on to hold the territorial franchise rights for Farrell's for the Pacific Northwest.

Accountant Dale Belford approached Bob Farrell and Ken McCarthy in 1965 and was offered an ownership interest in Farrell's in exchange for his expertise. He brought his business acumen and was able to set Farrell's up with a multiunit bookkeeping system and improve the franchise program. Farrell and McCarthy then set out to design their prototype store with their second Portland location.

By 1969, Portland was built out. Farrell's expanded into California and began to franchise to Minnesota and Michigan. With overlapping duties, the three partners worked out an agreement designating the duties of each partner. Bob Farrell oversaw personnel, menu pricing, and promotions. Ken McCarthy had responsibility for construction, equipment, and ice cream. Dale Belford took on contracts, accounting, and financial projections.

The conception of each new location began with Bob Farrell and Dale Belford. They would scout a new site for both company-owned and franchised locations, putting together a lease and financing package. When this was completed, Ken McCarthy would take over and travel to that town. He would choose a building contractor and supervise the construction of the structure until it was completed.

Ken McCarthy would make appointments with local dairies and present their ice cream formulas. A dairy in the area had to be able to produce the ice cream to their specifications and at an agreeable price. A week before opening, a team of five trainers traveled to the new location. This crew would run advertisements in the local paper to staff the new location.

The training crew would interview between 100 and 200 people for all positions. Around 35 were hired for both full-time and part-time positions. From 6:00 p.m. to 10:00 p.m. each night for one week, the training crew taught the new employees. After the week of training, most were as good as the home-store employees. Ken McCarthy believed it was best to hire mostly high school and college students without any restaurant experience, as they did not have any bad habits to break.

Locations were opened quickly. There were times when three crews of five trainers were working at multiple new locations at the same time with a supervisor over all 15 teachers. Overlapping store openings kept one crew on the road and away from home for over two months. The crew stayed in a location until the trainers were convinced each employee knew his or her position completely. Only then would the trainer be able to go home.

Bob Farrell and Ken McCarthy were away from home for a month at a time. Between opening new locations and supervising franchise operations, neither partner saw much of their families. But they built a very profitable company.

By 1969, the disagreements between Bob Farrell and Ken McCarthy were putting a strain on their relationship. They arranged to hire two people to take over McCarthy's duties. One was a vice president of a restaurant chain, and the other was a building contractor. In January 1970, McCarthy stepped down and retired from the company. The partners agreed to sell the company as soon as possible.

Dale Belford contacted Kentucky Fried Chicken, Campbell Soup, and McDonald's to determine if they would consider purchasing Farrell's. None of those companies were interested. Ken McCarthy believed Farrell's was too complicated for other restaurant companies to understand.

Soon after Ken McCarthy retired from Farrell's, some of the locations began to lose money. As he was still an owner, McCarthy received monthly financial statements for each location and saw that sales volume was slipping. Farrell's was a novelty restaurant, and as the novelty wore off, sales declined. McCarthy knew there was not much time left to sell.

Ken McCarthy threatened to sell his ownership interest in Farrell's on the street. In response, Dale Belford was finally able to put a package together with Marriott Corporation. In June 1972, Marriott purchased the Farrell's Corporation from the three partners.

Farrell's never again achieved the financial success that Bob Farrell and Ken McCarthy created in the first nine years of operations. Changes in the sales mix of Farrell's, economic conditions, and declining customer visits resulted in lower profit margins. But perhaps it was just the unique combination of two stubborn Irishmen in Portland, Oregon, that resulted in the greatest success for the chain.

One

Beginnings

On Friday, September 13, 1963, Bob Farrell and Ken McCarthy opened the very first Farrell's Ice Cream Parlour at 103 Northwest Twenty-first Avenue near Burnside Street in Portland, Oregon. They had 32 employees, $1,300 in the bank, and owed $26,000. They had to work hard and make few mistakes. Each partner put $5,000 of their own money into that first location.

It took 18 months to find a landlord willing to take a chance on this concept. The first location originally sat 72 guests. After they were open for a while, a party room was added using space from the parking lot that increased the seating capacity by another 30 guests.

Ken McCarthy kept his job at Carnation Dairy in Portland, working 8:00 a.m. to 5:00 p.m. He would then come to Farrell's at 6:00 p.m. and get home around 2:00 a.m. At Carnation, McCarthy would work with new ice cream locations and assist in equipment selection and layout. His employer did not know McCarthy was a partner in Farrell's, but with Bob Farrell's help, he did manage to get himself assigned to the Farrell's account. This made it much easier to explain why he spent so much time there. In May 1964, McCarthy was finally able to quit his job at Carnation, and the Farrell's partners were able to cut their hours from 100 to 80 per week.

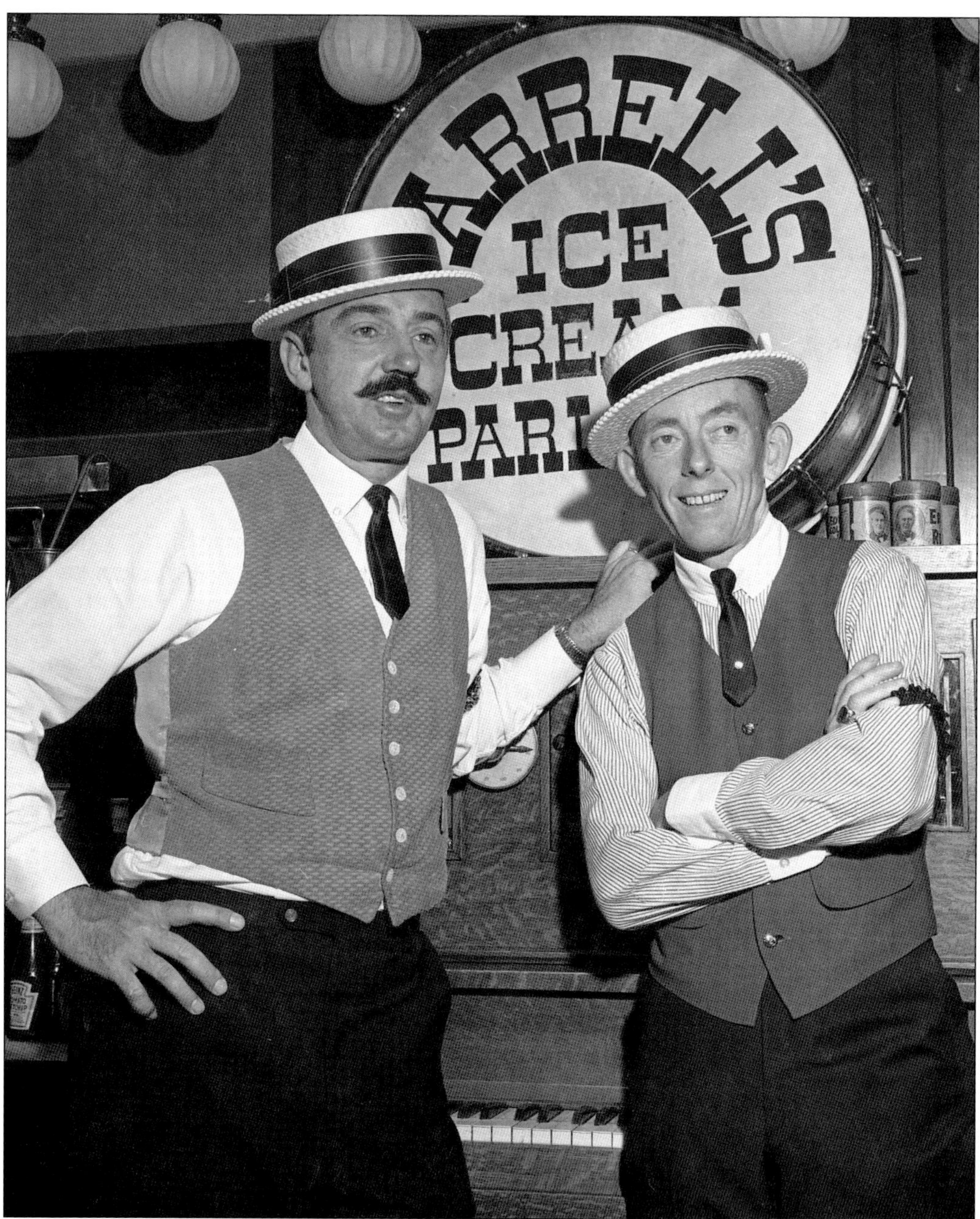

Farrell's cofounders Bob Farrell (left) and Ken McCarthy (right) are seen together with the bass drum and player piano in the very first location at 103 Northwest Twenty-first Avenue in Portland, Oregon, in 1965. The first Farrell's opened on Friday, September 13, 1963. As McCarthy still worked at Carnation, he could not tell them he was involved with Farrell's. He had Farrell approach Carnation for assistance and financing. Farrell asked to have McCarthy assigned to the Farrell's account. Carnation told McCarthy to give Farrell all the assistance he needed.

Insurance agent Jay Basher (seated on the right) of Standard Insurance is reviewing the blueprints for the second Farrell's location at 122nd Avenue and Halsey Street in Portland with Bob Farrell and Ken McCarthy in 1965. Farrell and McCarthy intended to use the second location as a prototype for future Farrell's spots, and this required a great deal of planning.

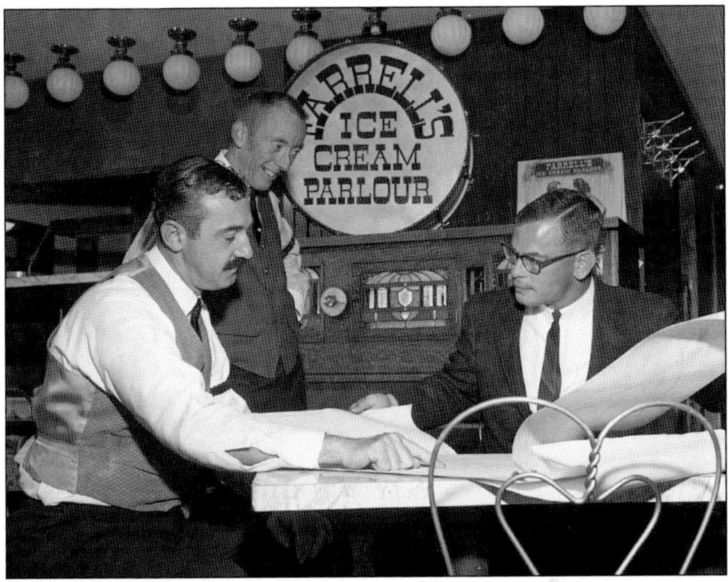

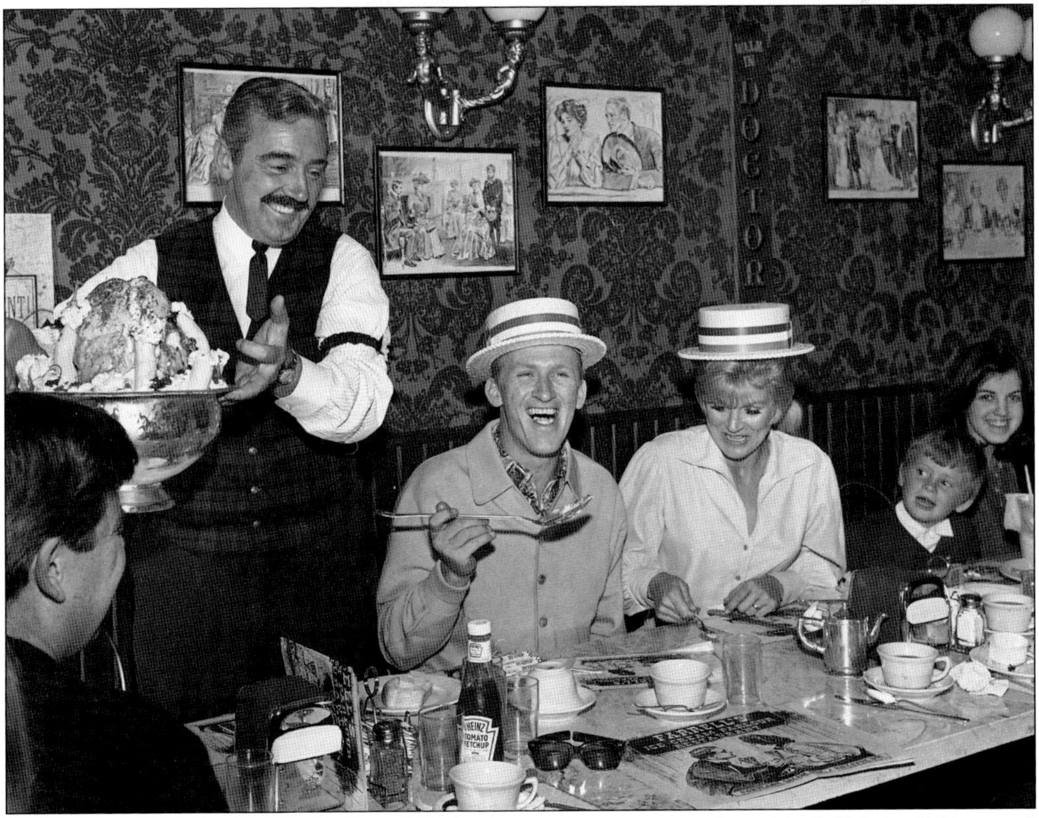

Bob Farrell is shown serving the Portland Zoo sundae to piano player Fred "Mickey" Finn and his wife, Barbara. Mickey was a popular entertainer and piano player. The Portland Zoo was a large sundae meant to serve 10 guests. It was made with seven different flavors of ice cream, three different flavors of sherbet, multiple toppings, bananas, whipped cream, nuts, and cherries. When Farrell's expanded to other cities, the sundae was renamed the Farrell's Zoo.

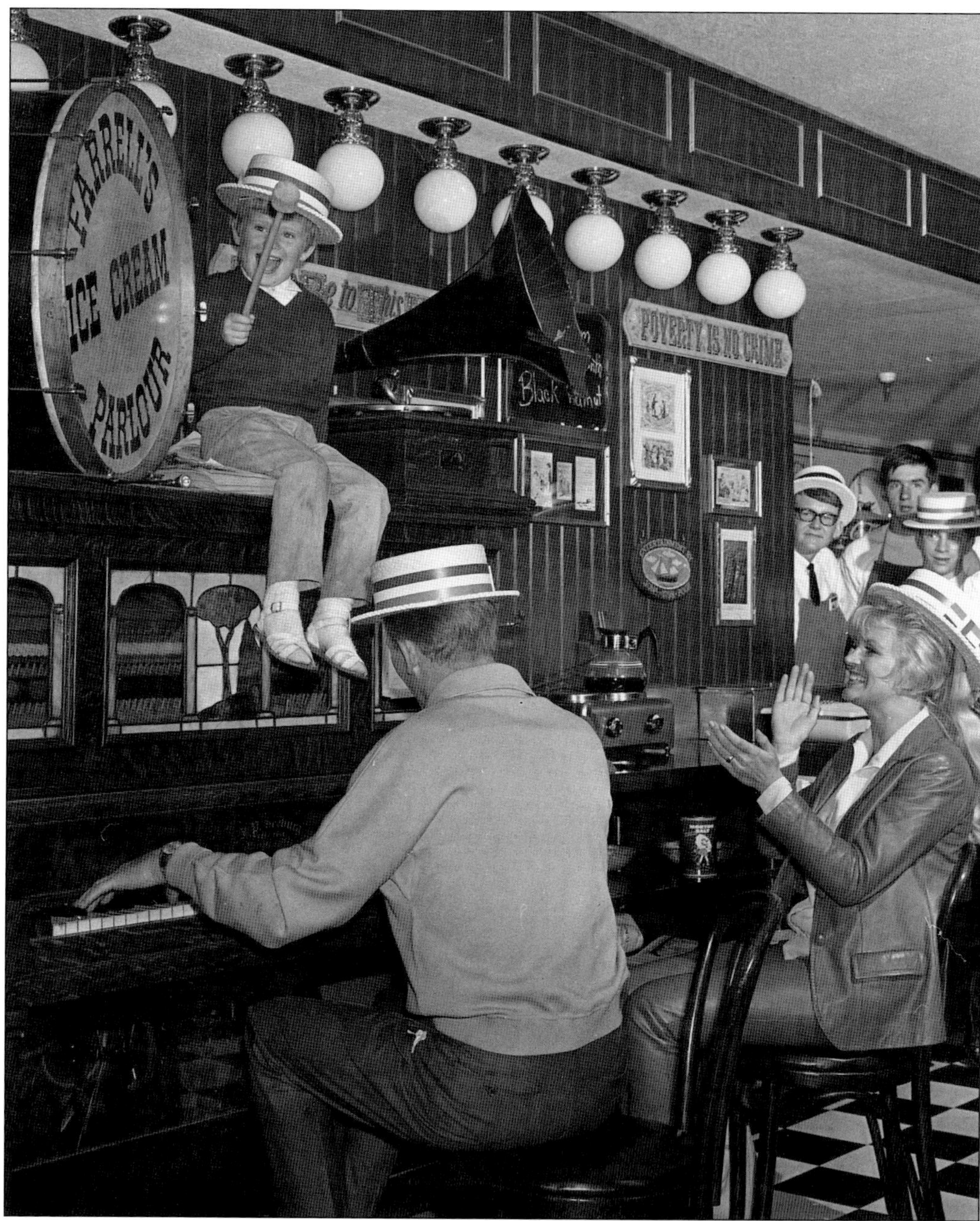

After enjoying the Portland Zoo sundae, piano player Mickey Finn put on a show for Farrell's guests and employees, performing ragtime and Dixieland piano favorites from his nightclub show. Finn was a popular entertainer and piano player. He opened the popular Gay 90s nightclub in San Diego in 1960. In 1966, he starred in an NBC musical variety television show featuring ragtime and Dixieland music.

Jim, a waiter at the Halsey store, is all smiles while delivering a tray full of sundaes to guests at the preopening party at the second Portland location. Bob Farrell and Ken McCarthy had invitation-only parties at new locations to train the staff.

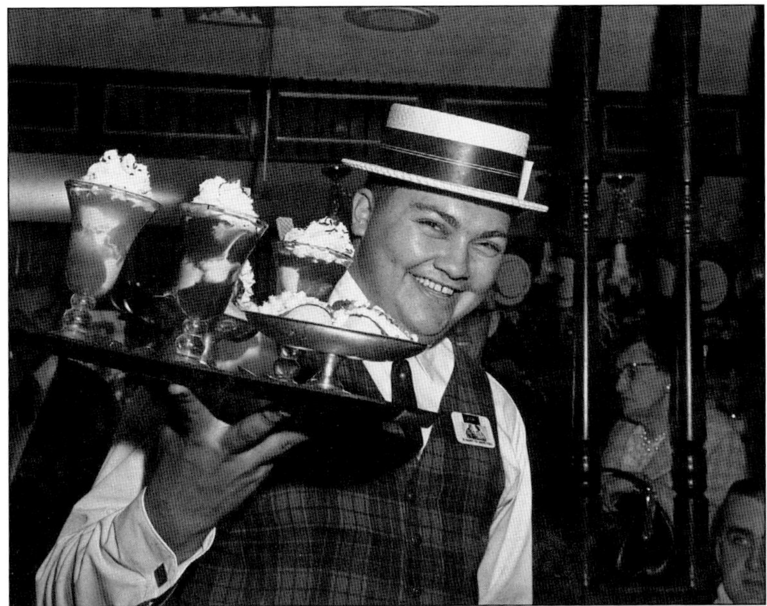

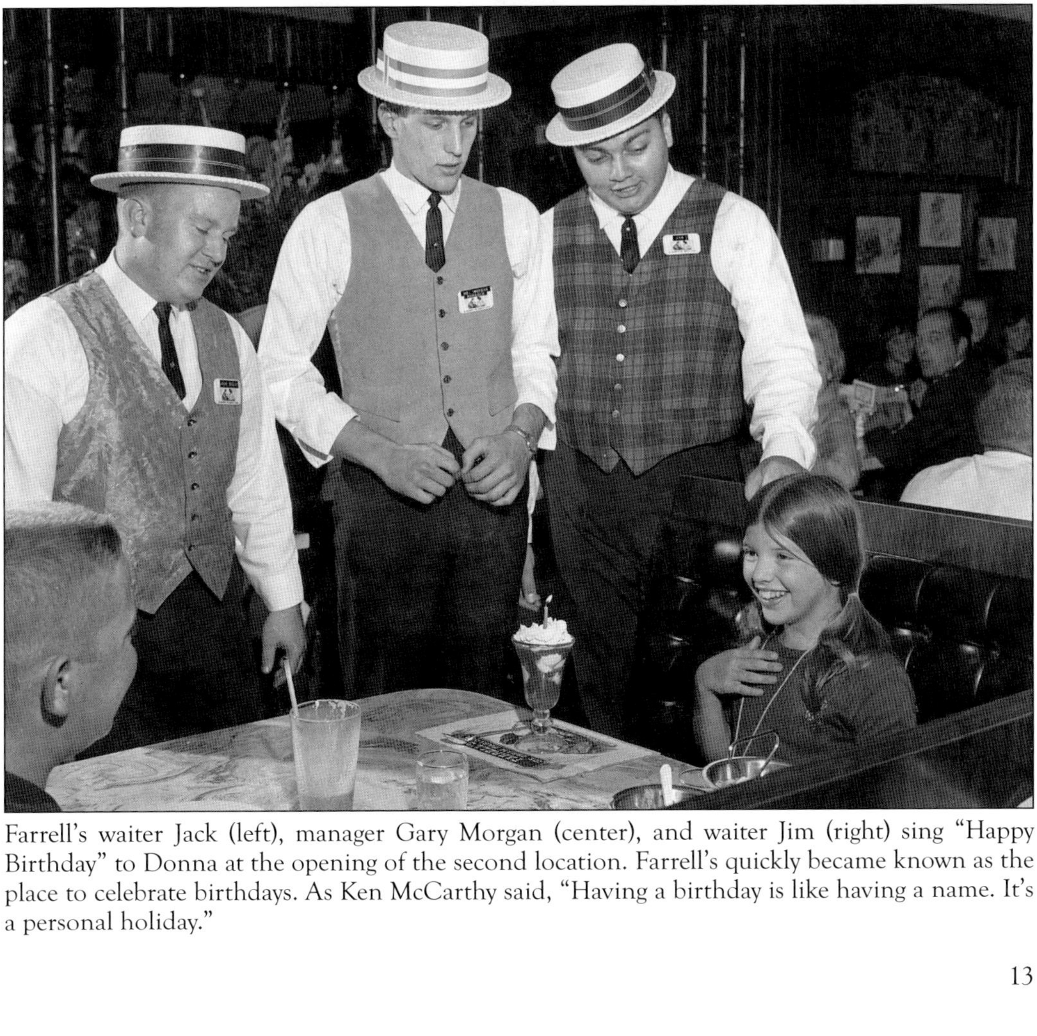

Farrell's waiter Jack (left), manager Gary Morgan (center), and waiter Jim (right) sing "Happy Birthday" to Donna at the opening of the second location. Farrell's quickly became known as the place to celebrate birthdays. As Ken McCarthy said, "Having a birthday is like having a name. It's a personal holiday."

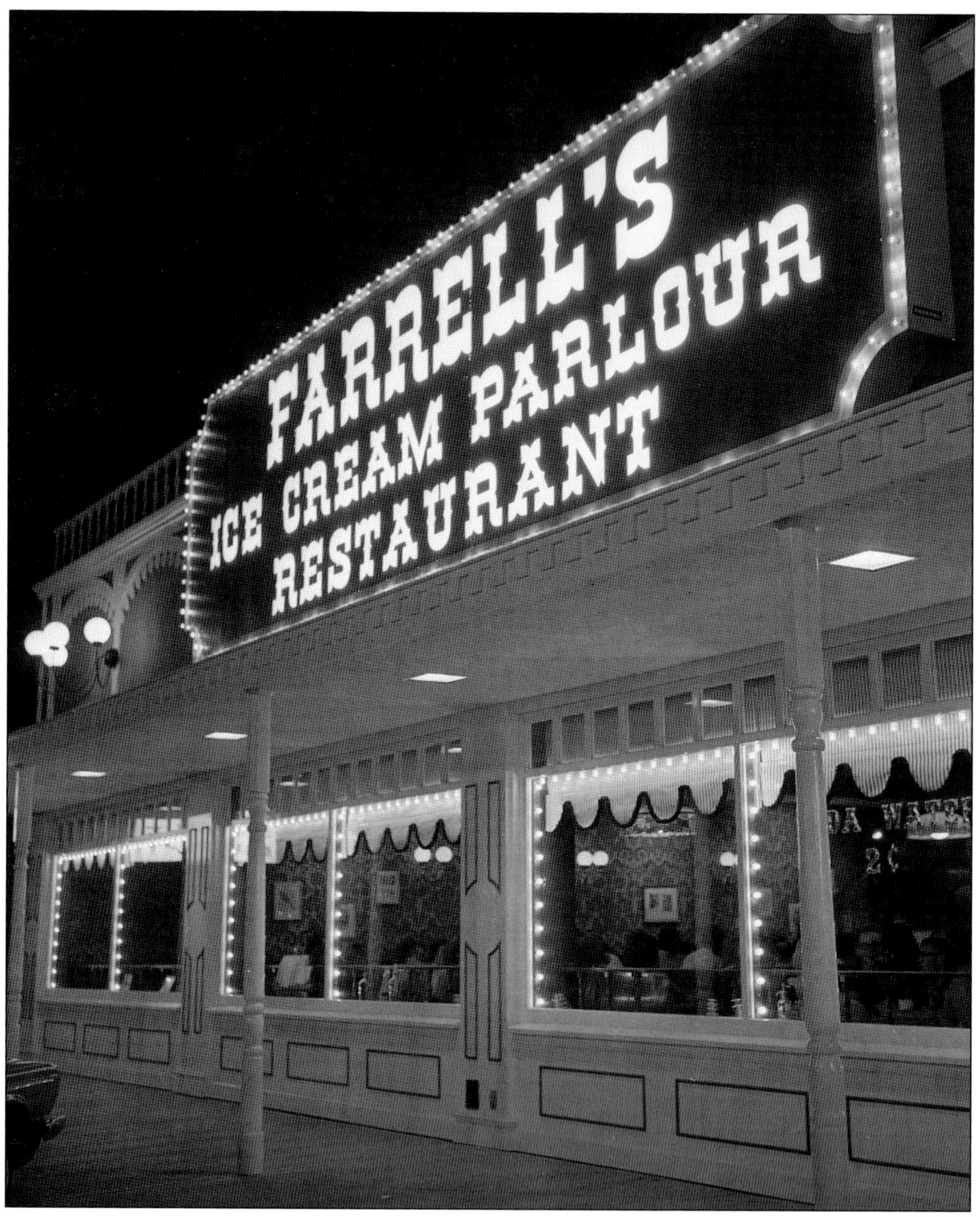

Bob Farrell and Ken McCarthy developed a very festive and distinct exterior for Farrell's. The bright red and white paint was enhanced with bright signs and marquee lighting to attract attention.

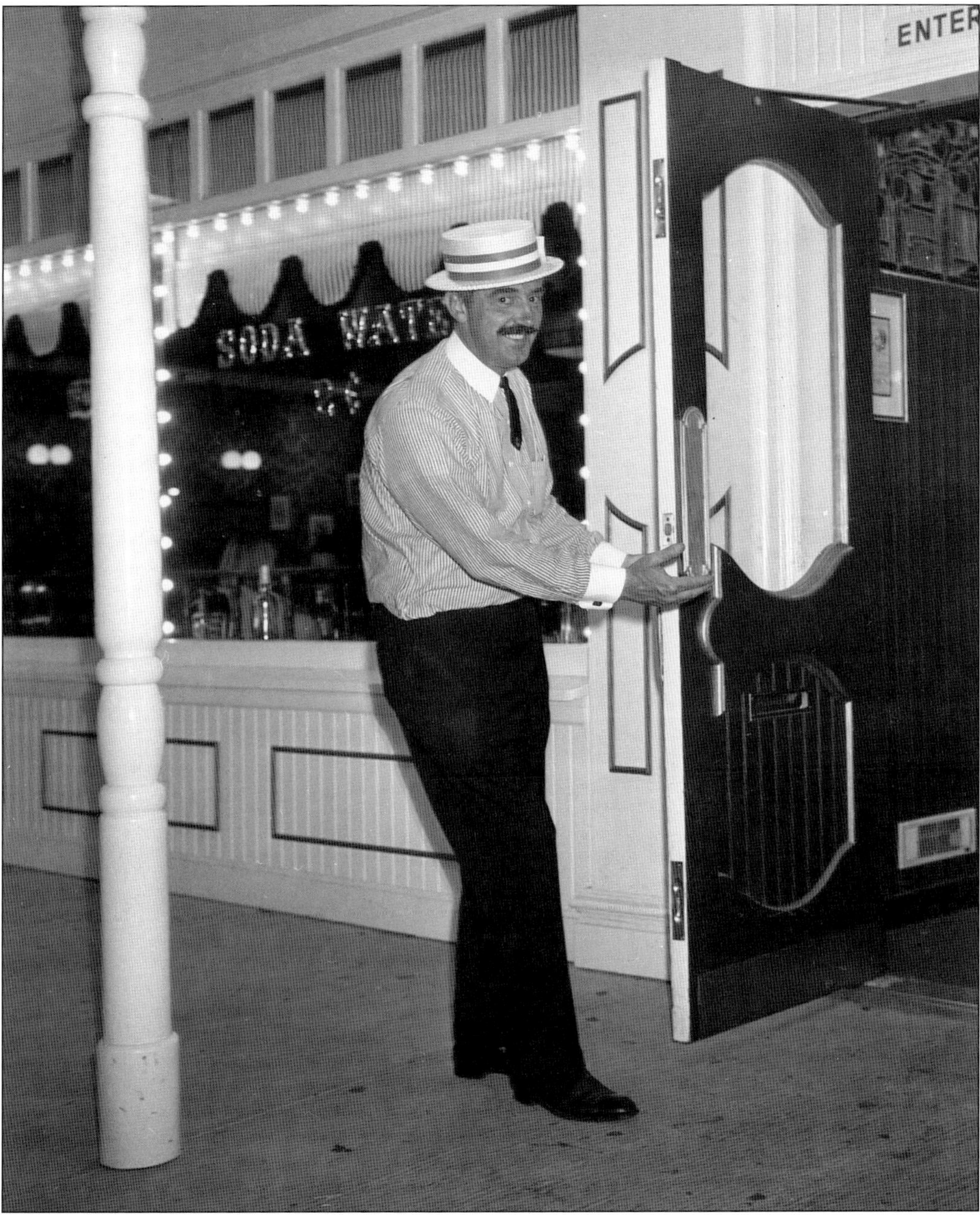

Bob Farrell holds the door open at the third Farrell's located at Northeast 122nd Avenue and Halsey Street in Portland, Oregon. Farrell quickly became the face of Farrell's, much to the displeasure of cofounder Ken McCarthy. As McCarthy could not tell Carnation that he was one of the owners of Farrell's, they had to keep his name out of the initial promotion.

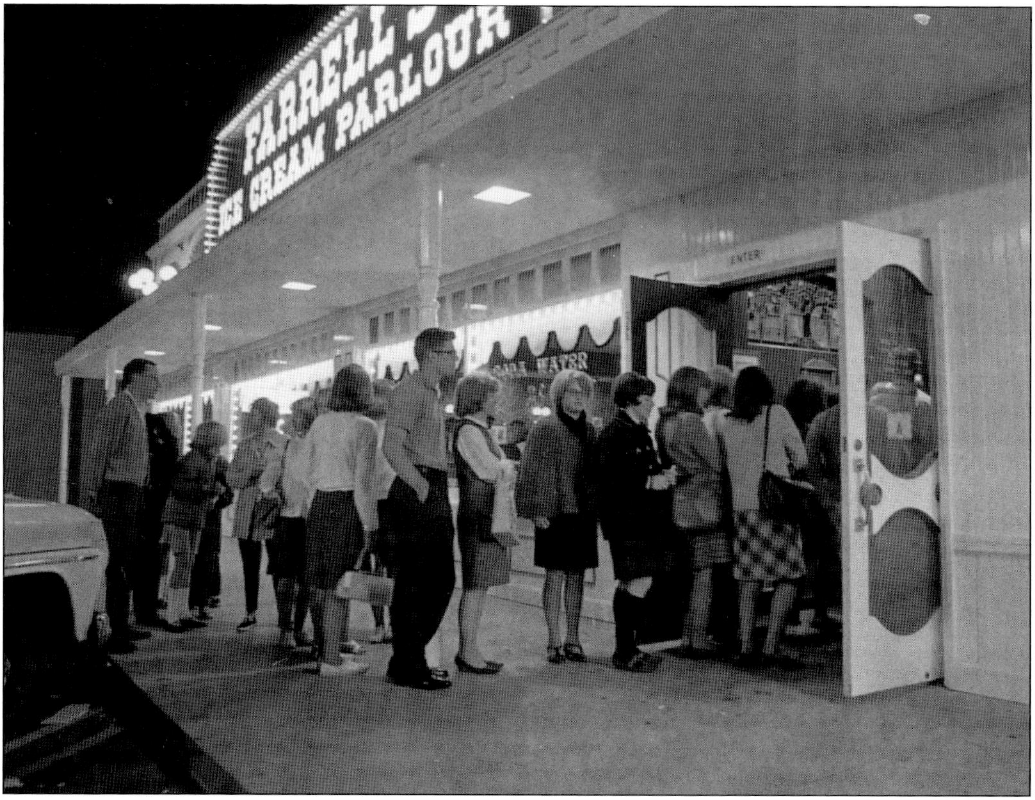

A line forms outside the Halsey location for the preopening night party. As new locations opened, lines became a common occurrence. Bob Farrell and Ken McCarthy became obsessed with efficiency as quick service resulted in faster-moving lines.

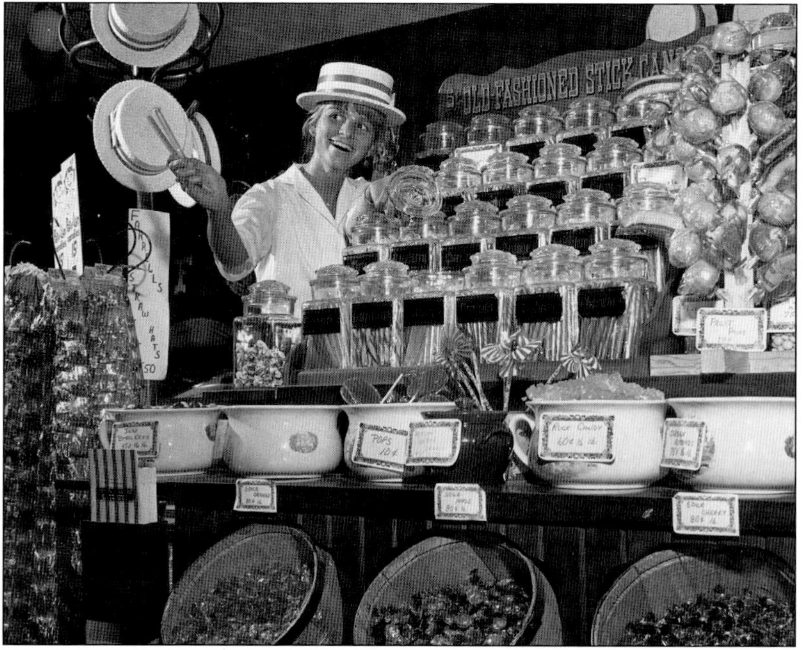

A cashier is seen showing off the candy selection at the Halsey location. Farrell's became known for old-fashioned candies. Customers would admire the candy as they waited in line and would exit through the candy shop on the way out. Candy and merchandise sales would eventually become 10 percent of total sales for Farrell's.

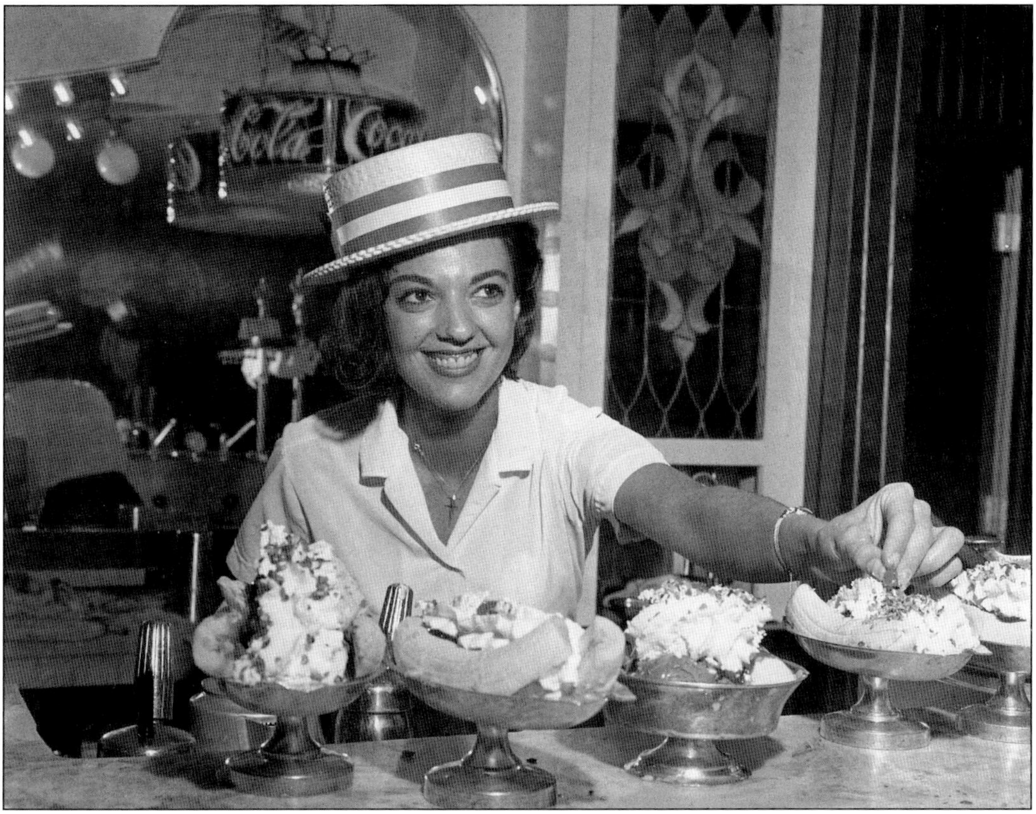

Rose Marie Law is seen displaying several of the classic sundaes from the fountain. Law was part of Farrell's from the opening of the first location in 1963 and became the training supervisor as the chain grew. She brought nine years of food industry experience to Farrell's and was responsible for quality and cost controls in the kitchen.

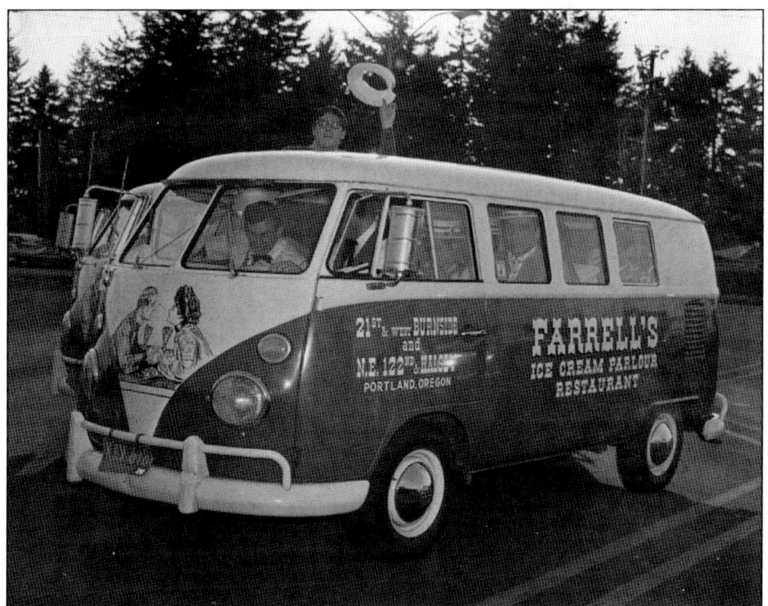

With the new locations in Portland, Farrell's needed transportation to move supplies between the stores. Farrell's added two Volkswagen microbuses with Farrell's logos and addresses painted on the side that would become traveling billboards on the Portland roads.

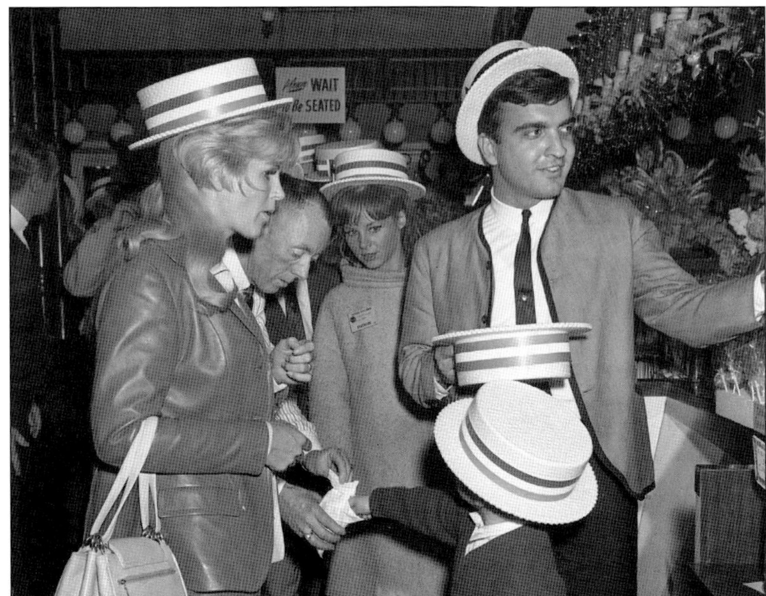

These guests are checking out the candy section on their way out. The skimmer hats became a popular novelty item to purchase. Farrell's would later put their name on the hat to better promote the restaurants.

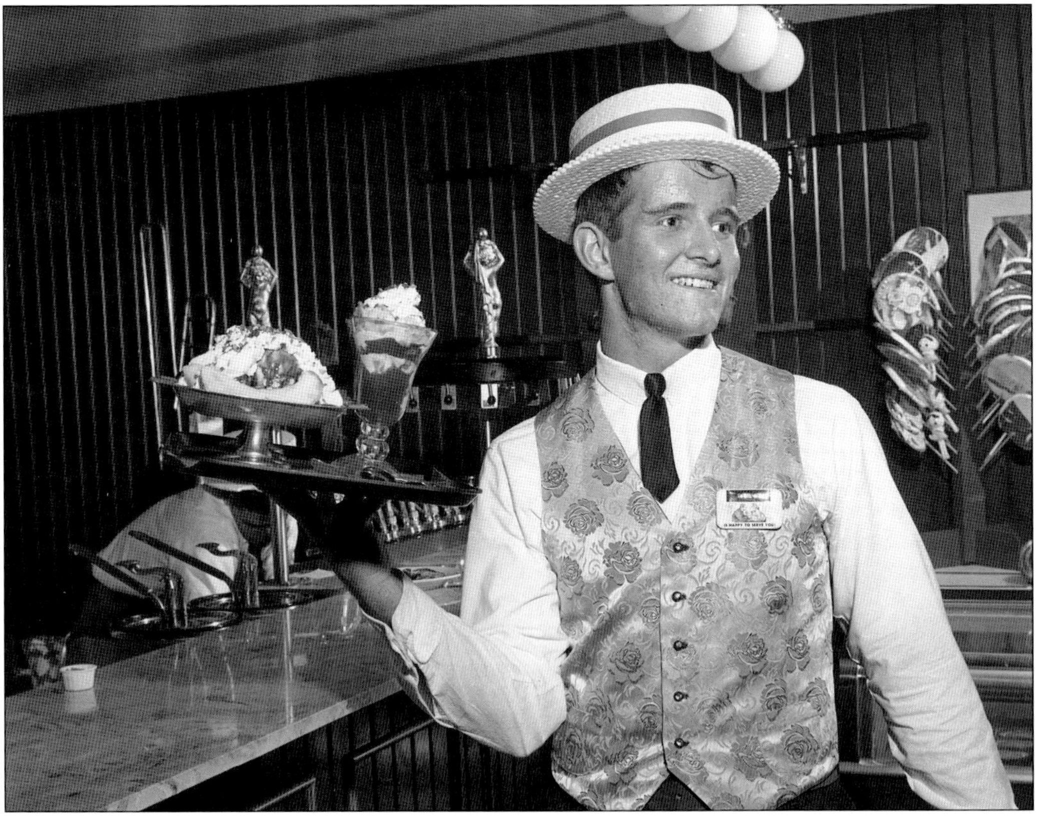

Each Farrell's location was designed with the soda fountain located where guests could watch while waiting in line for a table. Ken McCarthy believed the soda fountain was a stage where the fountain men would perform for guests while creating the sundaes. A guest entering the store would be greeted with a counter full of sundaes waiting to be delivered.

Two

EUGENE

With accountant Dale Belford as a partner, Farrell's was now better positioned to franchise the concept. After franchise locations in Salem, Oregon, and Bellevue, Washington, Bob Farrell and Ken McCarthy chose Eugene, Oregon, for the newest franchise location and fifth Farrell's in the chain. While the floor plan was smaller than later locations, it did have a separate party room.

As a college town, Eugene was suited to provide the newest Farrell's with plenty of young people as workers. Further, Farrell's would become the place to go to after sporting events. Eugene was also one of the smaller towns to have a Farrell's in the entire history of the company.

This location was the first to include bay windows for display purposes. And it was the first freestanding Farrell's in the chain. The Eugene location remained relatively unchanged over nearly four decades of operation, finally closing in 2006.

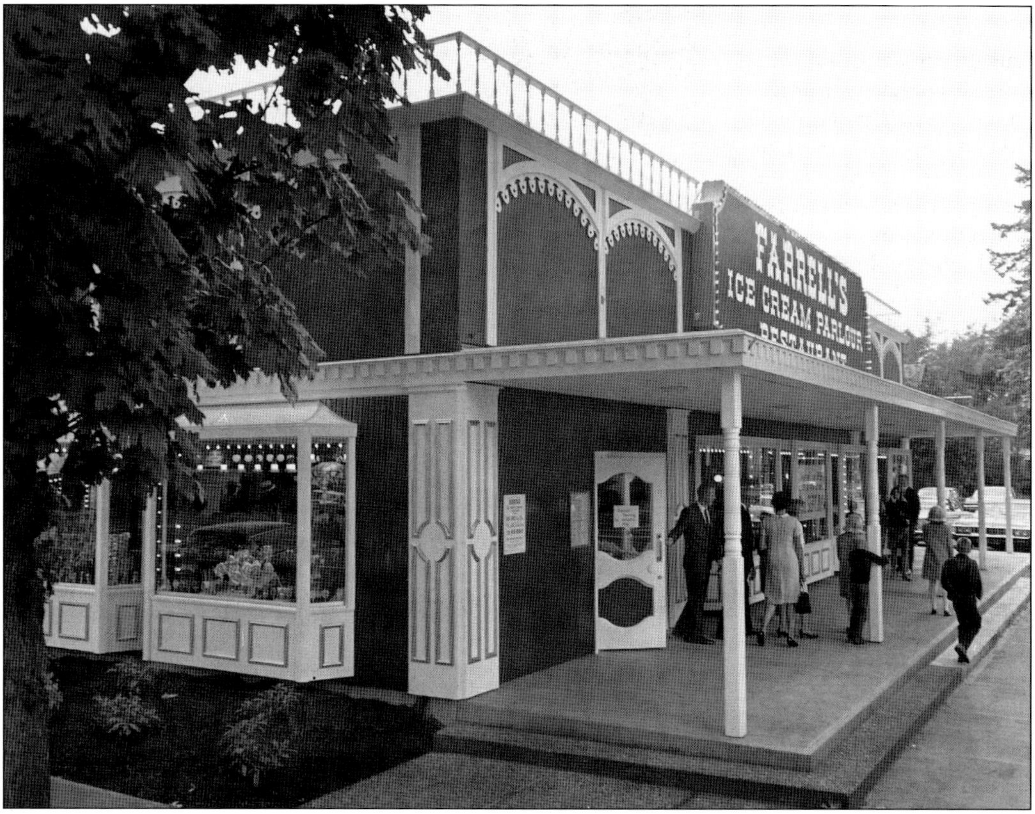

While the Eugene location was a franchise, it was the first freestanding Farrell's. Located at 1313 Pearl Street, this location opened in 1967. Ken McCarthy wanted to open a freestanding store in Portland, but they were not financially able to do so for the first several locations.

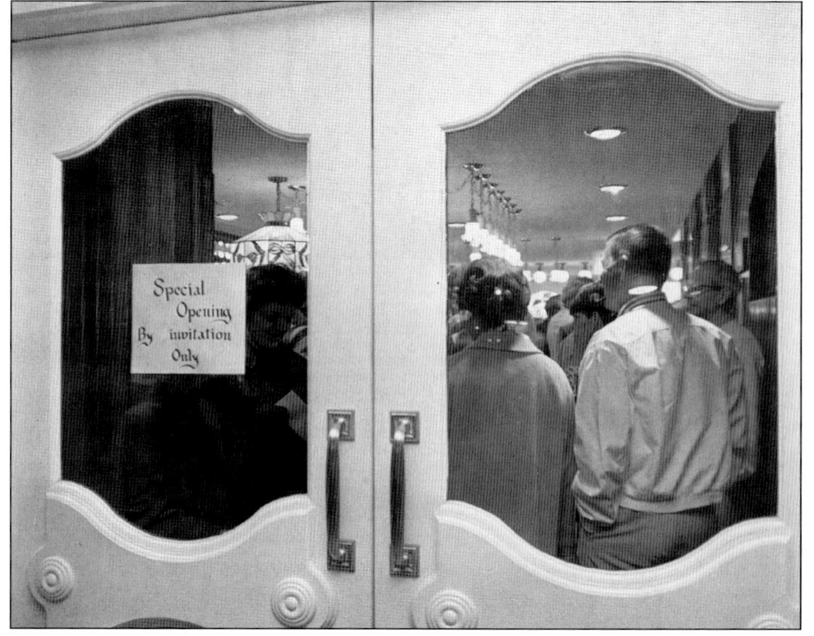

Just as they did for the Portland locations, Farrell's held an invitation-only preopening party to give the new staff a chance to test their training. While giving away ice cream for a night came at a cost, the Farrell's partners saw it as an investment for the experience it gave the new employees.

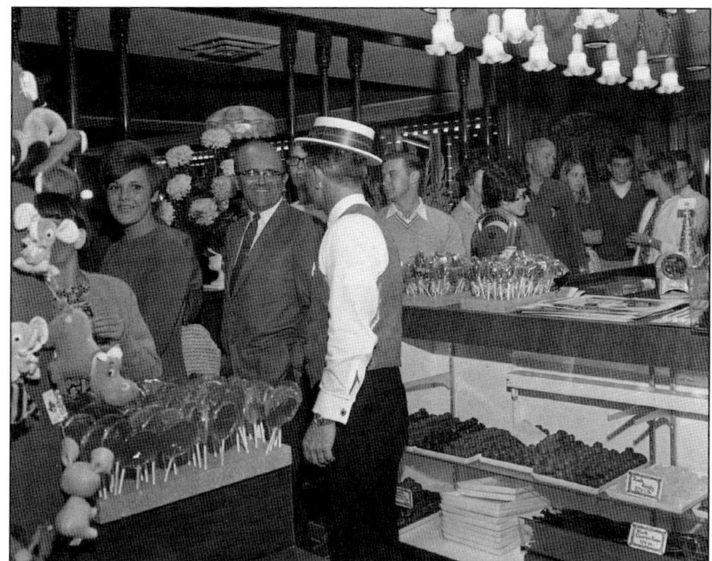

Greeting and seating customers was often the job of the manager or the franchise owner. This gave him the ability to control the number of parties per section, oversee the entire operations, and maintain the highest volume attainable. A manager must know what tables were open and be able to seat guests based on the strengths of the waiters and waitresses.

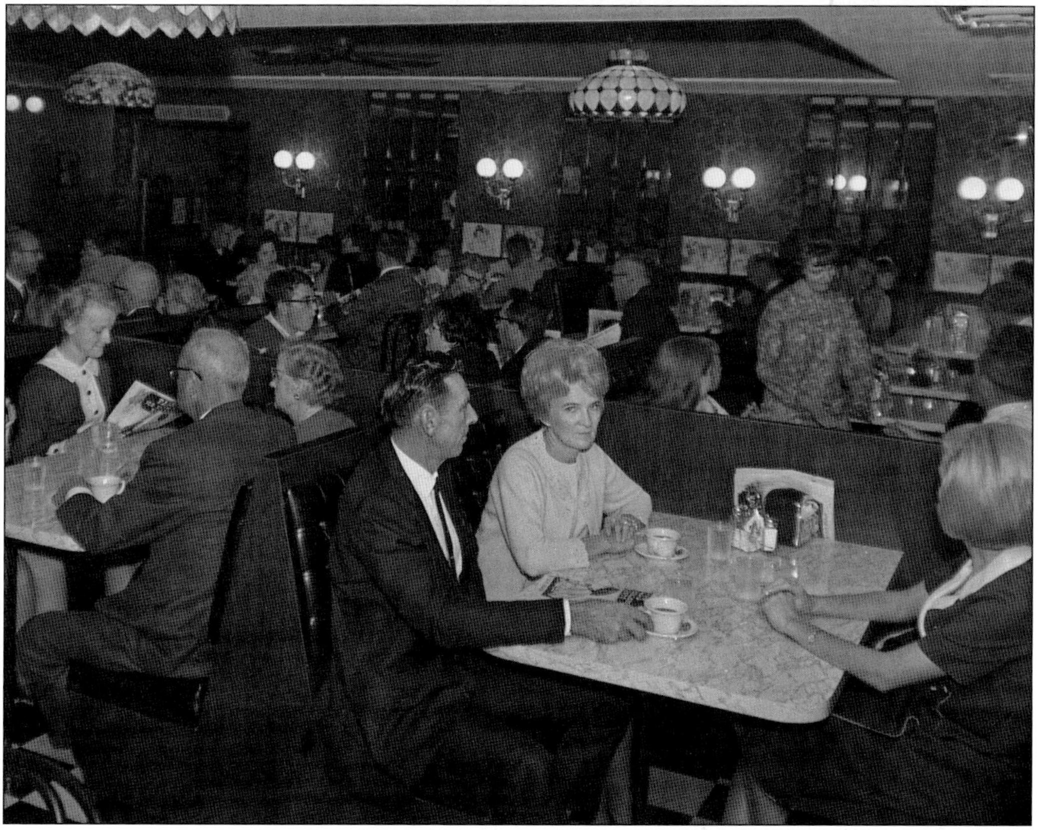

Bob Farrell modeled the booth layout after Jahn's Ice Cream in New York. Using a grid layout resulted in the greatest efficiency for service. Waiters were trained to clear dirty dishes as diners finished their meals and sundaes to make turning the table over faster. "Never go into your section empty headed and never leave your section empty handed" was taught to all Farrell's waiters and waitresses.

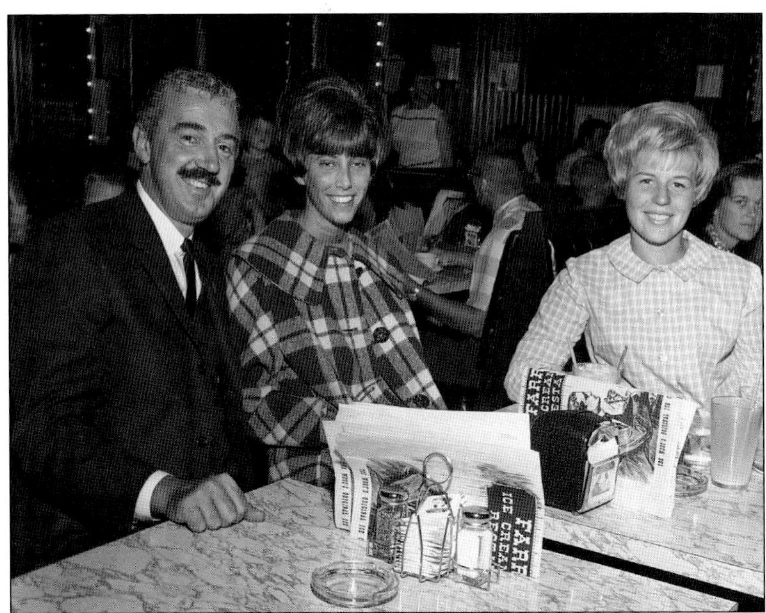

As seen in this photograph, Bob Farrell took the time to get to know the guests at the preopening parties. Prior to opening Farrell's, Farrell worked as a sales manager for Libby, McNeill & Libby selling a product line to restaurants and chain grocery stores. His inspiration for opening Farrell's came from disappointing service at a restaurant in Seattle when he took his family out for hot fudge sundaes.

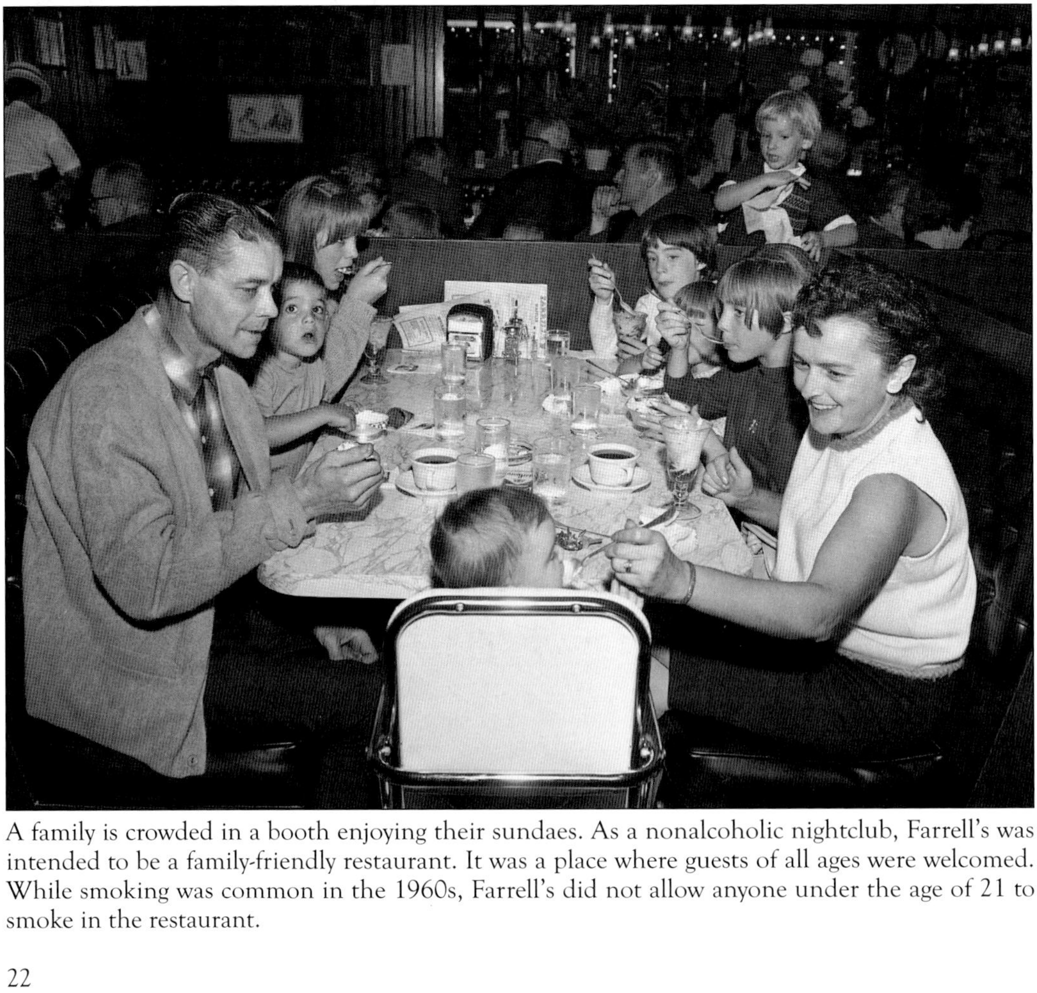

A family is crowded in a booth enjoying their sundaes. As a nonalcoholic nightclub, Farrell's was intended to be a family-friendly restaurant. It was a place where guests of all ages were welcomed. While smoking was common in the 1960s, Farrell's did not allow anyone under the age of 21 to smoke in the restaurant.

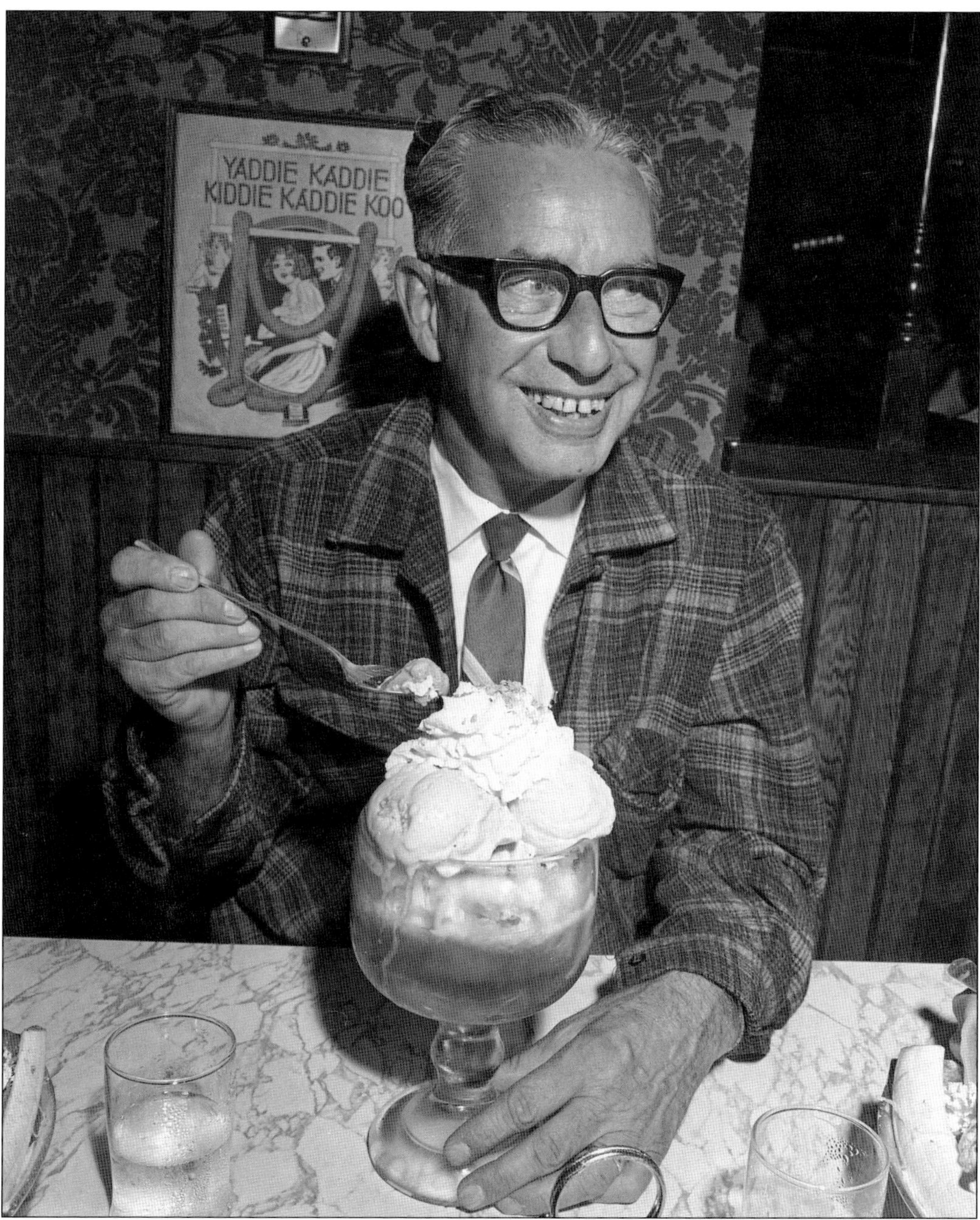

The Gibson Girl sundae brought a smile to many guests. The Gibson Girl was a popular six-scoop sundae with vanilla ice cream, three flavors of sherbet, and flavorful syrups served up in a large glass goblet. It was one of several large sundaes intended to attract attention as it was delivered to a waiting guest.

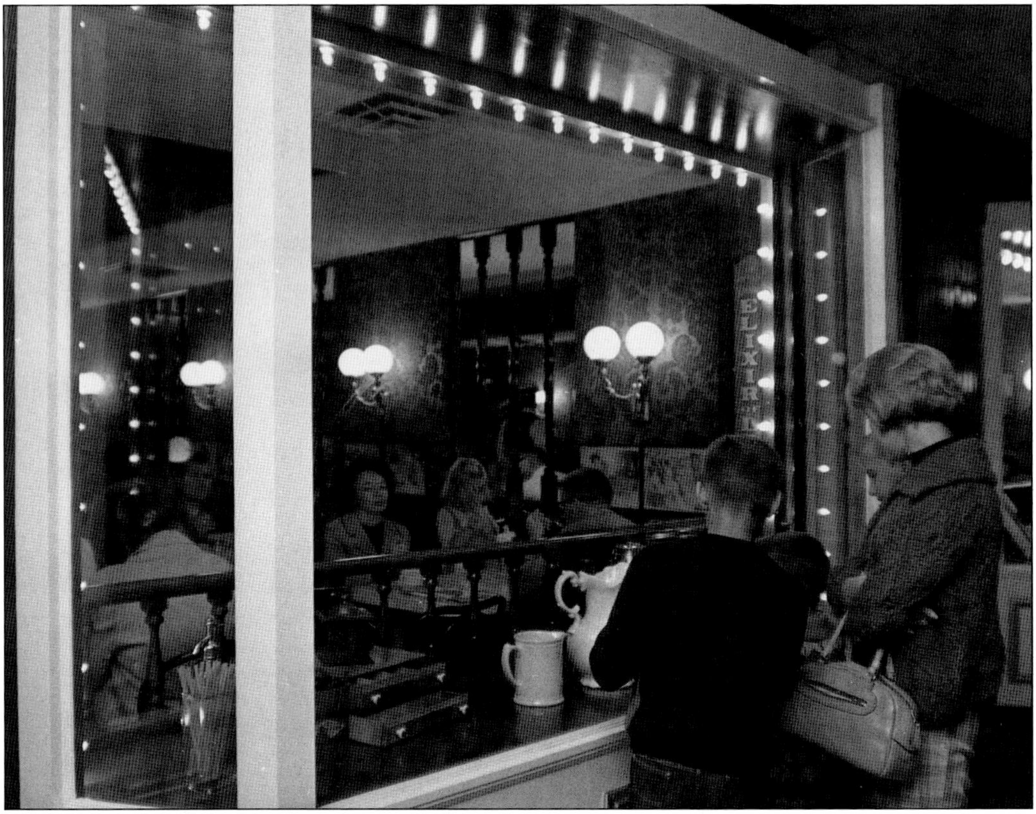

Guests are shown checking out the antiques on display in one of the windows. The Eugene store was the first Farrell's location with bay windows. These windows provided additional visual space for the store to use for promotional displays.

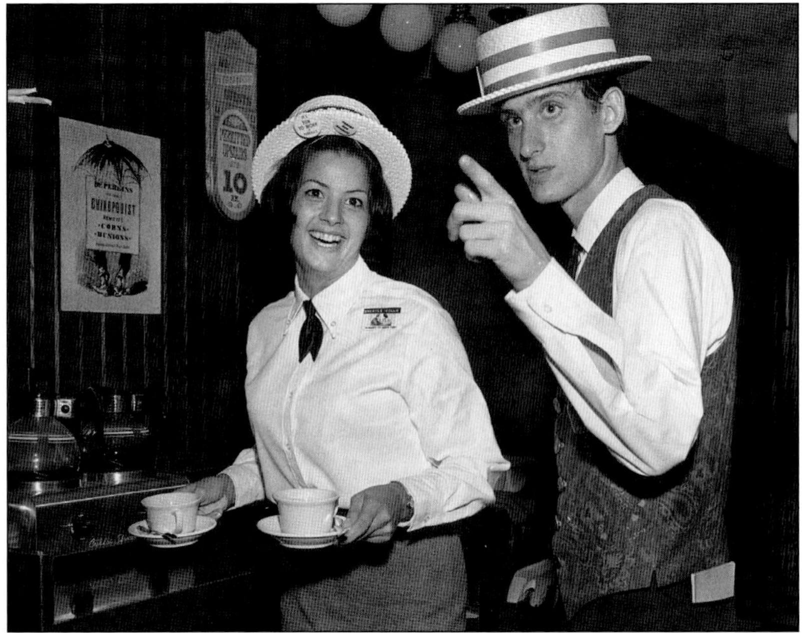

A training supervisor provides new employee Sheryle Hills guidance on how to deliver coffee to her customers. Ken McCarthy believed it was best to hire employees without restaurant experience so there would be no bad habits to break. As new locations were opened, the Farrell's training program increased in effectiveness.

Another family is seen enjoying their sundaes. For most of the first decade of Farrell's, fountain sales accounted for 60 percent of total sales as most guests visited Farrell's after supper or after a school function. Farrell's became known as the "after place" since customers often came in after something.

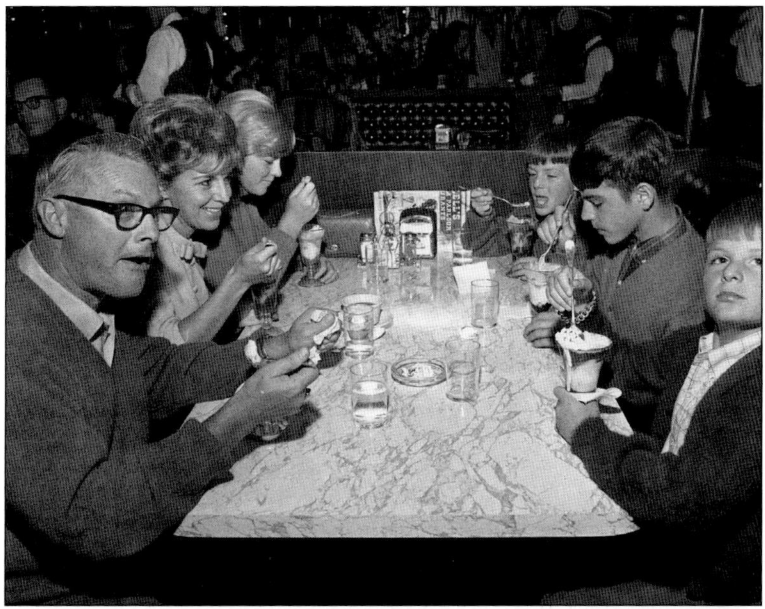

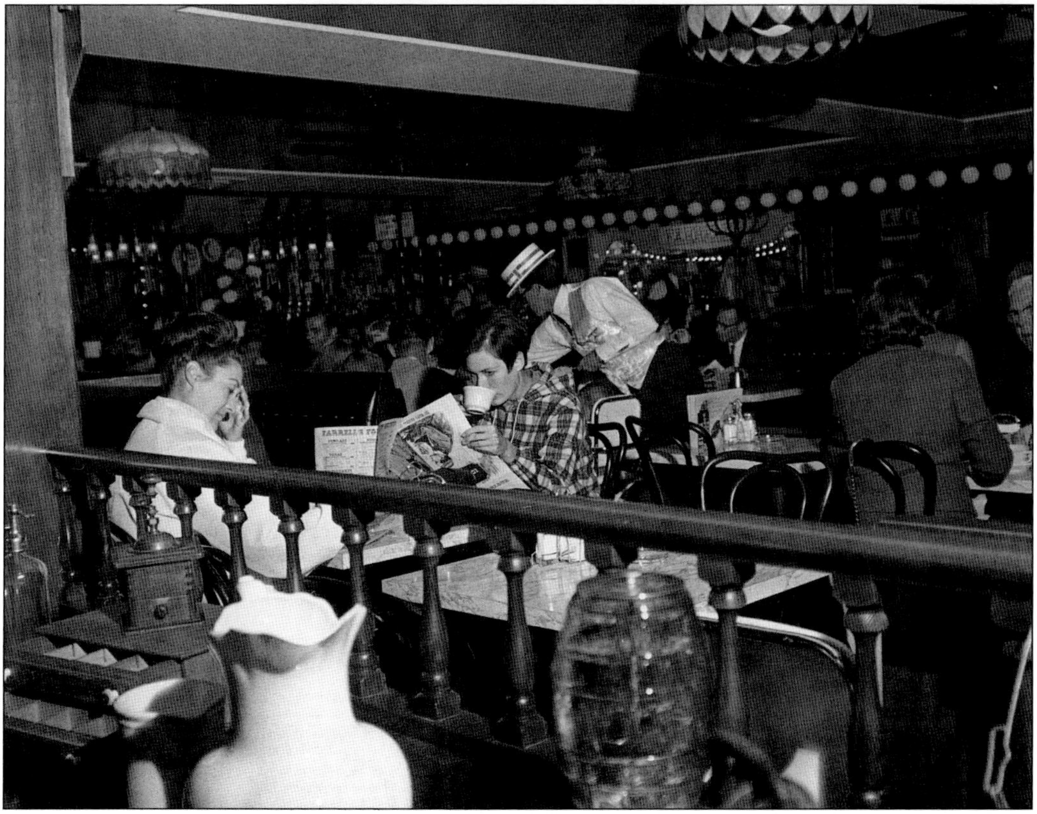

The main dining room is seen through one of the front windows. Farrell's were often located in high-visibility locations so a bustling dining room would attract more attention from those passing by. After several years, marquee strip lighting was installed in new and existing locations to attract more attention and enhance the festive atmosphere.

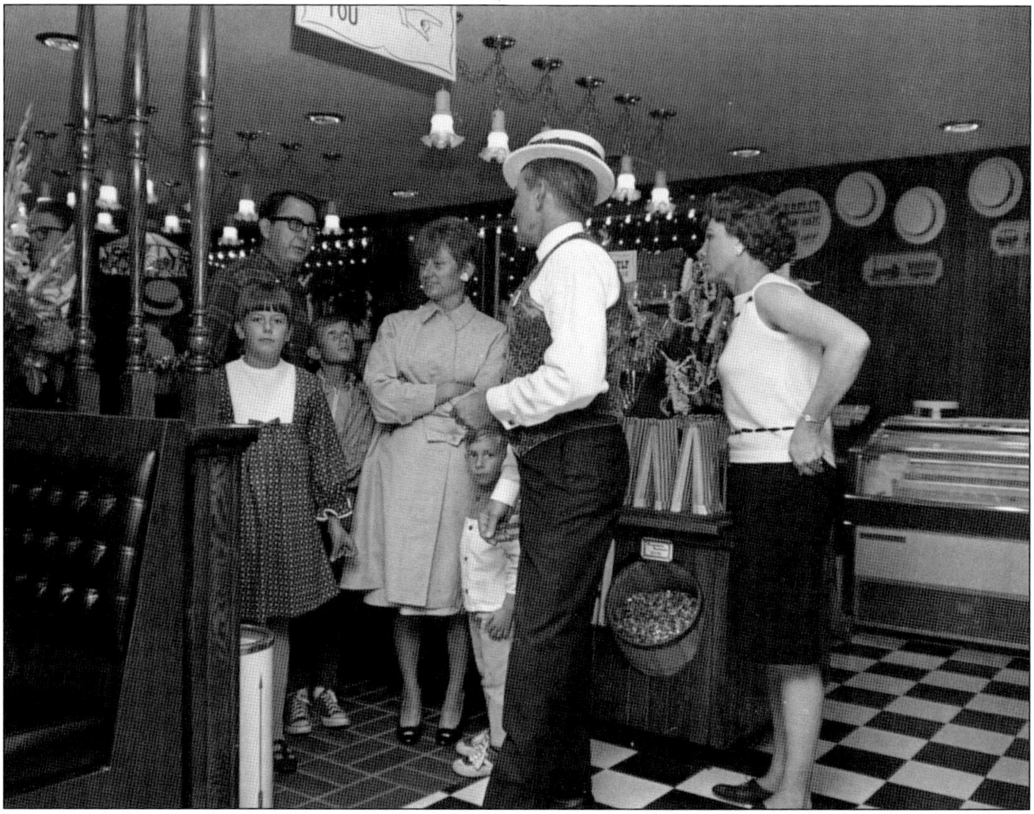

Another family is greeted for the preopening party. A display freezer for carryout was included in the candy section to sell hand-packed pints and quarts of Farrell's ice cream. For the first couple of years, Farrell's used Carnation ice cream. As Farrell's became too large for Carnation to supply ice cream, Ken McCarthy developed proprietary ice cream formulas that were produced by local dairies for Farrell's.

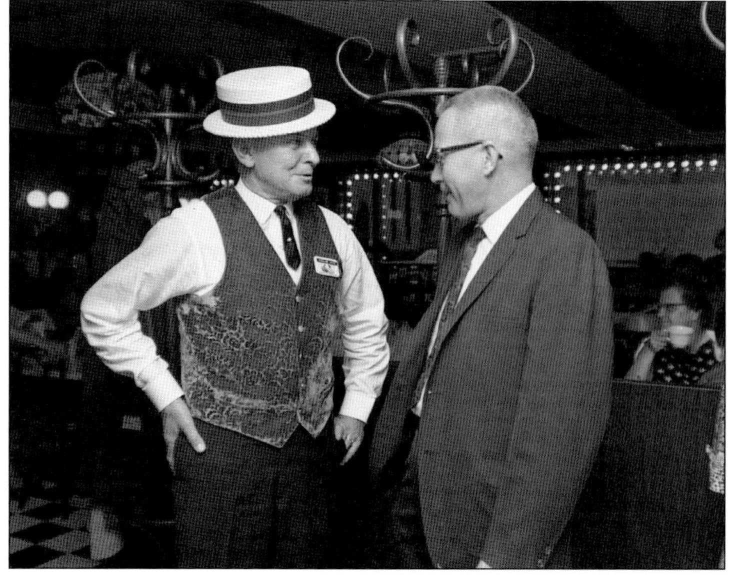

Two Eugene, Oregon, businessmen network at the preopening celebration for Farrell's. While the two Portland stores were better known by 1966, the Eugene location was still a new concept. Local business owners were curious to see how this new restaurant concept would work out.

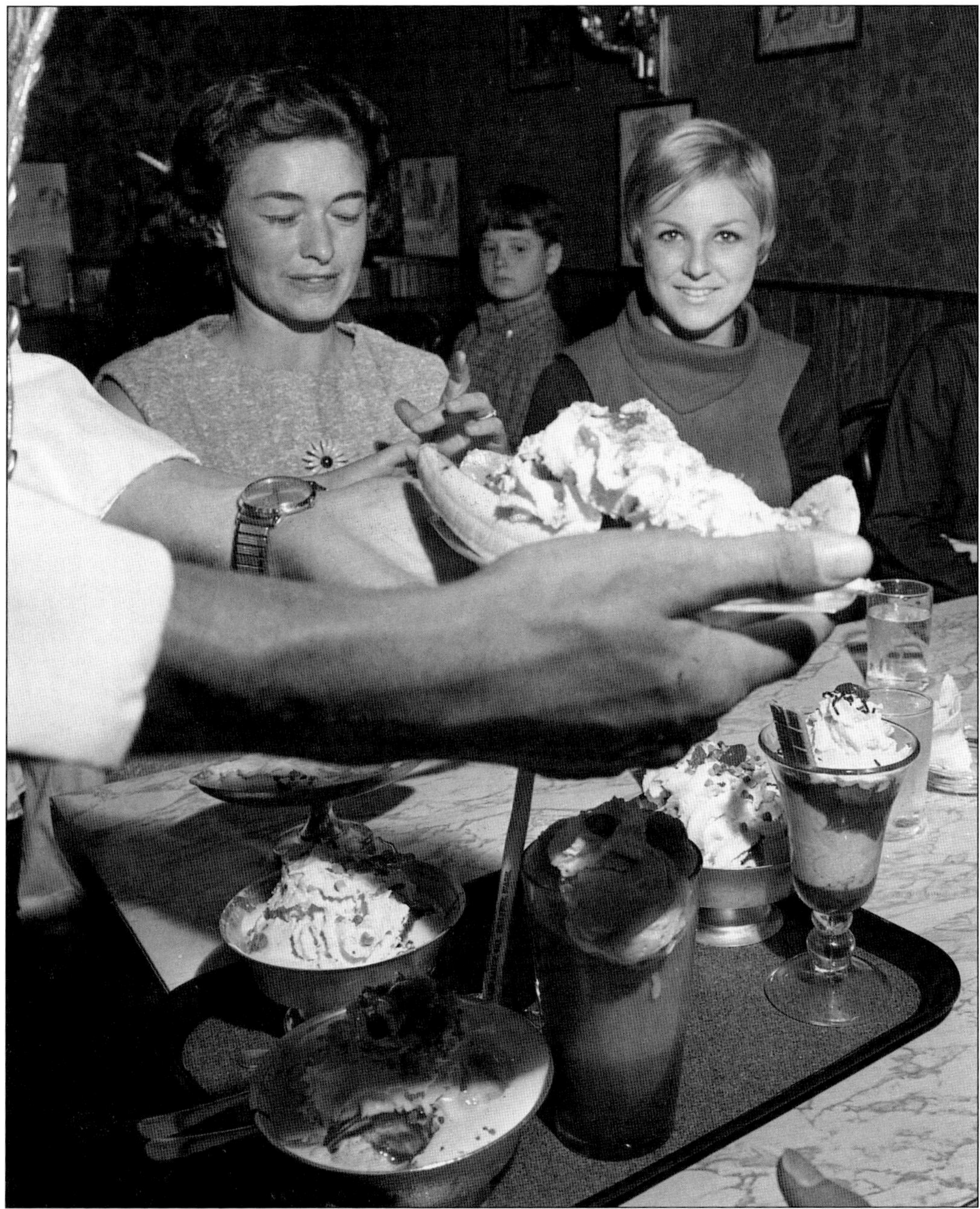

A waiter is seen delivering a banana split to a guest. As a classic American sundae, the banana split was made with vanilla, strawberry, and chocolate ice cream topped with strawberry, chocolate, and pineapple toppings served in a split banana.

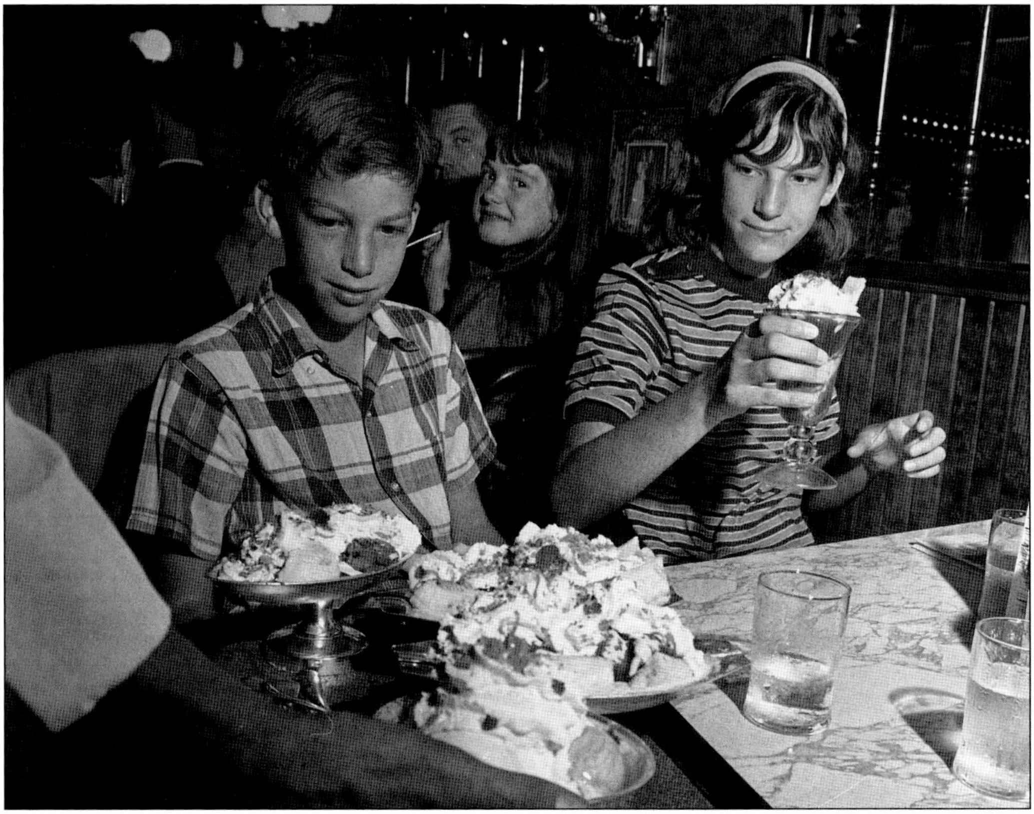

While Farrell's originally used all glass dishware, it switched over to silver dishes made by Grand Silver Co. for many of its sundaes. The type of dish was identified by the sundaes served in them. In this photograph are the split dish, twin dish, and "girl" dish. This pedestaled split dish was used for banana splits.

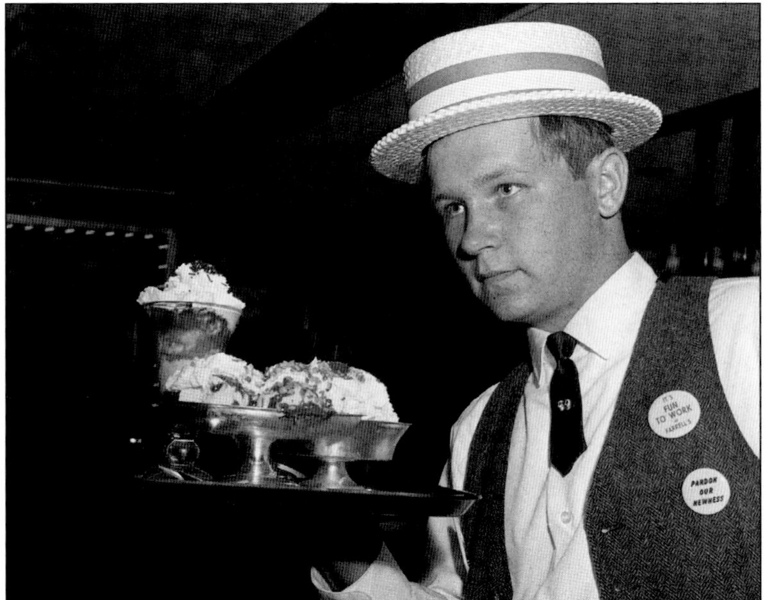

The twin dish was used for the hot fudge twin sundae. The girl dish was named after the four girl sundaes. Three sundaes were named after Bob Farrell's daughters Kathy, Colleen, and Kristie, and one sundae was named after Ken McCarthy's daughter Sharon.

A guest enjoys a sundae served in a glass tulip dish. These were two scoop sundaes, including the Fudge-ana, Straw-ana, and the Farrell's Old Fashion sundaes.

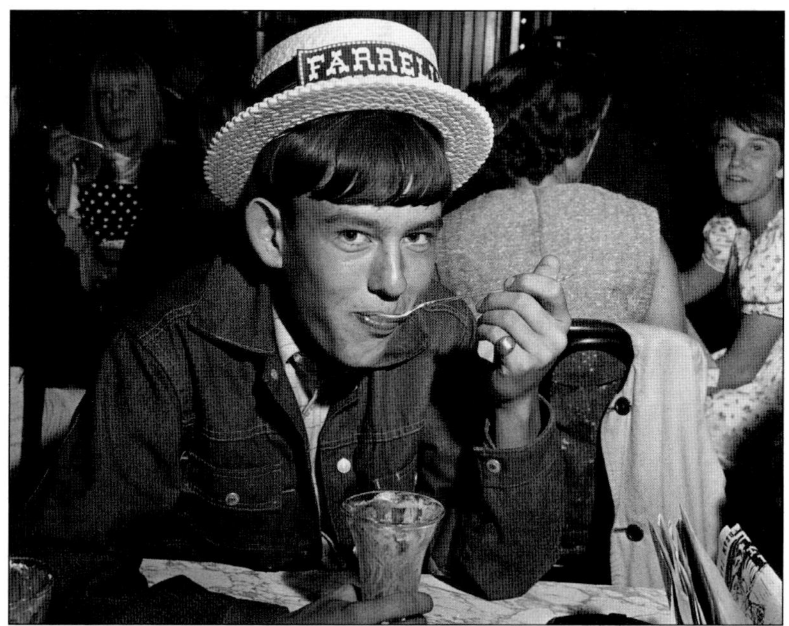

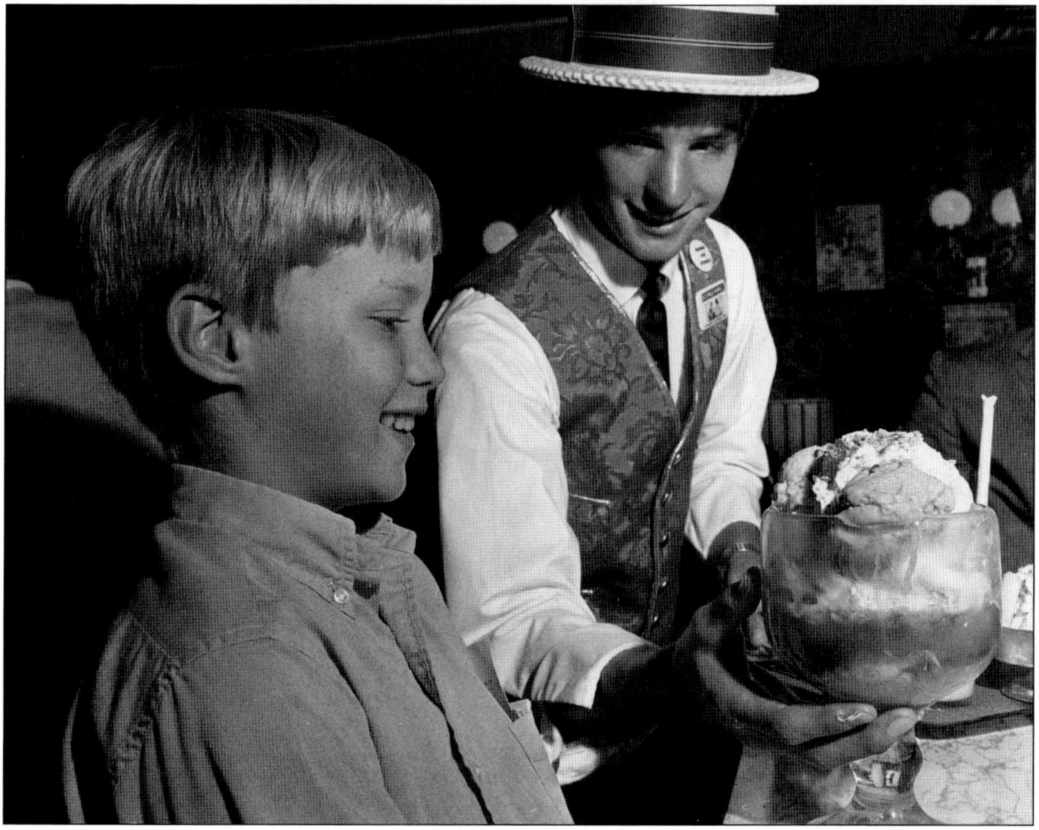

The Gibson Girl sundae was served in a large glass goblet used for super-duper floats and shakes. It was one of two six-scoop sundaes Farrell's was known for. In later years, Farrell's added more large sundaes as they became known for oversized ice cream concoctions.

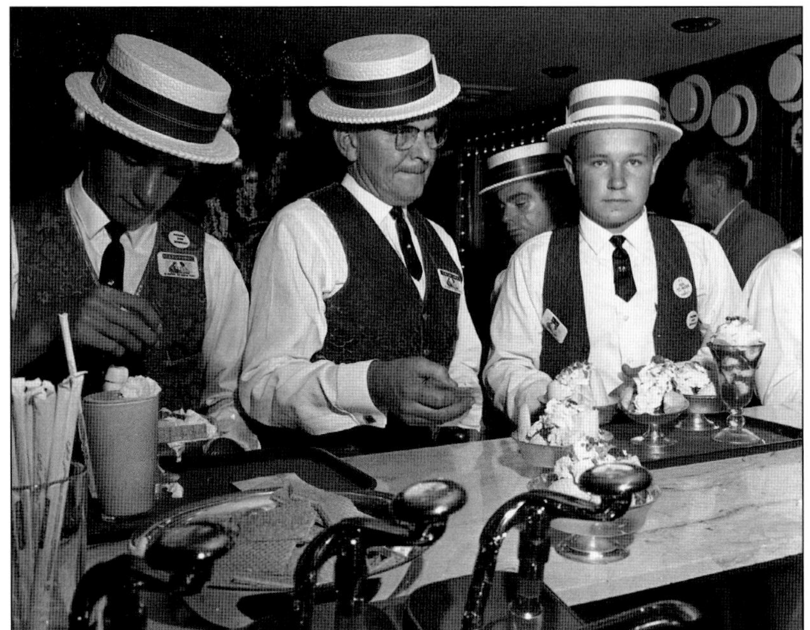

Three waiters are seen crowding the fountain counter to pick up their sundae orders. It was expected that fountain orders would be delivered to the guests within one minute of preparation. Ken McCarthy never wanted customers to see sundaes melting on the fountain counter while they waited to get their order.

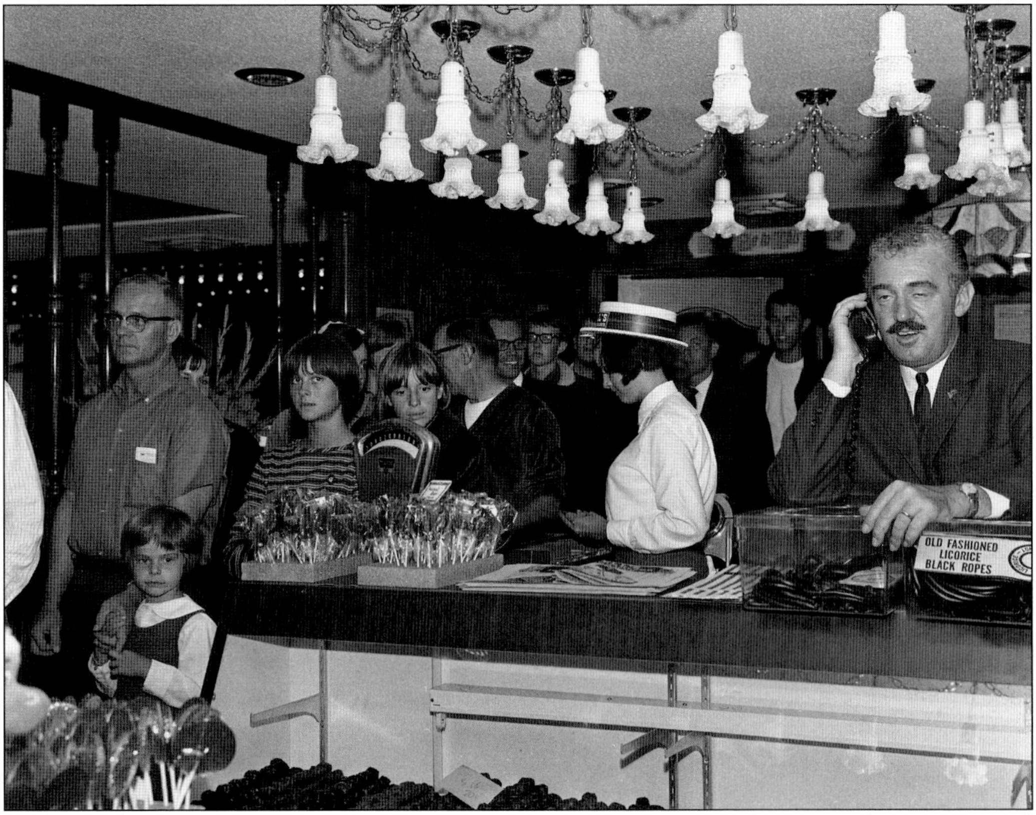

Bob Farrell is seen taking a phone call during the preopening party of the Eugene location. Farrell often used his sales background to promote Farrell's. As his name was on the store, he became the public face of Farrell's.

These college students are seen attempting to eat a Zoo sundae. The Eugene location was close to the University of Oregon and often catered to crowds in town for a game. It also gave them a steady supply of youthful workers to staff the location.

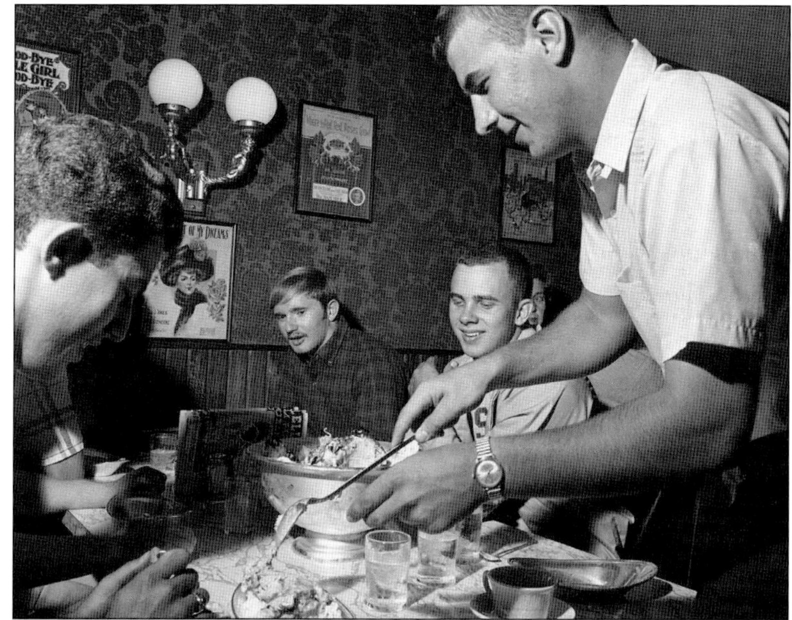

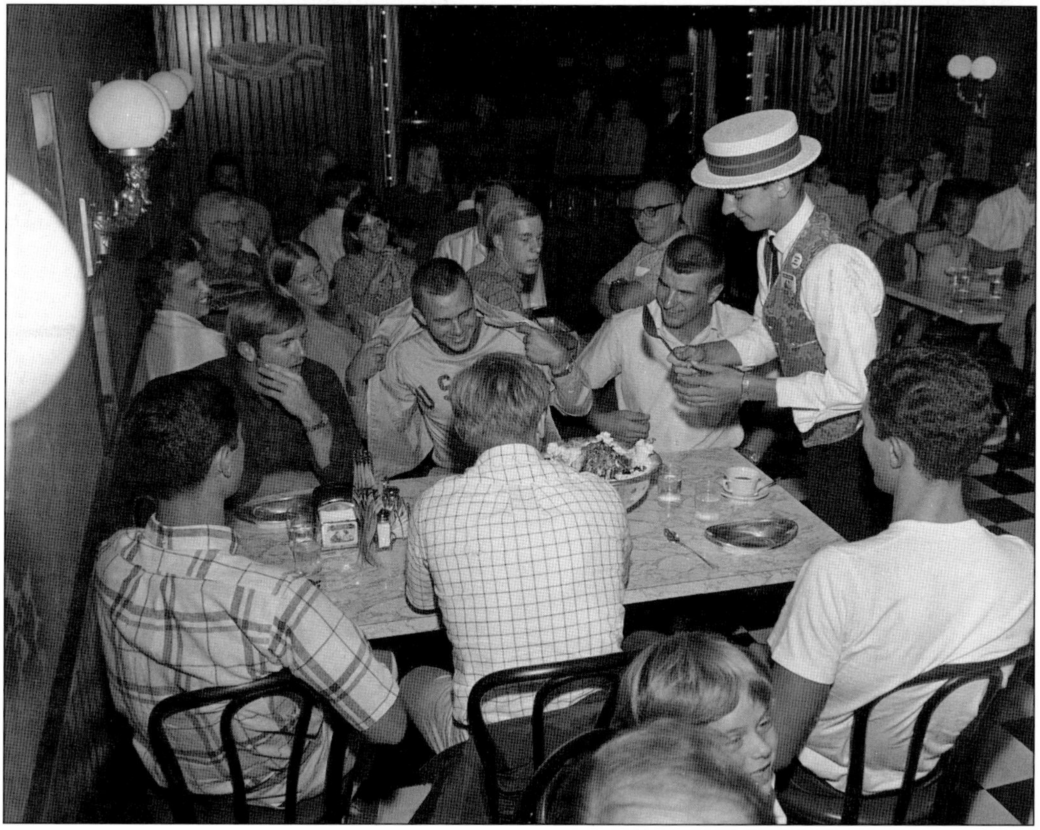

A waiter is shown serving the Zoo sundae to college students. Even though the sundae was designed for 10 people, it was not unheard of to have smaller groups finish the Zoo. Some individuals have finished a Zoo by themselves.

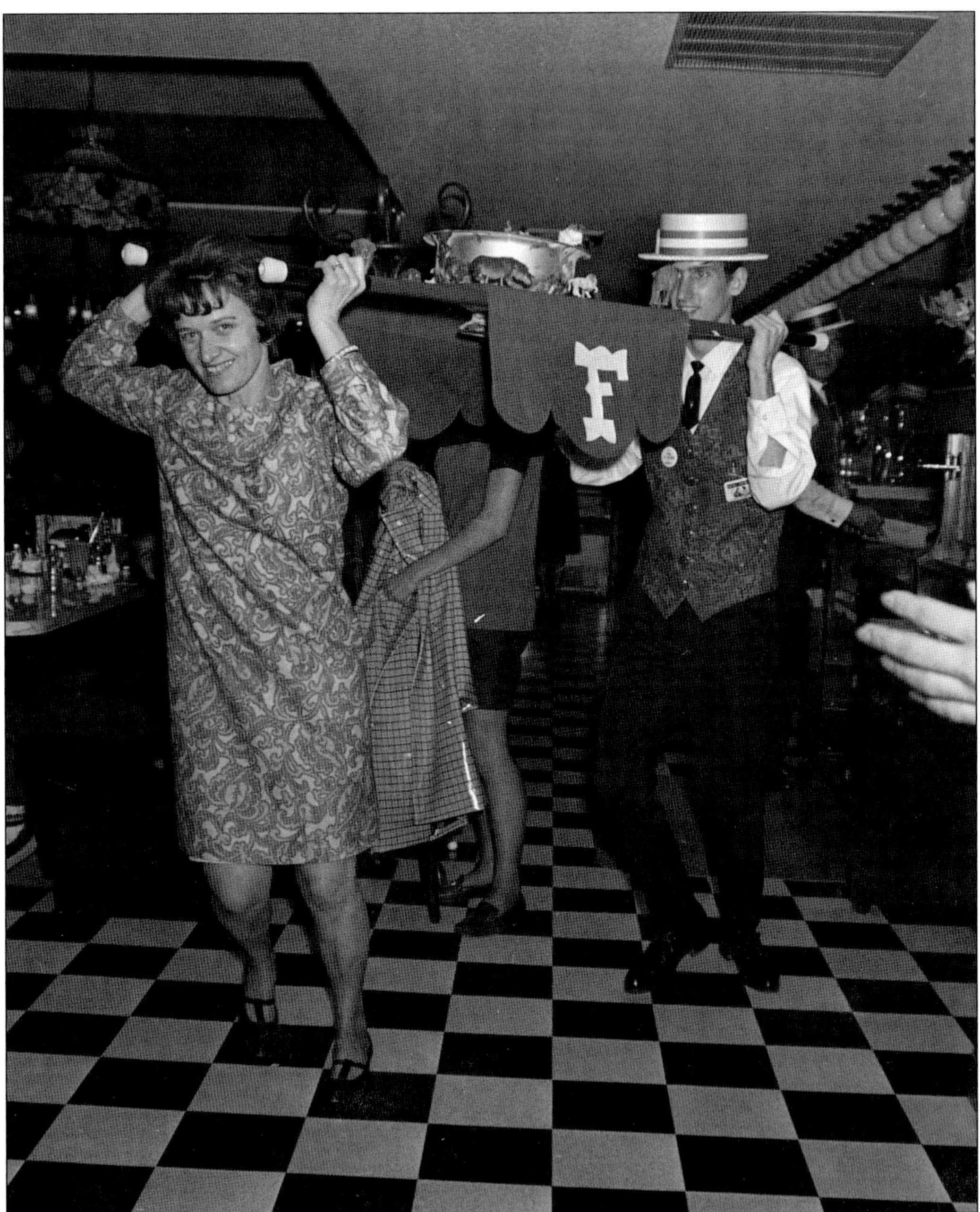

Farrell's became known for delivering the Zoo sundae to guests on a stretcher. While the sundae could just be delivered on a tray, watching two employees running around the dining room with the stretcher while other employees sounded a firehouse siren was far more entertaining.

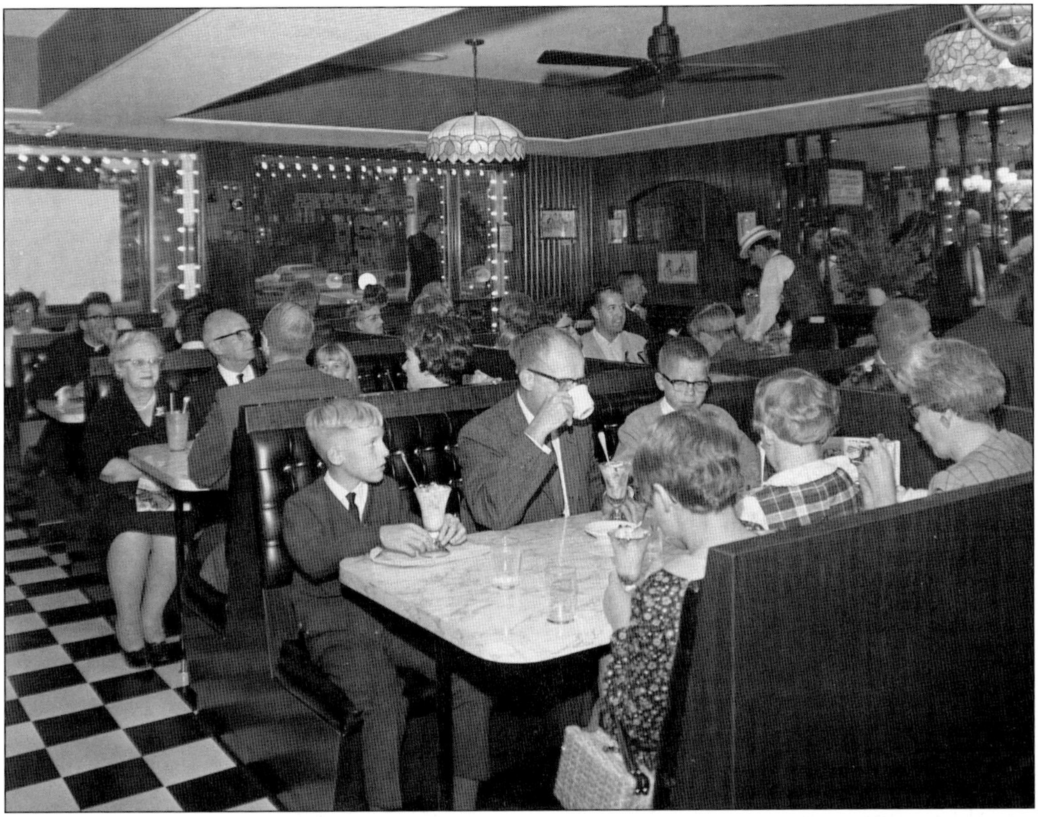

A full dining room was a very common sight during the early years of Farrell's. More so on Friday nights and Saturday nights as guests came in after movies, shows, or school functions. Until mall-based locations became more common in the 1970s, most Farrell's saw their biggest sales after 8:00 p.m. at night.

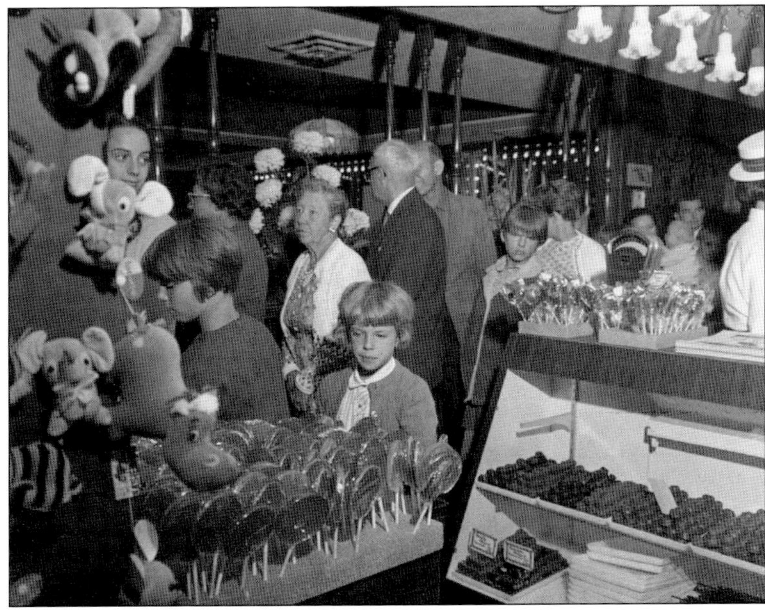

Here, a young guest is seen eyeing a candy display. Even after enjoying ice cream sundaes, many parents would purchase candy for their children as they exited through the candy store. While Farrell's stocked many larger candy items, there were also penny candy options that made the impulse purchase more likely.

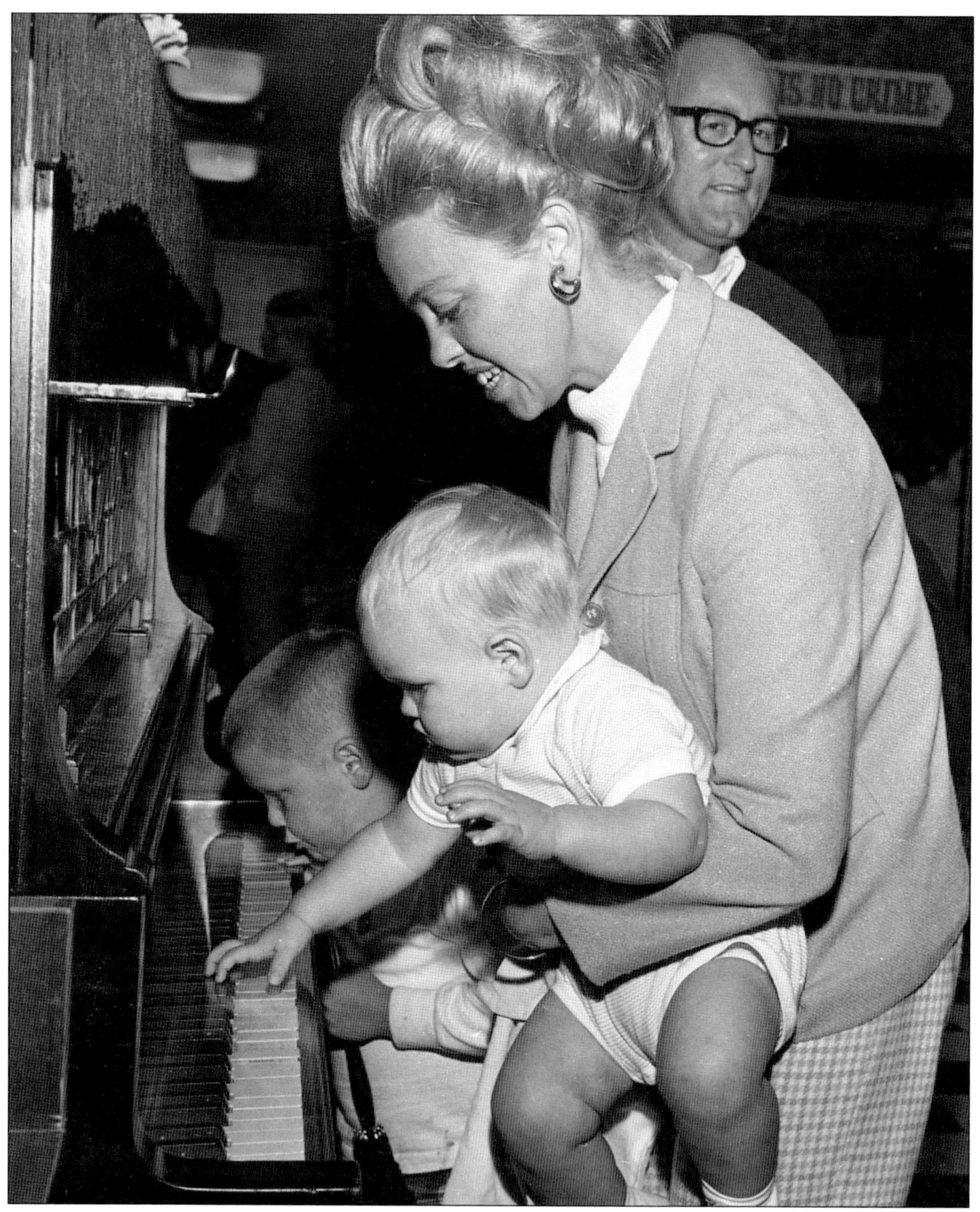

A mother is seen showing the player piano to her children. To enhance the old-time atmosphere of Farrell's, coin-operated player pianos were given prominent placement in each location. As these were often old pianos, the maintenance of the pianos gave managers more grief as the years went on.

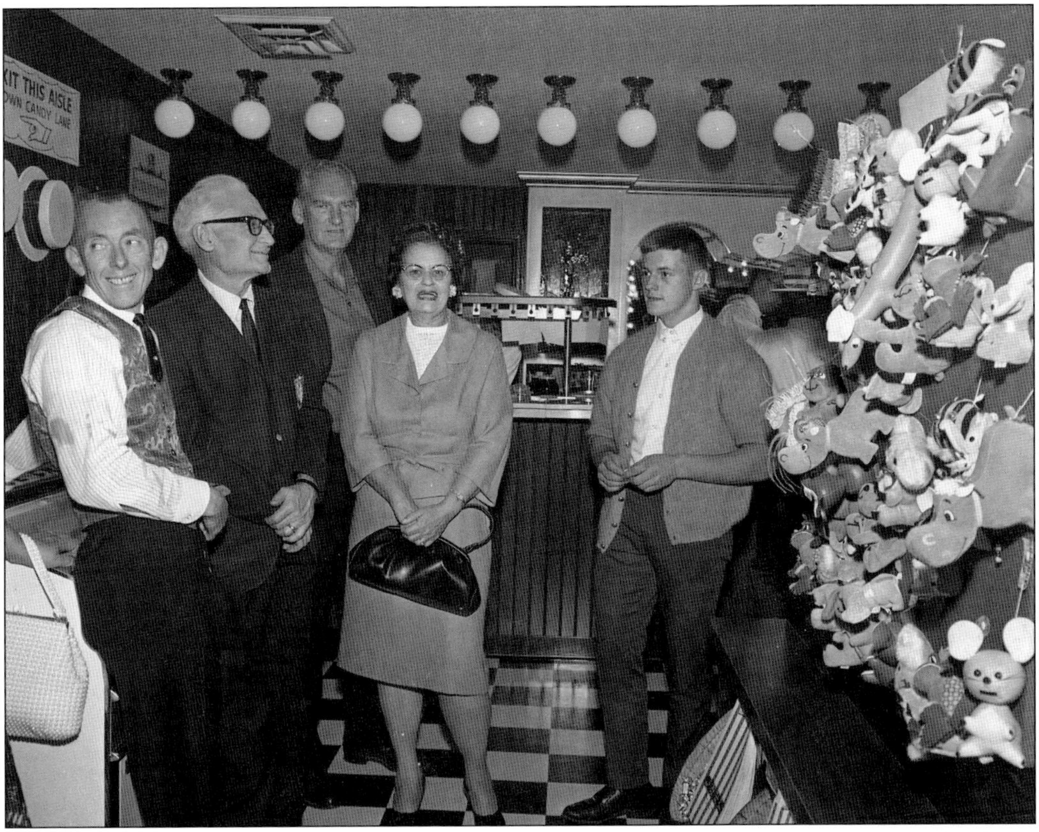

Ken McCarthy and Dale Belford are having a conversation with departing guests at the preopening party. Belford became one of the owners of Farrell's when he brought his accounting expertise to the company. Belford established a centralized accounting system that provided a statistical analysis of monthly records. This meant Farrell's could provide simplified, comprehensive reports for the individual restaurant owners and managers. The franchise package was designed for amateurs in the restaurant business. The accounting procedures were designed to track down opportunities for increased profits.

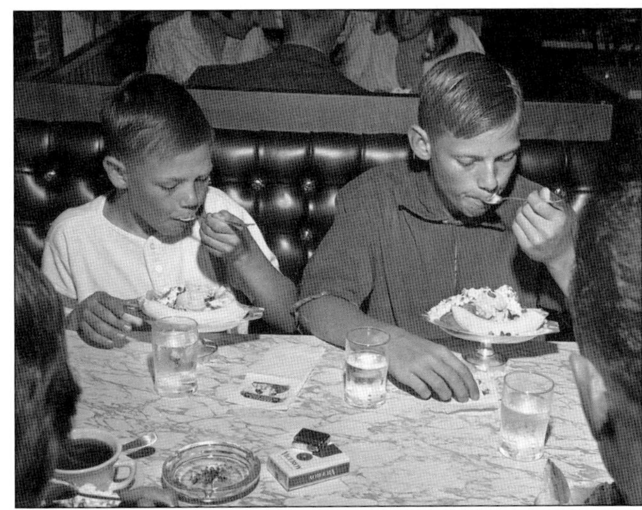

It was Bob Farrell's idea to use a 1905 theme for the restaurant. Ken McCarthy said Farrell was an idea man, and the turn-of-the-century theme became a success.

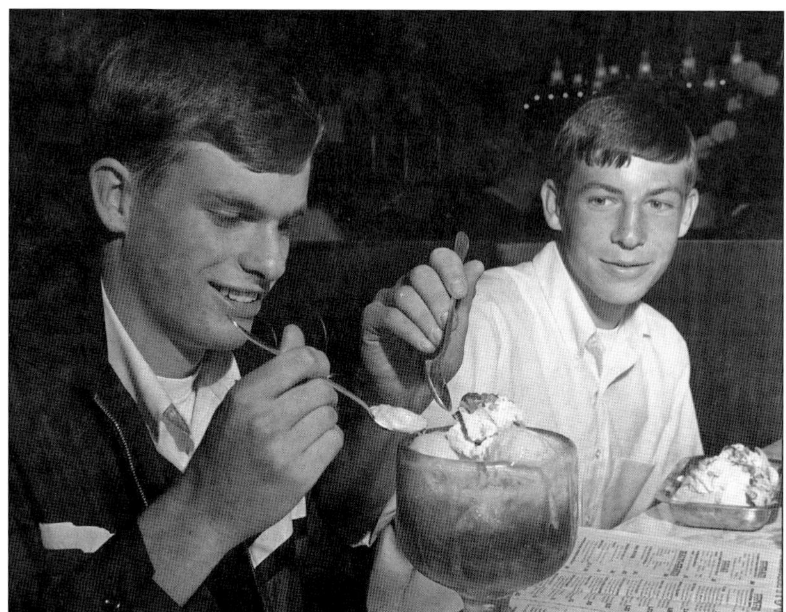

Despite having a dish full of ice cream in front of him, this young man is stealing ice cream from his brother's supersized float. Several of the Farrell's sundaes were large enough to share.

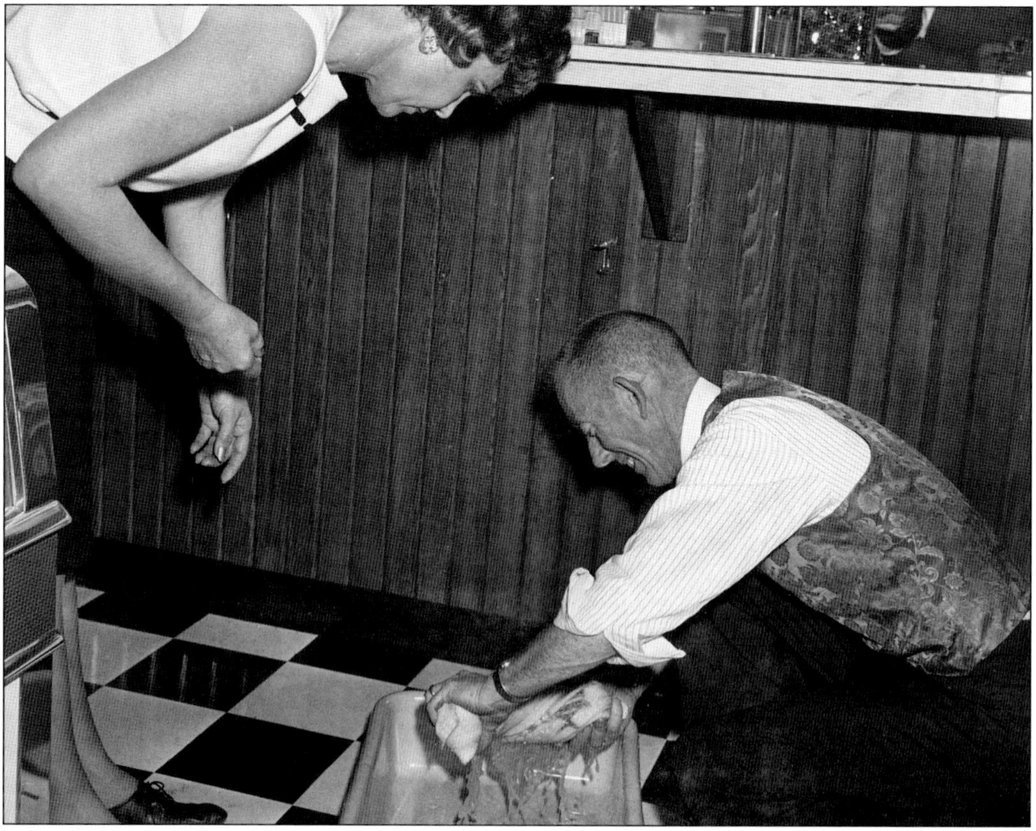

Ken McCarthy is seen helping cleanup a mess in front of the fountain counter. McCarthy believed nobody was above cleaning up after customers and was critical of managers or franchise owners who were unwilling to help.

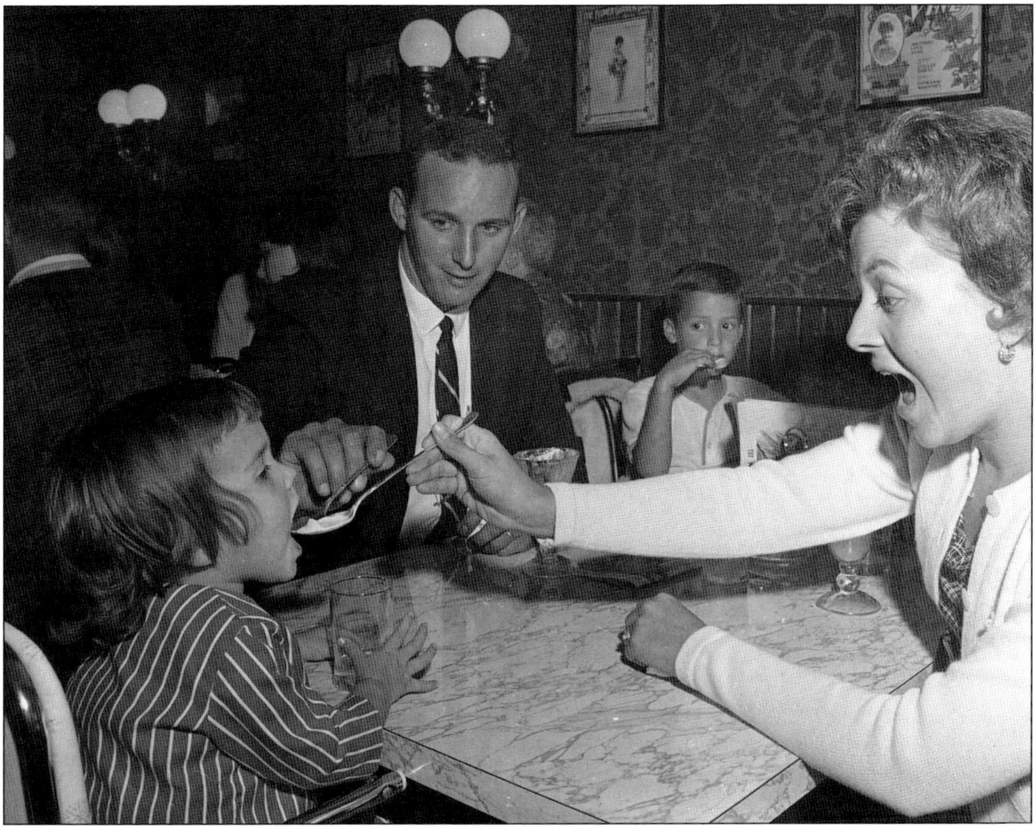

Generations of children grew up going to Farrell's with their parents. Farrell's was known as the place to go for families and became a favorite hangout for teenagers and young adults.

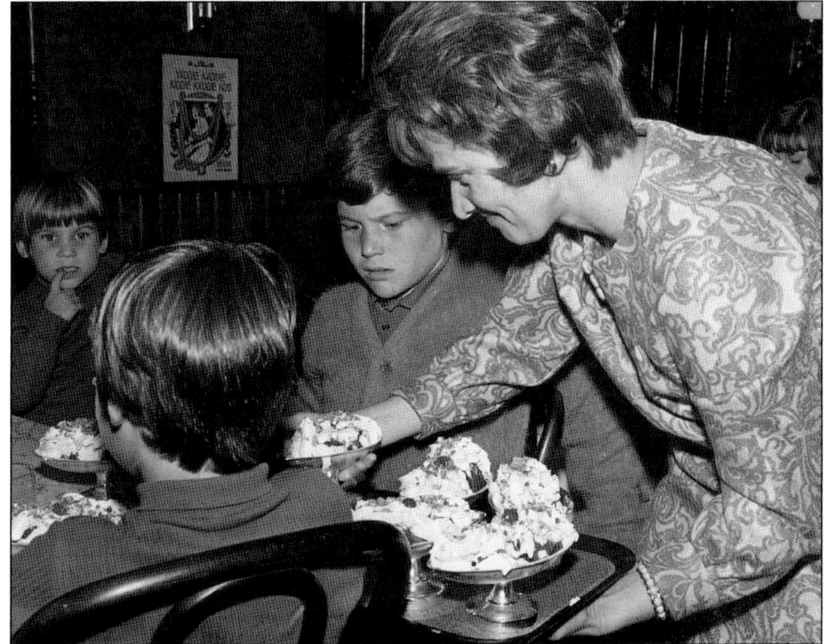

Waiters at Farrell's were well-trained to provide the highest levels of customer service. Ken McCarthy developed a comprehensive training program for all departments.

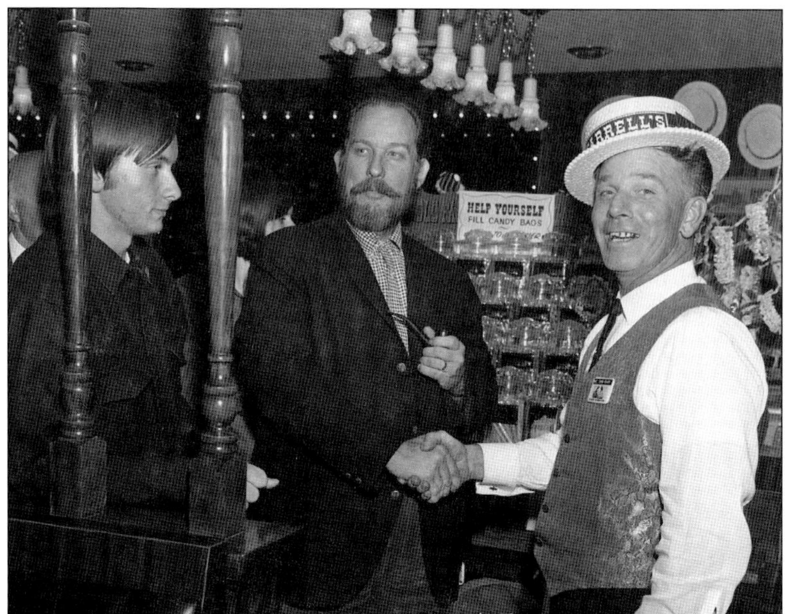

Don East (right), the owner of the Eugene franchise, is seen taking time to greet guests at the private preopening party. It was expected that franchise owners be directly involved in their stores.

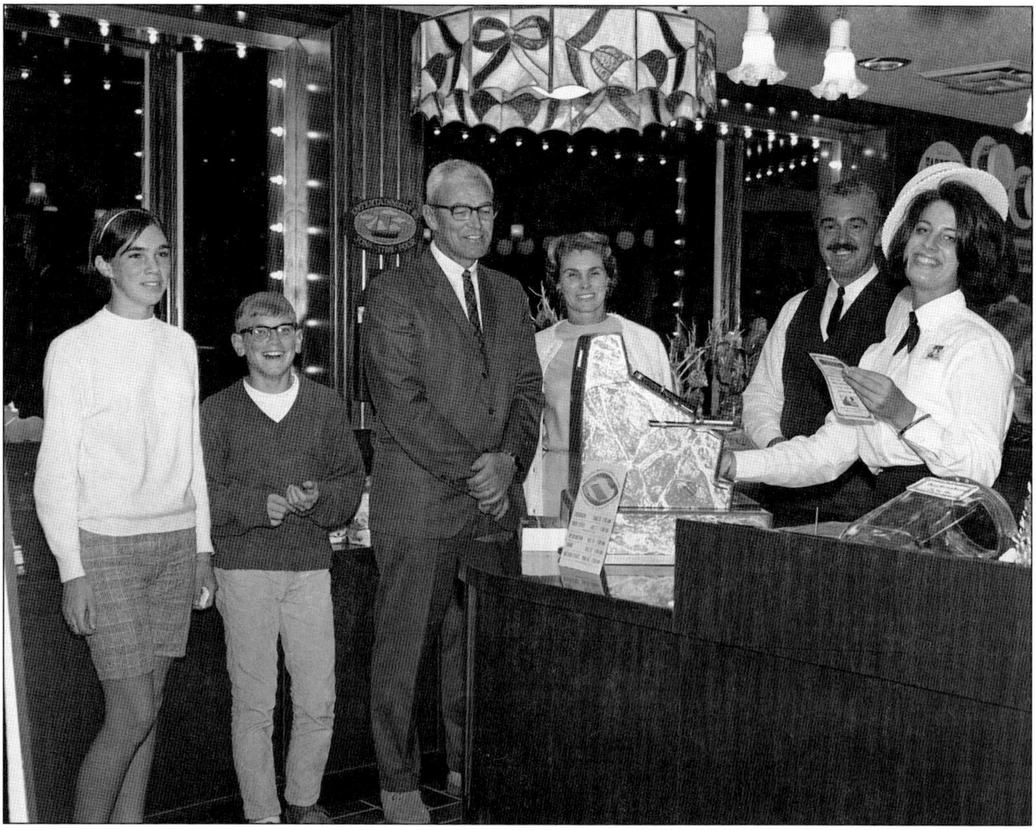

Bob Farrell (second from right) spends some time with departing guests at the cashier stand during the preopening party. Even after they sold the chain to Marriott Corporation, Farrell was often present at the opening of new stores.

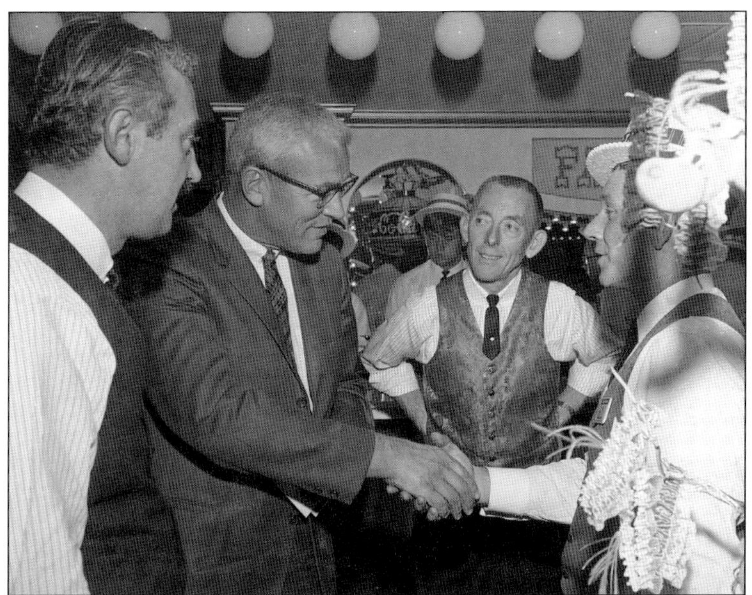

Bob Farrell (left), Ken McCarthy (center), and Don East, the Eugene franchise owner (right), are seen networking with a local businessman at the preopening party. Inviting prominent local business owners often increased word of mouth when opening a new Farrell's location.

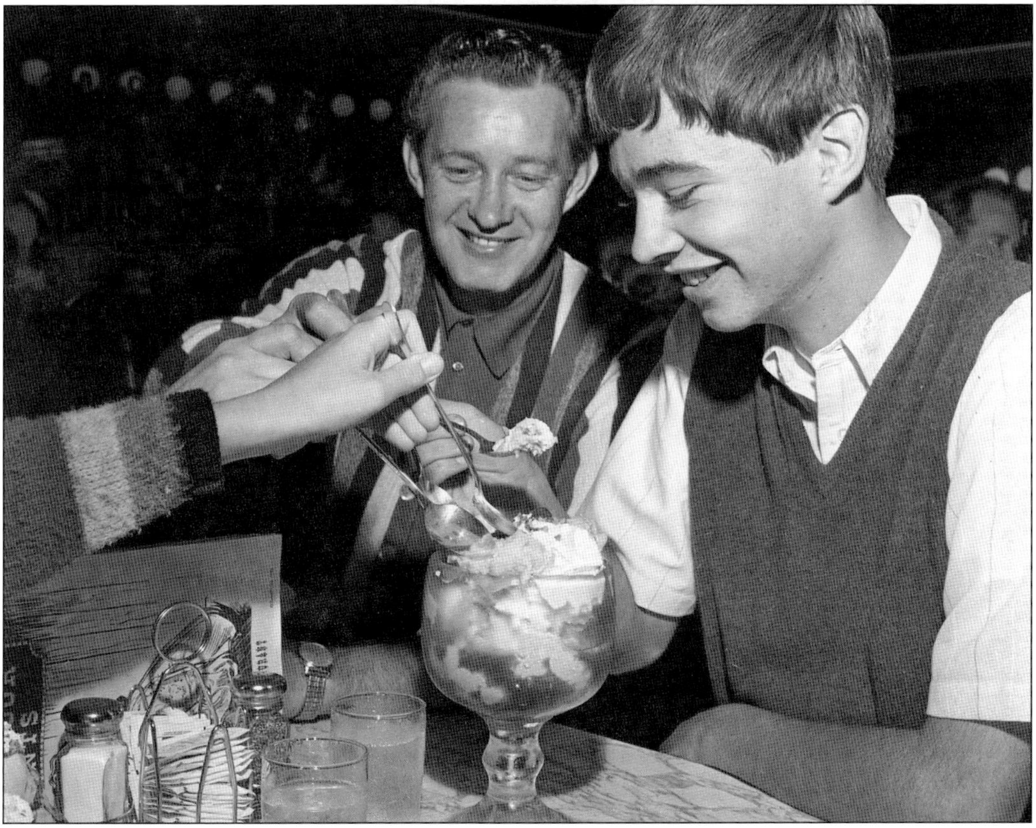

While some of the larger sundaes could be shared, customers often wanted to accomplish the task of eating them on their own. Some Farrell's locations hosted ice cream–eating contests as a promotional tool. While he was the attorney general of Arkansas, Bill Clinton won a Pig's Trough eating contest at a Farrell's in Little Rock in 1978.

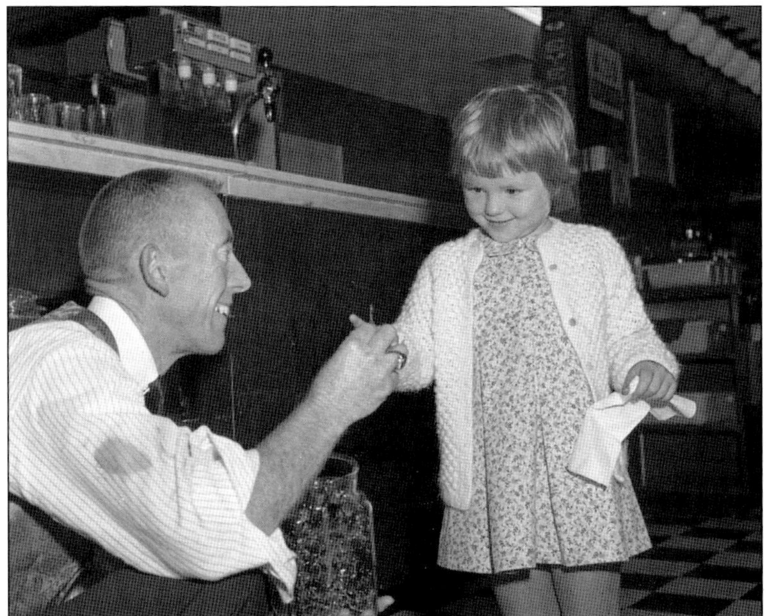

Ken McCarthy is shown giving a young guest a plastic animal pick as a souvenir. Shaped as different animals, these plastic picks were placed in the Zoo sundae as well as one of the four girl sundaes.

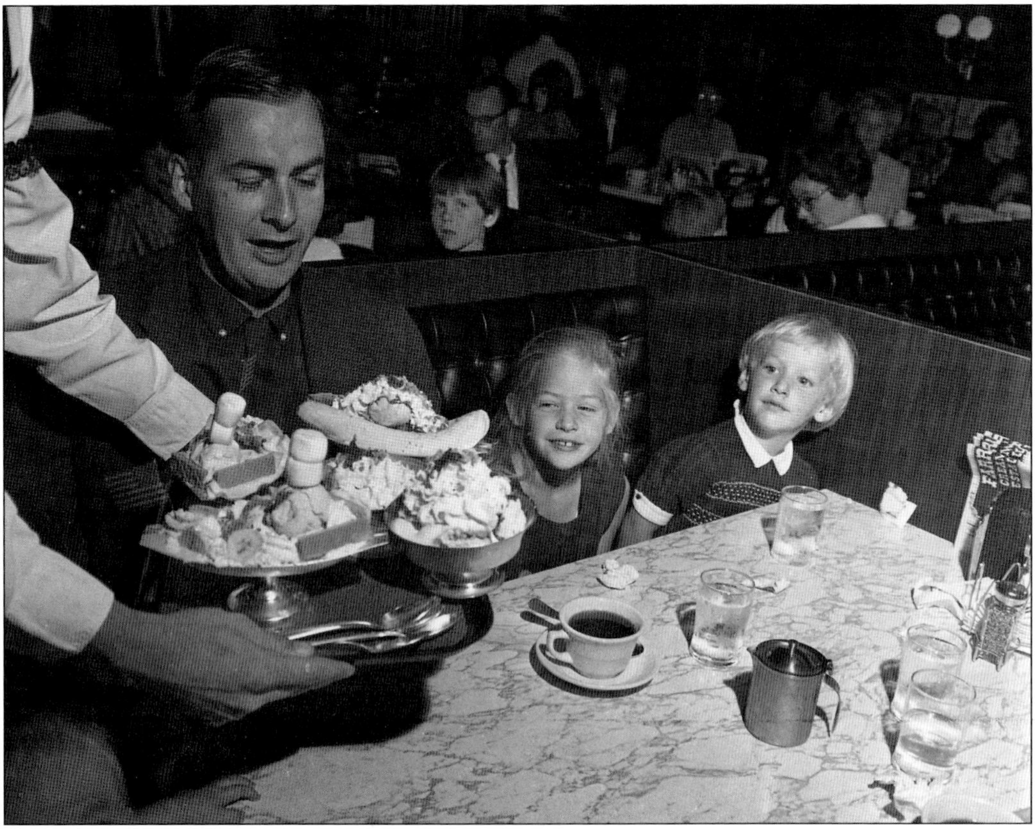

A server delivers a tray of sundaes to a family. This batch of sundaes included the Union Station Locomotive sundae. This was a creation designed to look like a train engine with marshmallows stacked to simulate the smoke from the engine.

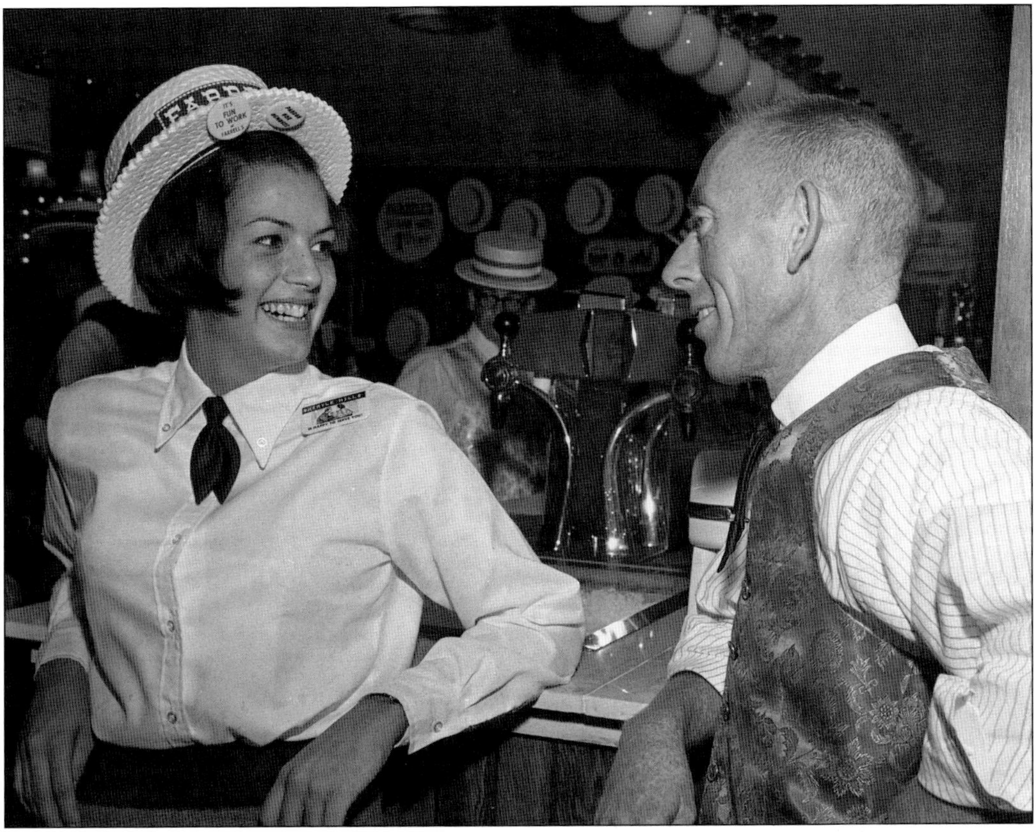

Ken McCarthy is seen taking a break during the preopening party with Farrell's employee Sheryle Hills. McCarthy hired people for their personality and believed one could train for the job.

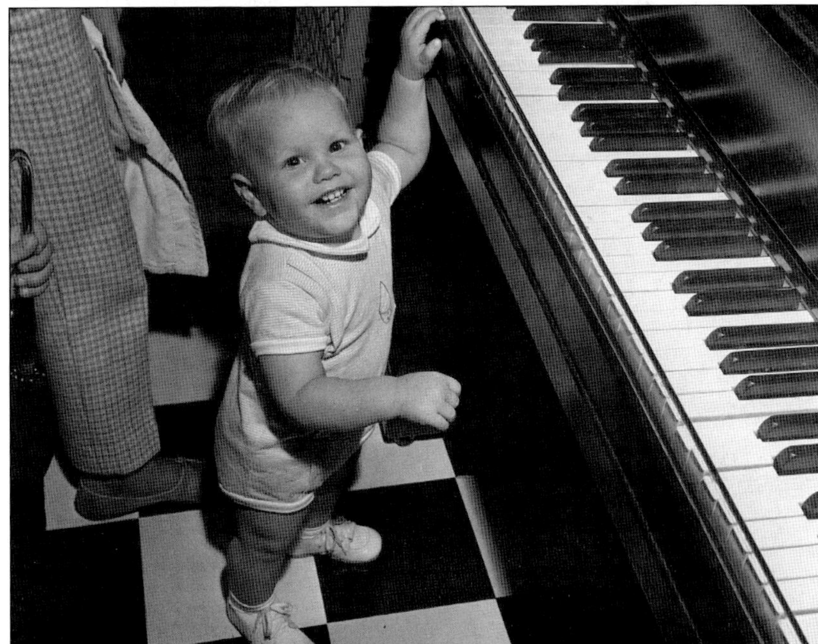

A young guest tries to play the piano at the opening. A plastic cover was installed on the player pianos to keep the young guests from banging on the keys.

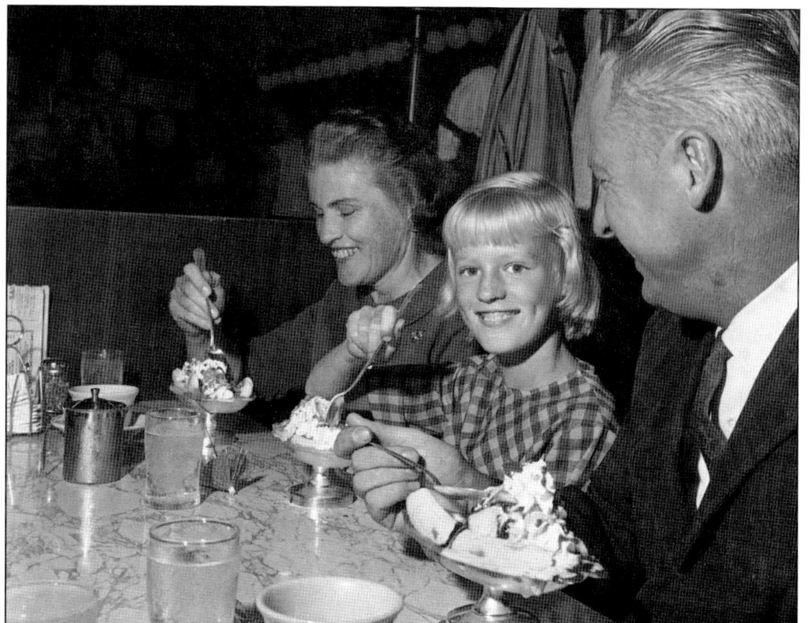

Happy guests are seen enjoying banana splits. Banana splits were one of the most popular sundaes on the Farrell's menu. During the opening day of the very first Farrell's, Bob Farrell and Ken McCarthy ran out of bananas.

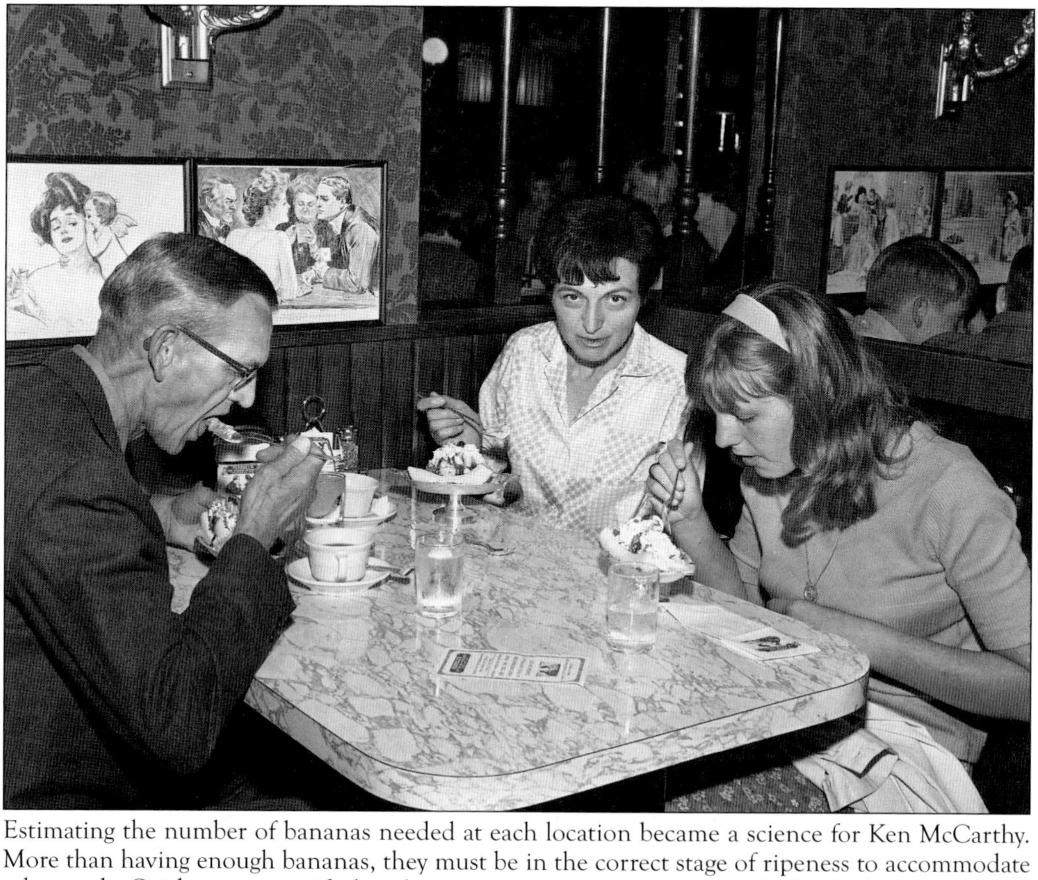

Estimating the number of bananas needed at each location became a science for Ken McCarthy. More than having enough bananas, they must be in the correct stage of ripeness to accommodate sales needs. Guides were provided to the restaurant managers to gauge the level of ripeness.

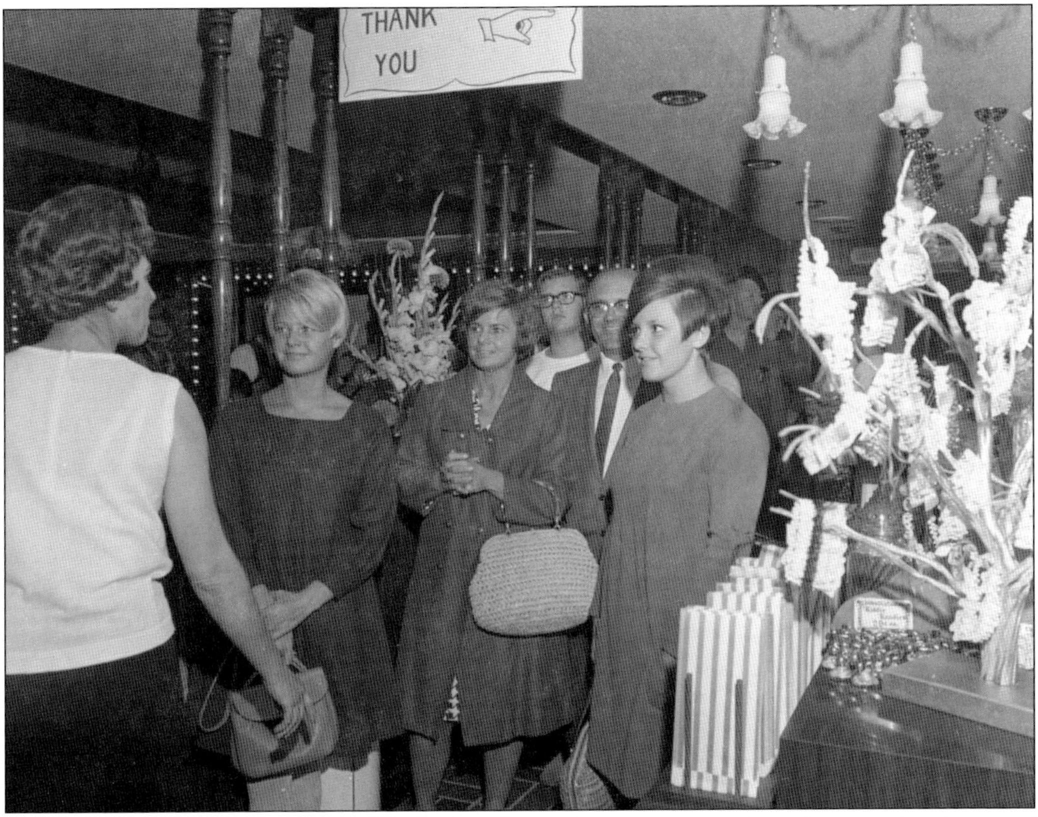

Most new Farrell's locations would have long lines of customers in their first couple of years of operations with Friday and Saturday nights being the busiest. The novelty of Farrell's attracted a lot of interest from guests when each location was opened.

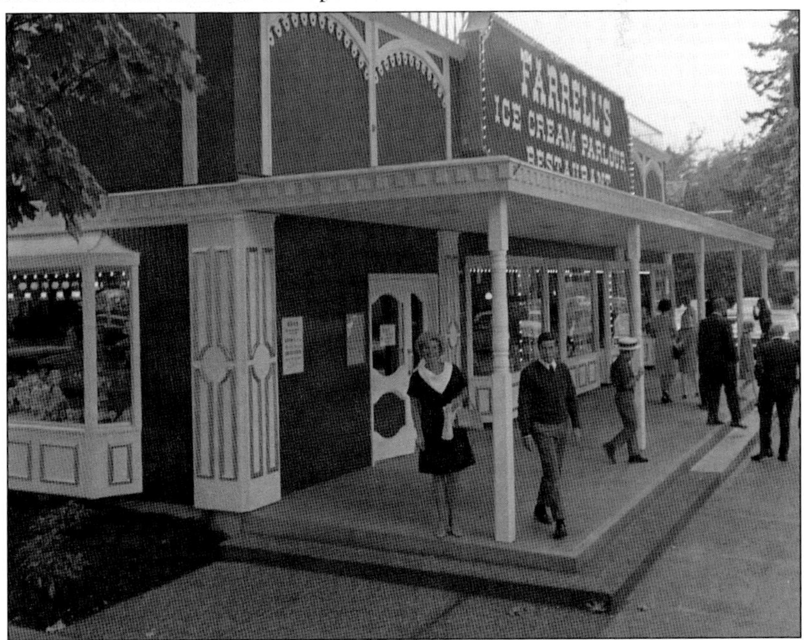

Guests are seen leaving Farrell's after the preopening party. The Eugene location was on a prominent corner of Pearl Street. With the bright red exterior and well-lighted signage, this store was one of the longest-lasting locations in the chain.

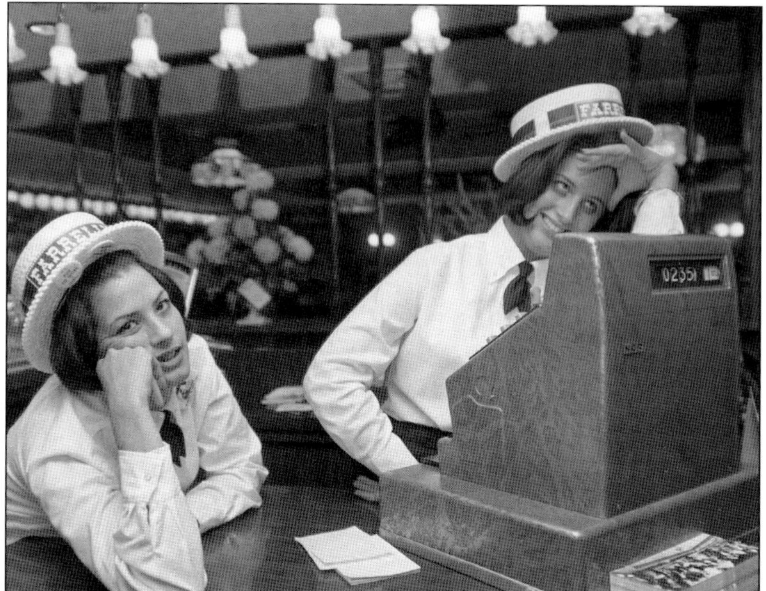

These two cashiers are finally getting a rest after the preopening party. While the sundaes were free to the invited guests, the cashiers were busy with candy sales and tracking the guest checks for the free sundaes.

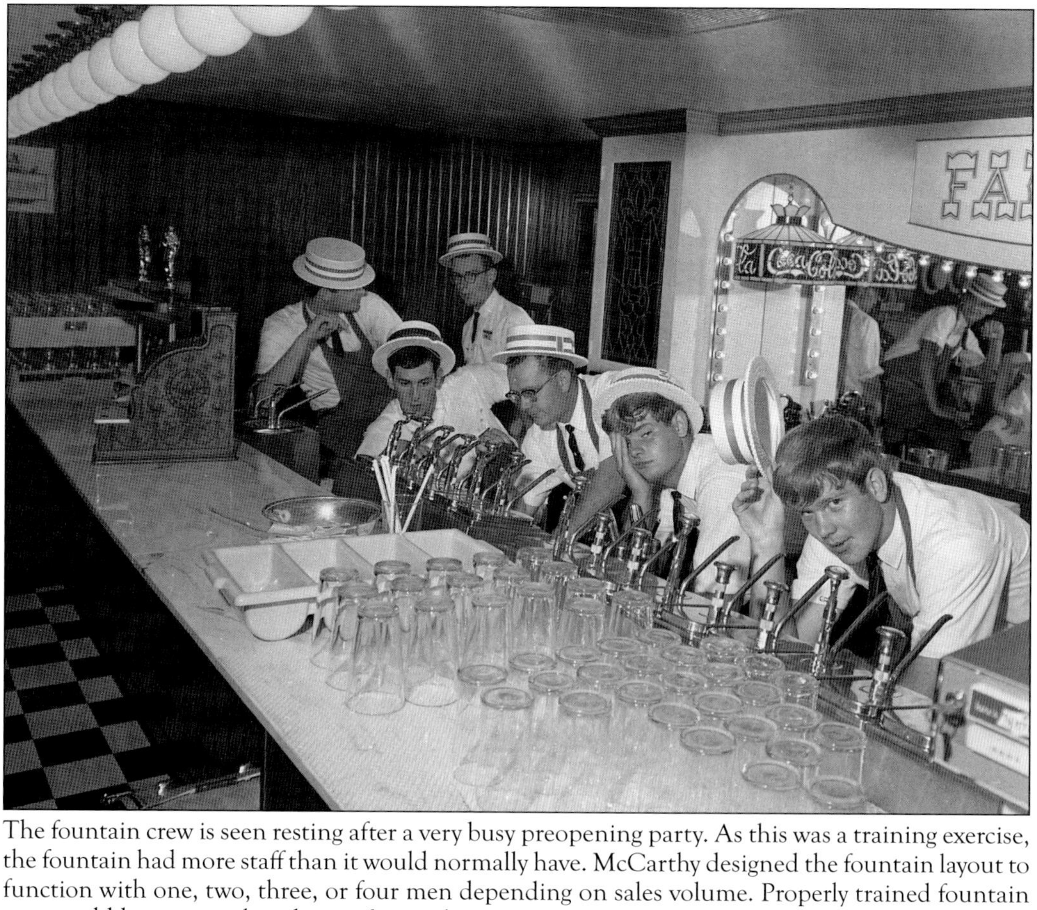

The fountain crew is seen resting after a very busy preopening party. As this was a training exercise, the fountain had more staff than it would normally have. McCarthy designed the fountain layout to function with one, two, three, or four men depending on sales volume. Properly trained fountain men could keep up with orders as fast as they came in.

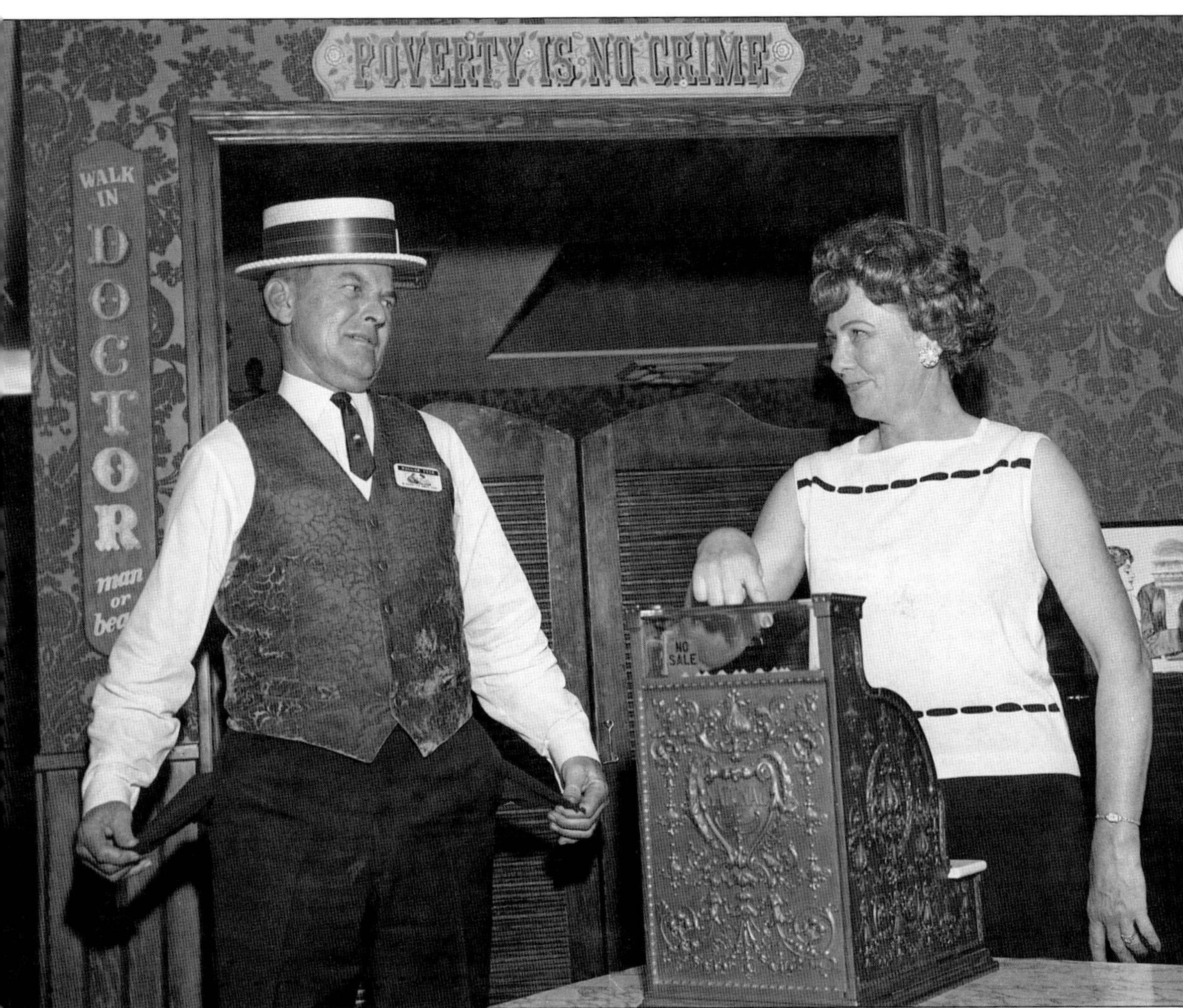

While the franchise owners did not make any money during the preopening party, the experience it provided the staff with was valuable. Further, it served as a promotion for the newly opened restaurant, as the happy guests shared their experiences with others.

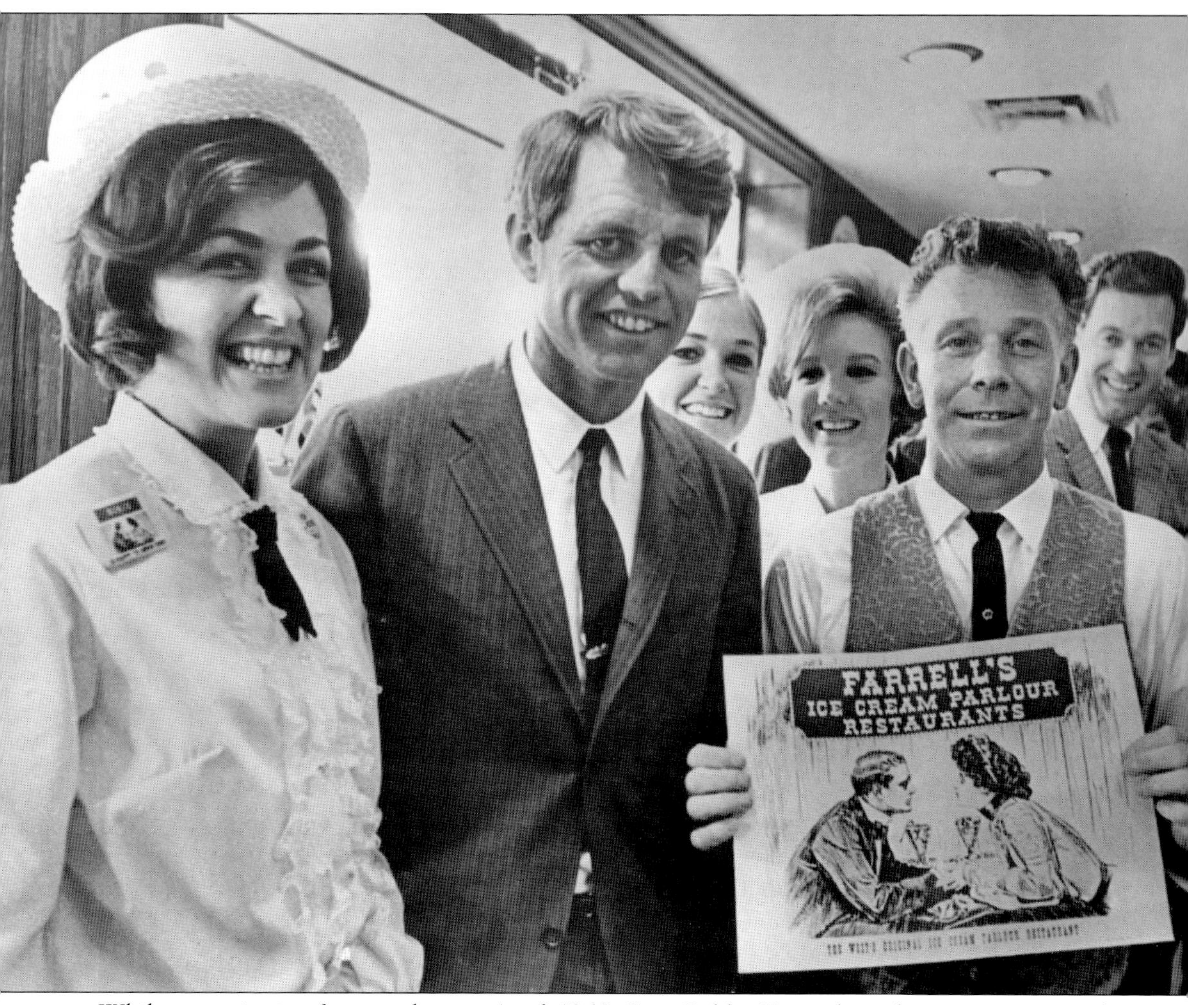

While campaigning for president in April 1968, Sen. Bobby Kennedy is shown stopping at the Eugene Farrell's to ask for votes in the upcoming primary election.

Three

Raleigh Hills

After opening the Eugene store in September 1967, the Farrell's partners returned to the Portland area to open their third company location in November 1967. A new retail center in Raleigh Hills was selected for the new site. This location became the first Farrell's with two dedicated party rooms.

While the chain was growing, in 1967 few landlords were ready to take a risk on a relatively new restaurant concept. Bob Farrell and Ken McCarthy would have to adapt their plans to the space available in buildings owned by willing developers. And with three franchised locations and three corporate locations, it became clearer that the franchise development program required stricter quality controls and training. To be able to franchise the concept, McCarthy believed that there must be frequent visits by corporate staff and extensive oversight.

While preparing for the Raleigh Hills store opening, Bob Farrell would begin working with franchisors in California to expand the concept. Ken McCarthy would spend more time at the Richardson & Holland plant in Seattle to work on developing ice cream toppings and flavorings to use in ice cream production.

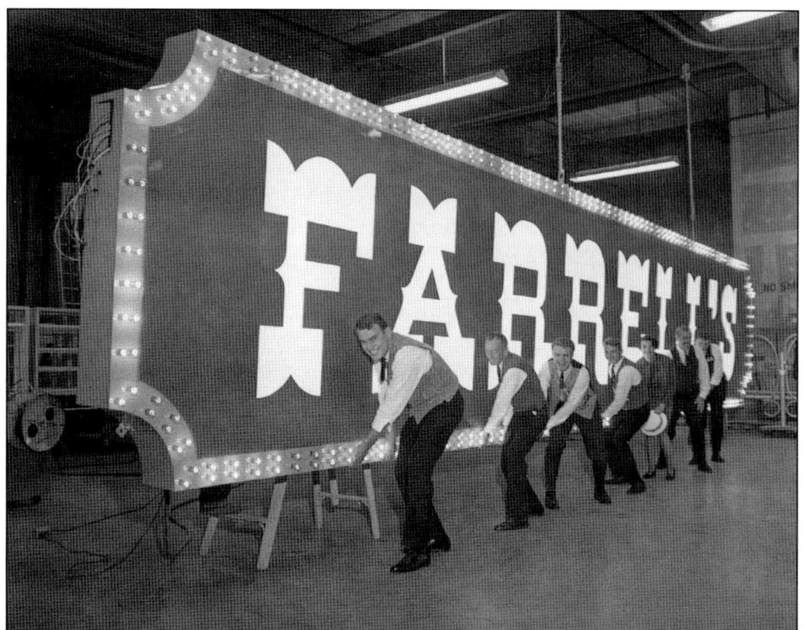

While at the Federal Sign Company in September 1967, Ken McCarthy (second from the left) and Bob Farrell (second from the right), along with their team of managers, are attempting to lift the sign for their next location under construction in Raleigh Hills.

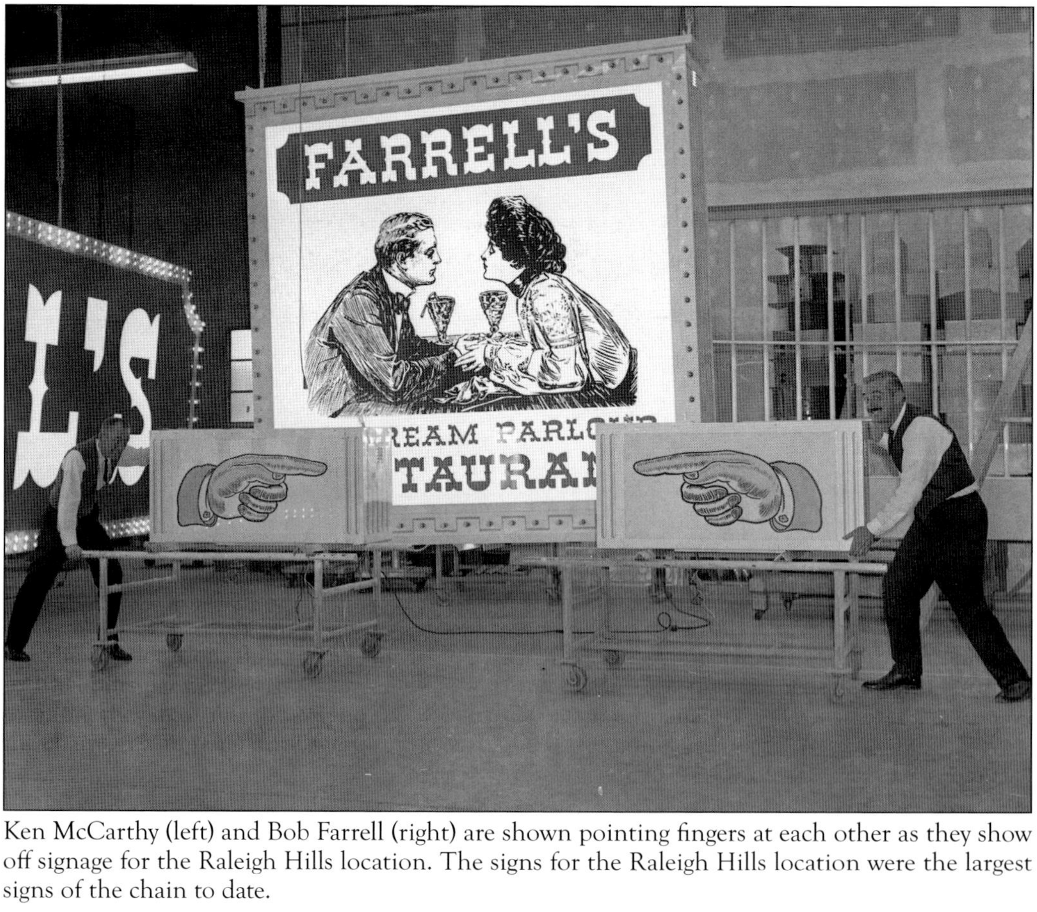

Ken McCarthy (left) and Bob Farrell (right) are shown pointing fingers at each other as they show off signage for the Raleigh Hills location. The signs for the Raleigh Hills location were the largest signs of the chain to date.

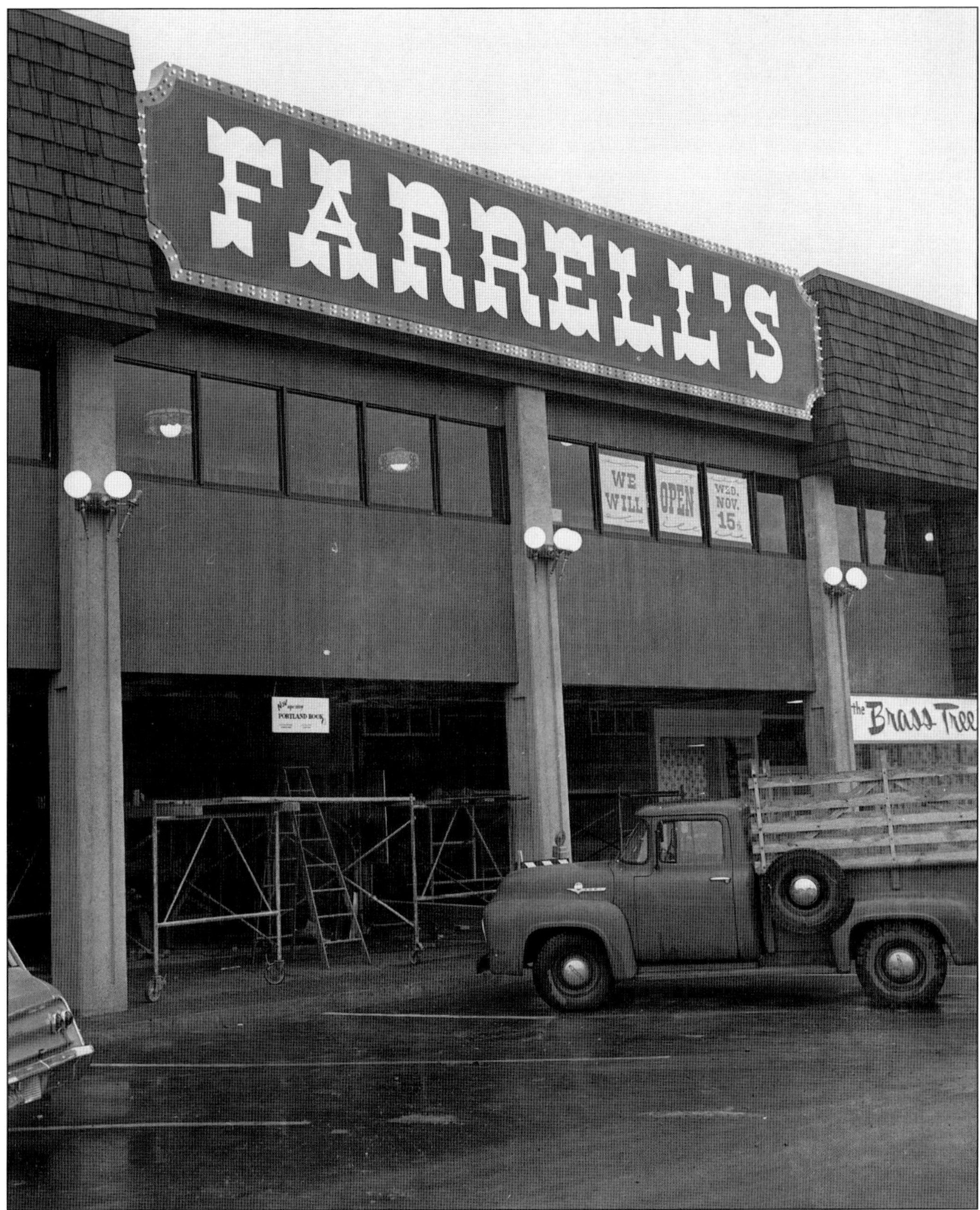

While the construction of the building was still in process, the Farrell's sign was installed a week before the scheduled opening. With the success of the original Farrell's at Twenty-first Avenue and Burnside Street as well as the Halsey store, Raleigh Hills would be bigger than the earlier locations.

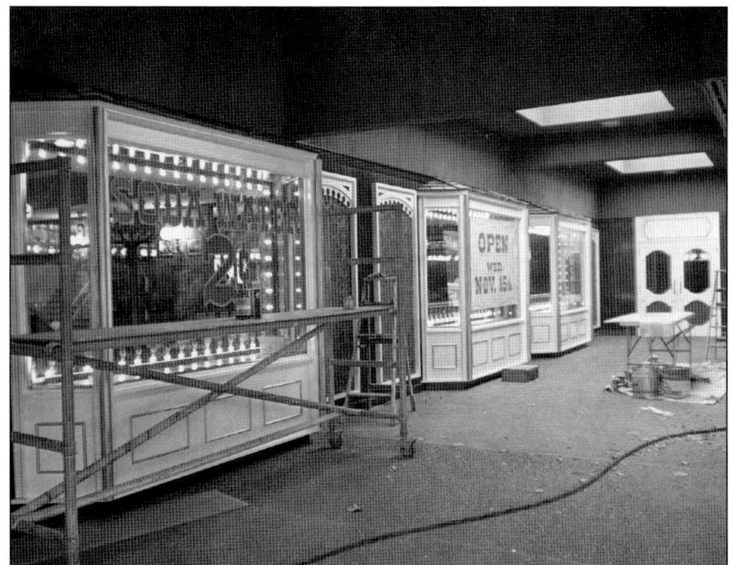

The interior hallway of the Raleigh Hills location is shown while construction is nearly completed. Unlike the two prior Portland locations, this building had an enclosed entrance hallway for some of the stores. Design elements of this location would become more common when Farrell's expanded to enclosed malls in the 1970s.

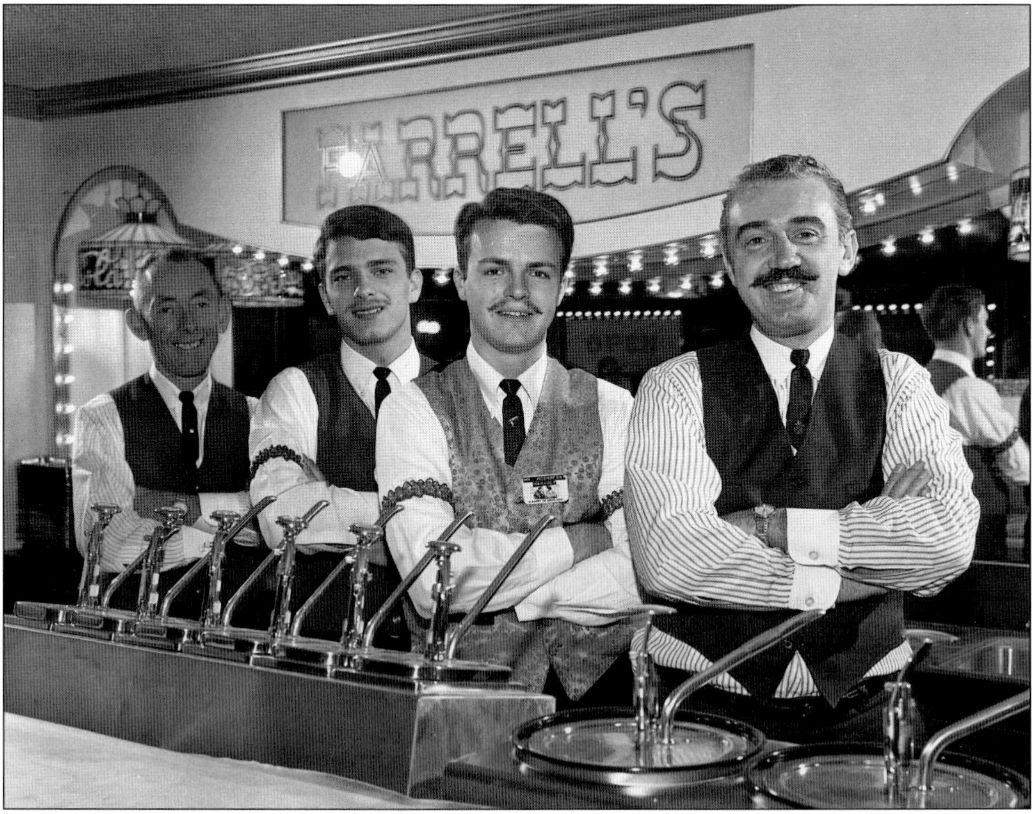

Ken McCarthy (left) and Bob Farrell (right) are seen posing with two of their managers, Gary Morgan (center left) and Wayne Hagoes (center right), in the fountain of the Raleigh Hills store. As a popular and expanding chain, Farrell's began to attract young talent in the restaurant industry. Many of the early managers rose to become regional managers for Farrell's, and some would go on to create their own restaurant concepts.

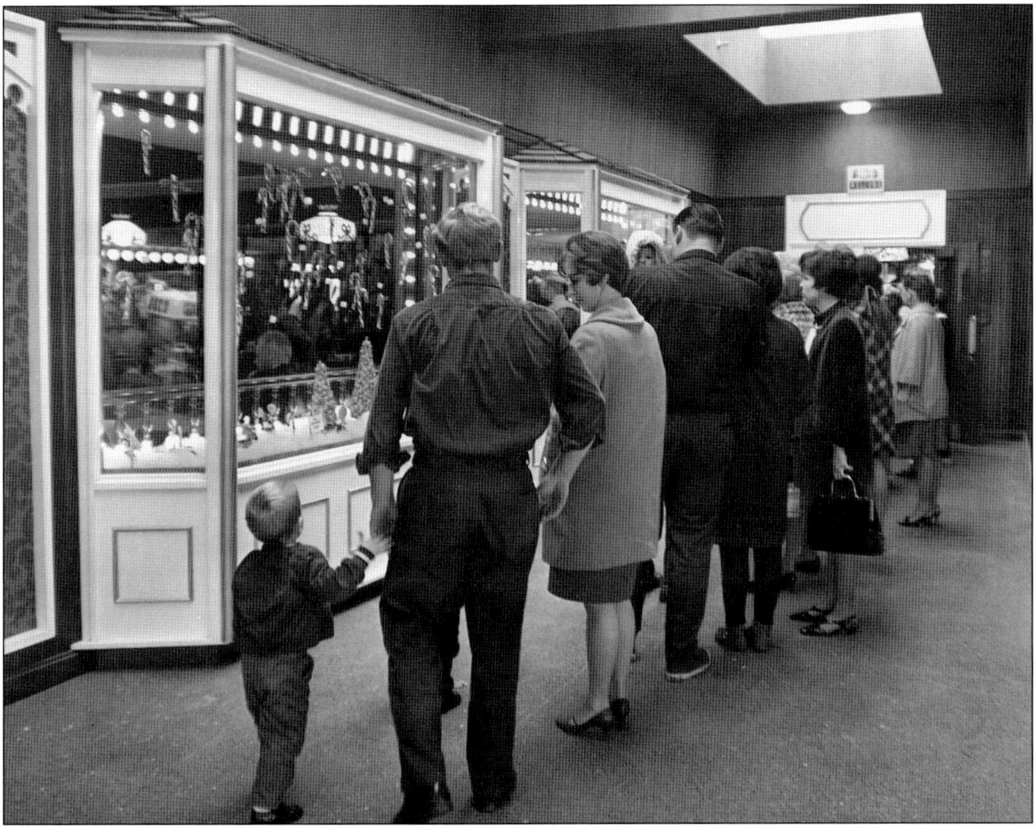

The private preopening party on November 12, 1967, at the Raleigh Hills location attracted a long line of customers. This location was at 4955 Southwest Seventy-sixth Street in Raleigh Hills, Oregon.

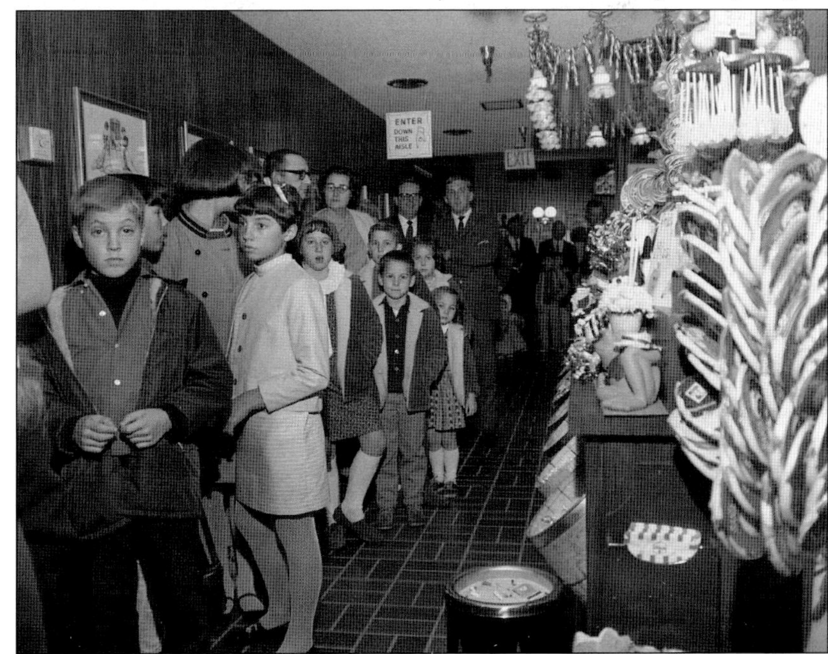

The long line from outside the store continued inside. With access to this location through an indoor hallway, guests were not exposed to the weather while waiting.

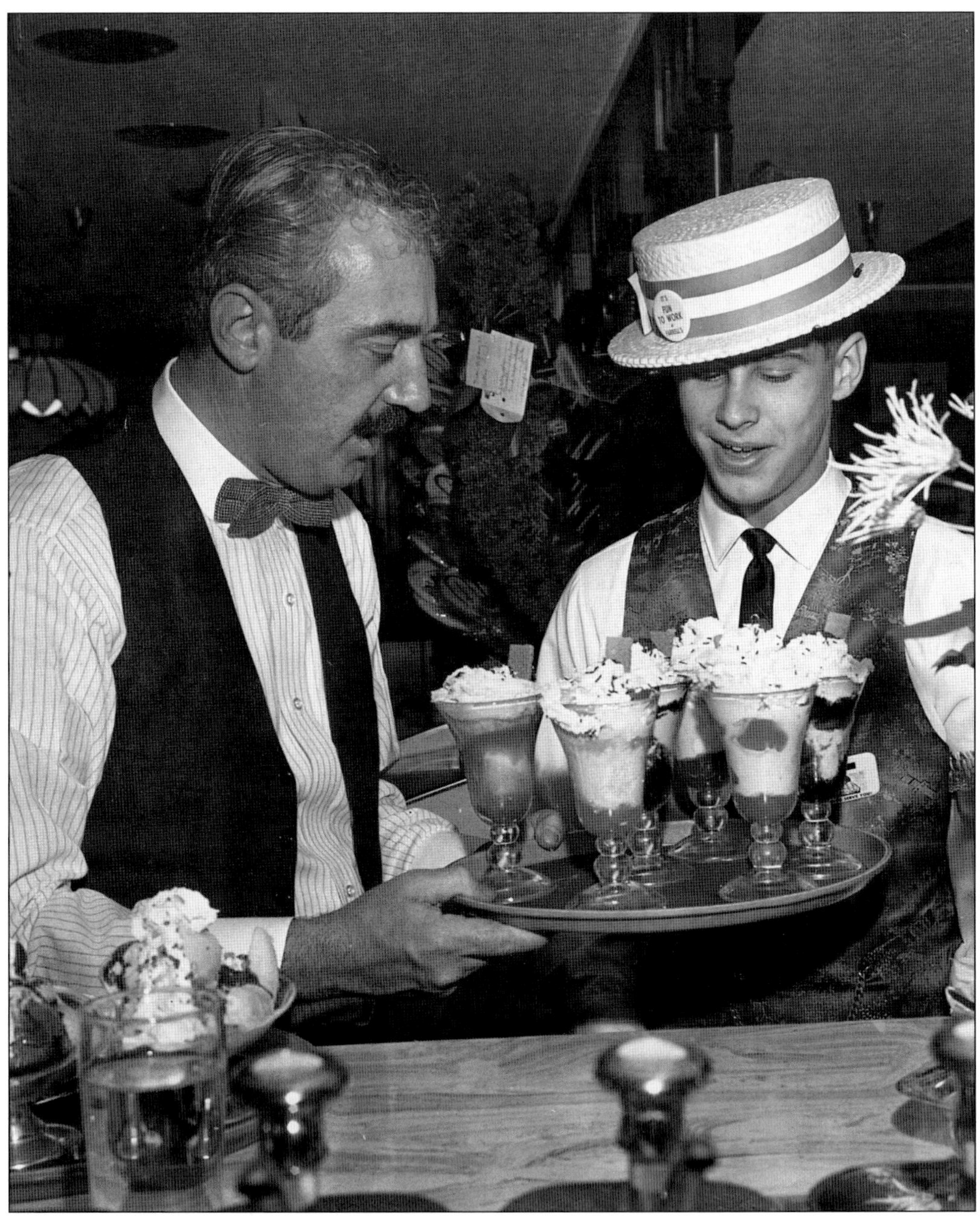

Bob Farrell is seen showing a new waiter how to properly handle a tray full of ice cream sundaes. A waiter must know the order in which he will be serving the sundaes to know how to tray them up. Further, he must know what sundaes he will take off the tray first to avoid having a tray full of sundaes spill onto guests.

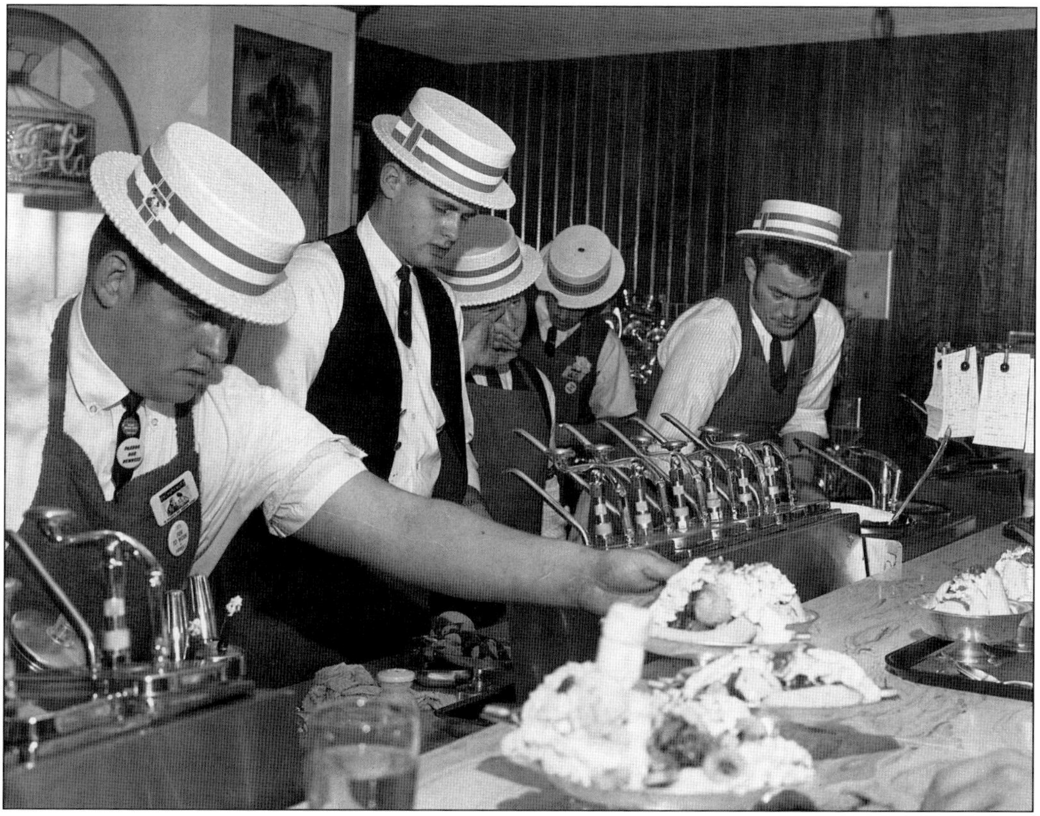

A group of fountain men are working on sundae orders as part of their training. Ken McCarthy's fountain design resulted in up to four stations, creating an efficient assembly process. The first station was the scooper. He would read the tickets and scoop the sundaes. The second station was the topper. He would get the dishes ready for the scooper and pump toppings on the scooped ice cream. The third station was the whipper. He would put bananas on the sundaes and add the whipped cream, nuts, and cherries. He would also coordinate the drinks and call the waiters or waitresses. At the fourth station was the drink man. He would prepare the ice cream sodas and the shakes as well as assist in Zoos and Pike Peaks.

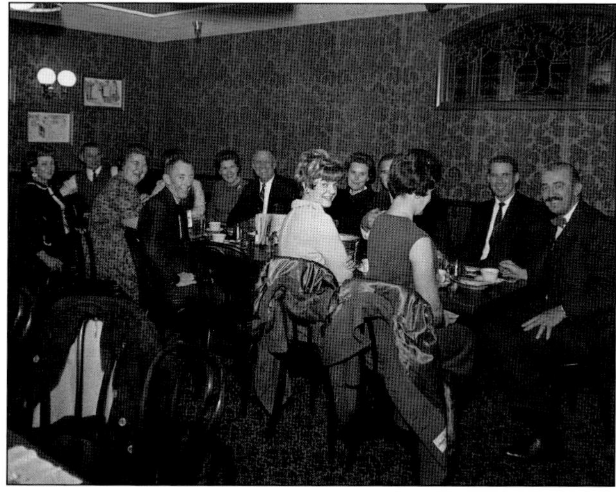

Ken McCarthy (fourth from left) and Bob Farrell (right) are enjoying some opening-day downtime with a group of local business leaders. With more managers involved in the training of new store staff, Farrell and McCarthy did not have to be as involved in the training process for the Raleigh Hills location.

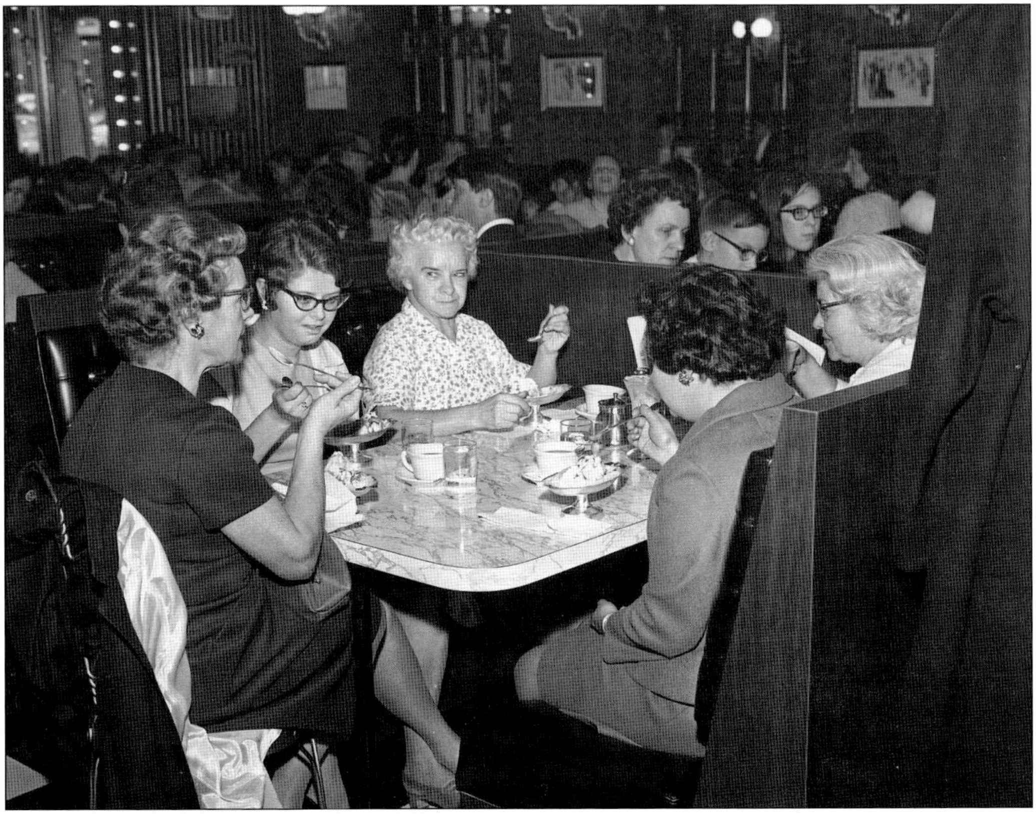

With the Farrell's chain growing, Ken McCarthy found himself working more to develop the training team and protocols for new location openings. McCarthy put together 300 slides to be used for training new employees. Later, Bob Farrell had those slides converted to short films that could be distributed to new locations for training.

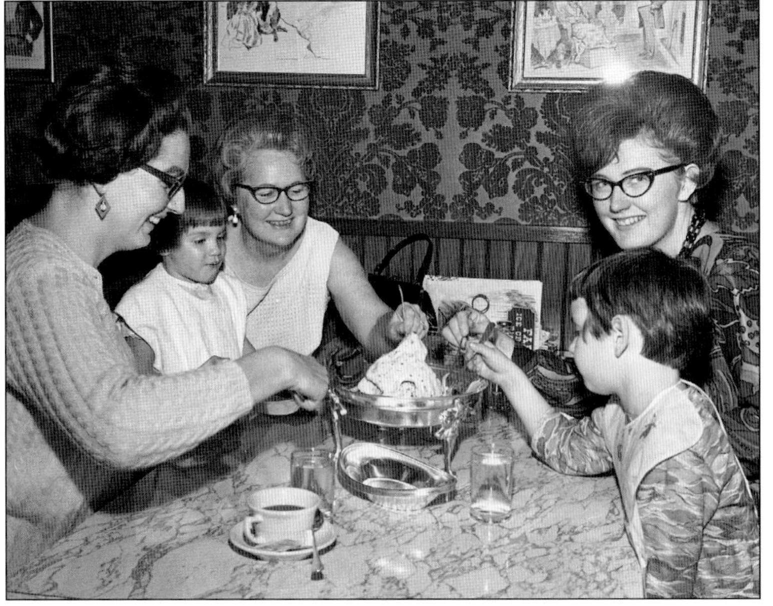

A family is seen digging into a Mount Hood sundae. This sundae was a mountain of five flavors of ice cream topped with hot fudge and marshmallow toppings, whipped cream, bananas, nuts, and strawberries and was served in a special pedestal dish.

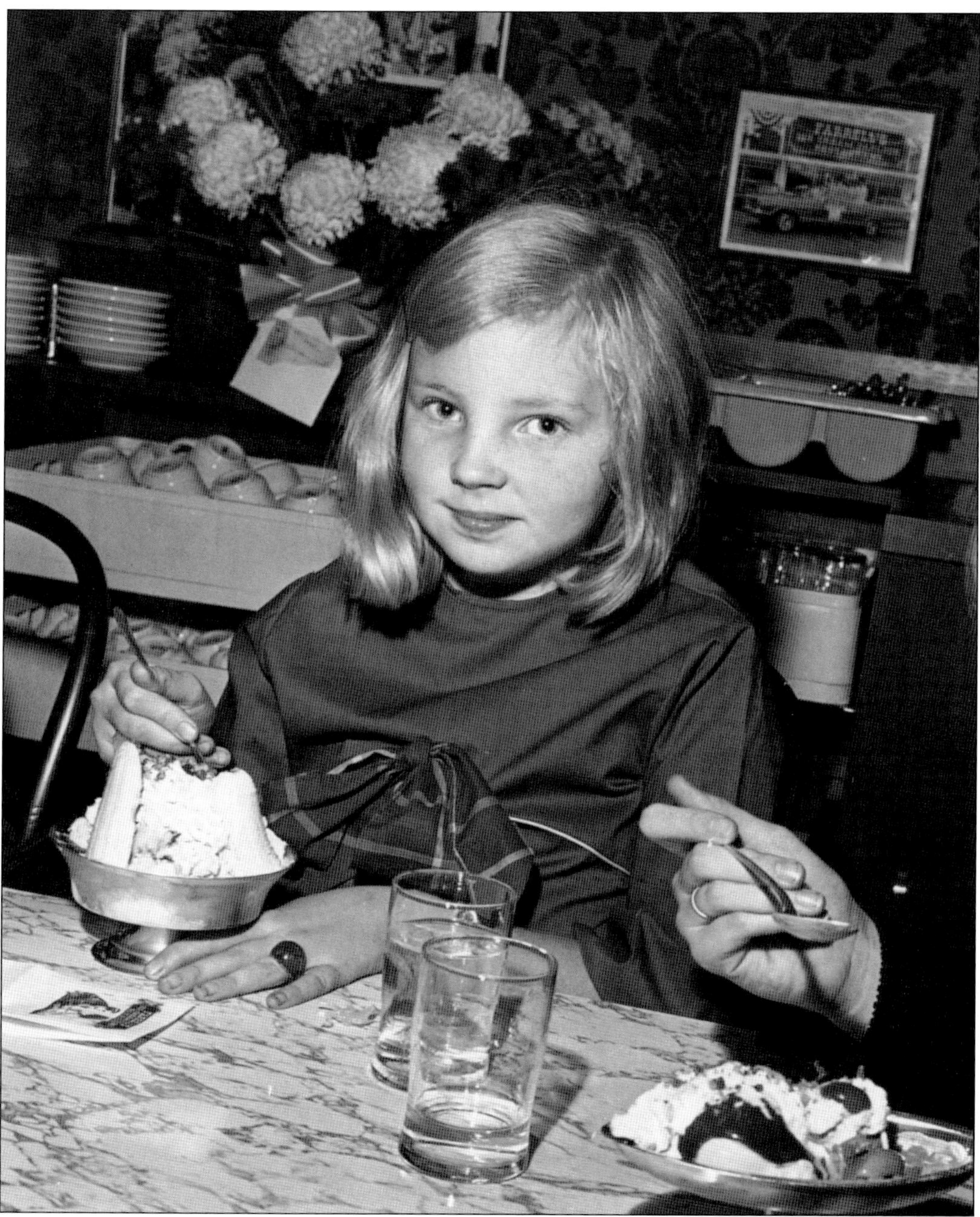

A young customer is shown enjoying her Kathy's Pink Surprise sundae. This sundae was named after one of Bob Farrell's daughters and was made with vanilla ice cream, bananas, and strawberry topping. Two other sundaes were named after Farrell's daughters: Colleen's Salute and Kristie's Delight. A fourth sundae called Sharon's Dish was named after Ken McCarthy's daughter. Collectively, these sundaes were known as "the girl dishes."

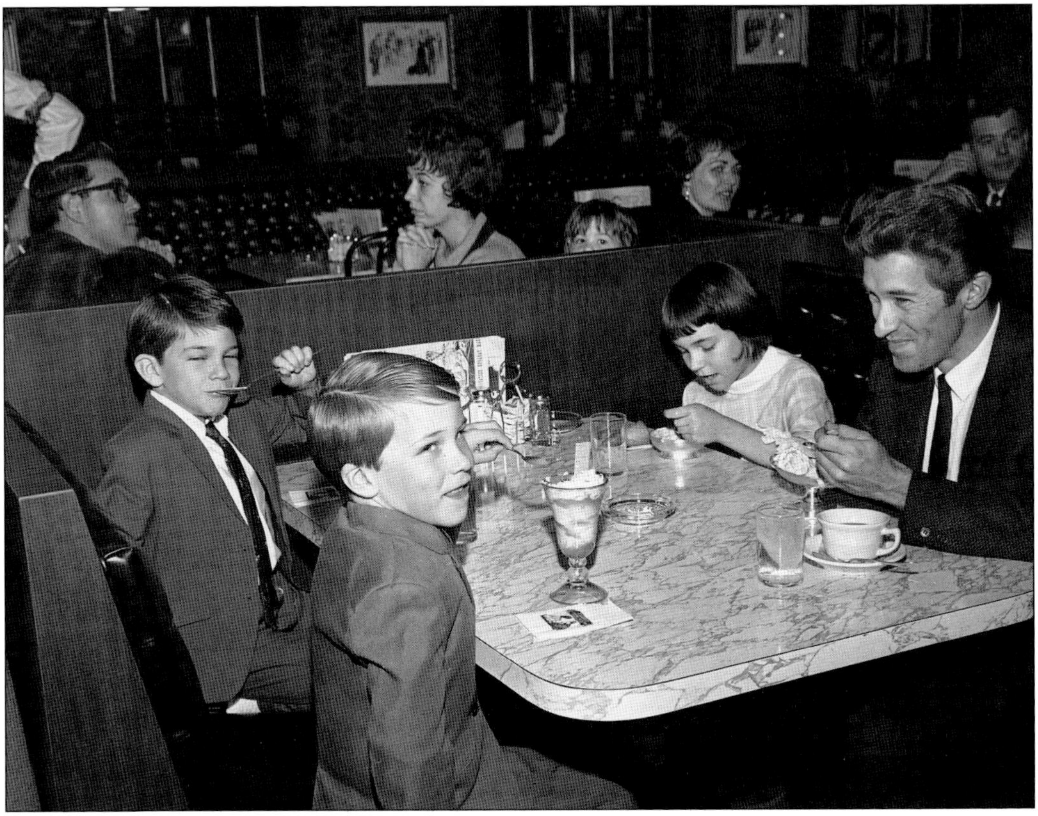

By the opening of the Raleigh Hills location, Ken McCarthy had developed proprietary ice cream formulas. When a new store location was identified, McCarthy would contact local dairies to find one that could produce the ice cream in the necessary quantities. To help decide which dairy produced the best ice cream, a scooping contest would be set up to determine which ice cream yielded the most scoops.

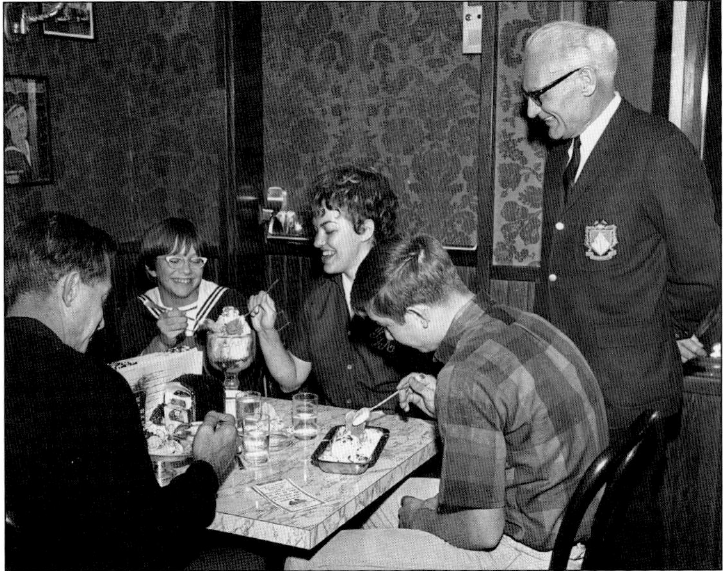

A Two on A Blanket sundae was a scoop of vanilla ice cream topped with hot fudge topping and a scoop of chocolate ice cream topped with marshmallow topping on two slices of pound cake. It was served in the same dish as the Trough, which later became known as the Pig's Trough.

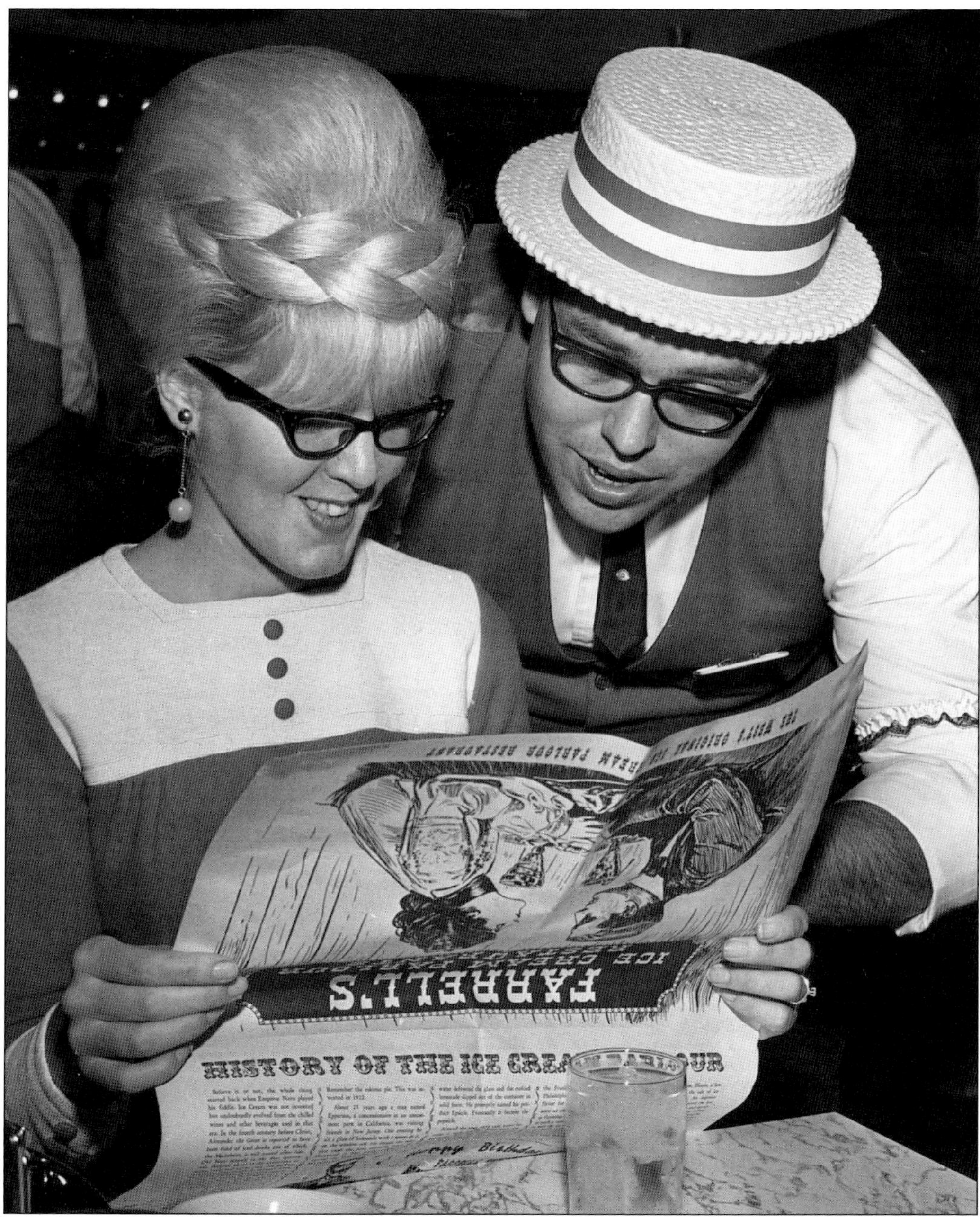

Farrell's became known for its newsprint-style menus, which were meant to be taken by guests. A new location would go through 50,000 or more in the first year of operation, as guests would take them when leaving. The menus became some of the best marketing for Farrell's.

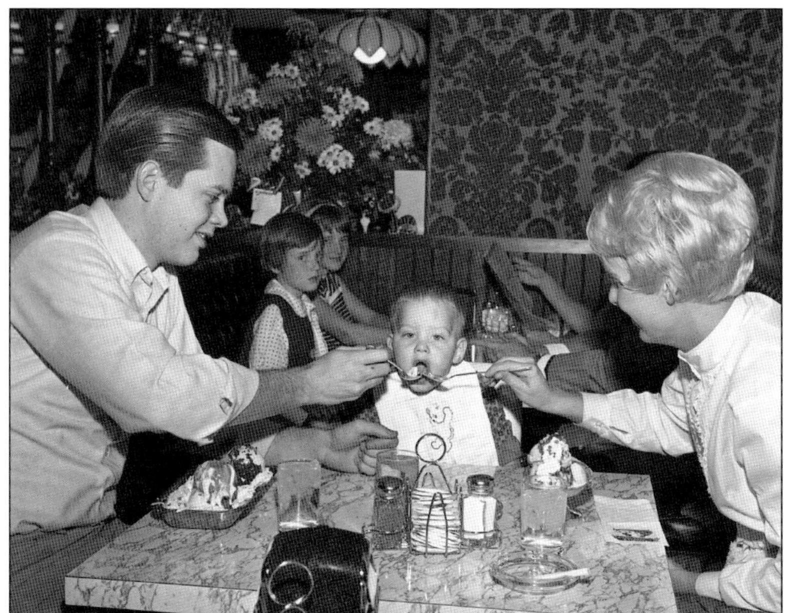

With a variety of different sundaes, sharing became a tradition at Farrell's. Sometimes, there was no need to order an ice cream treat for a little boy if the parents were willing to share their sundaes.

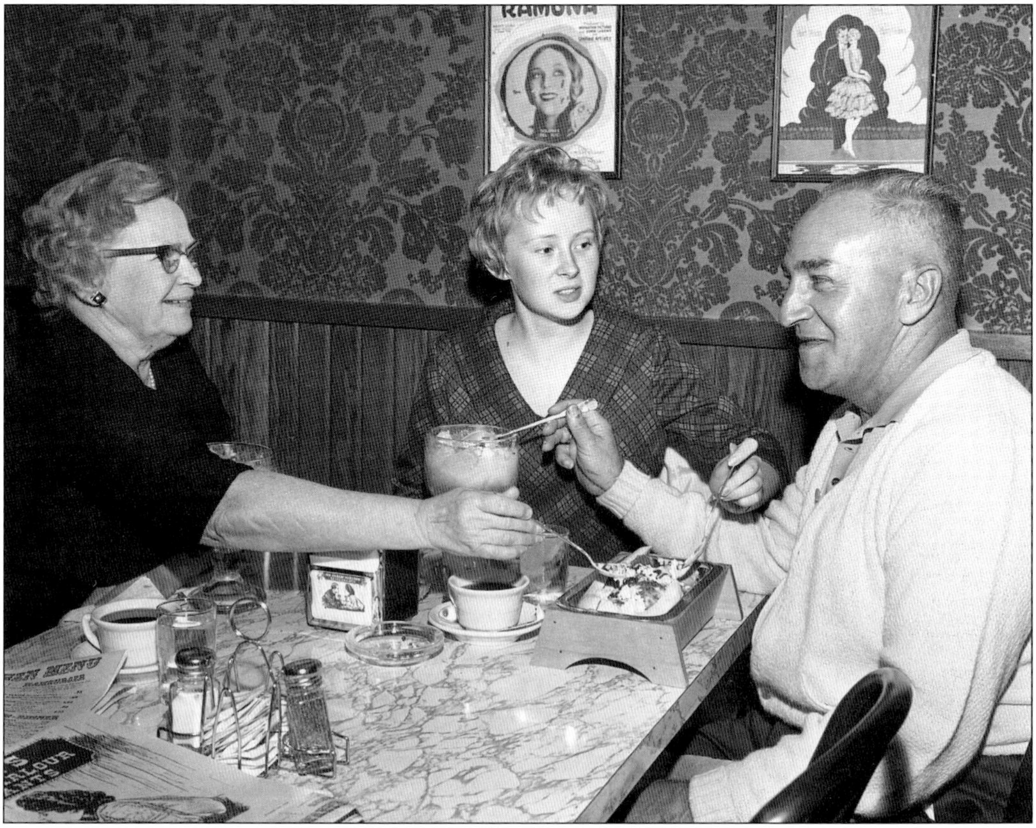

One of Farrell's best-known sundaes was the Pig's Trough, served up in a wooden trough. Originally called the Trough, it became one of the signature sundaes for Farrell's. A guest would receive a ribbon if they ate the sundae by themselves.

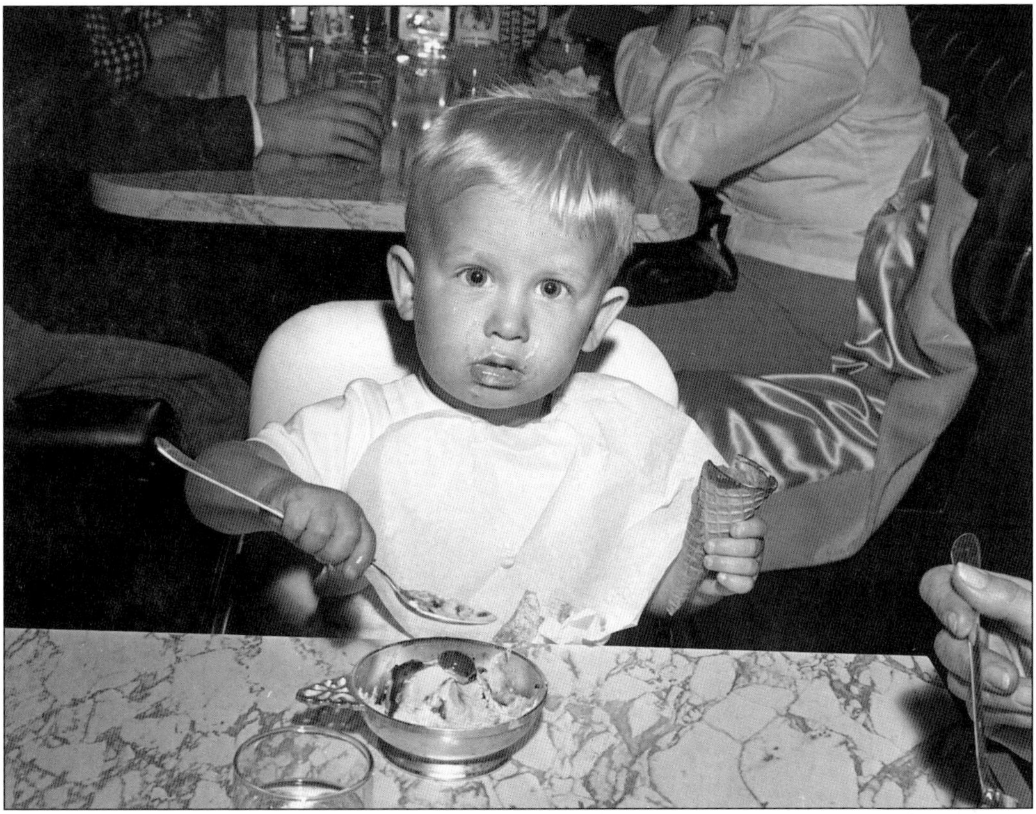

The Clown sundae became a favorite for young children at Farrell's: one scoop of vanilla ice cream topped with chocolate or strawberry topping, whipped cream for clown hair, a half cherry for a nose, and a sugar cone for the clown hat.

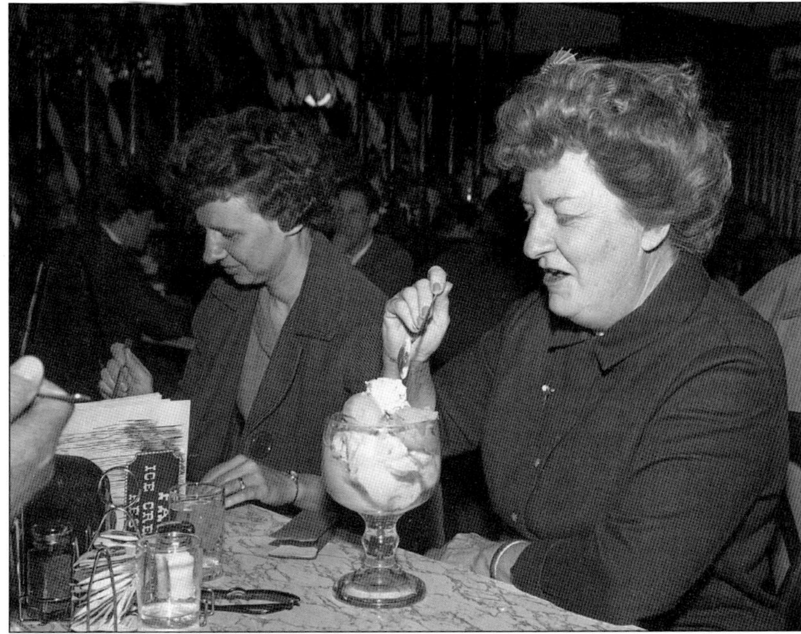

A guest enjoys the Gibson Girl: a six-scoop sundae made with vanilla ice cream, sherbet, and sweet syrups. The Food Network later featured this sundae as one of the best ice cream dishes.

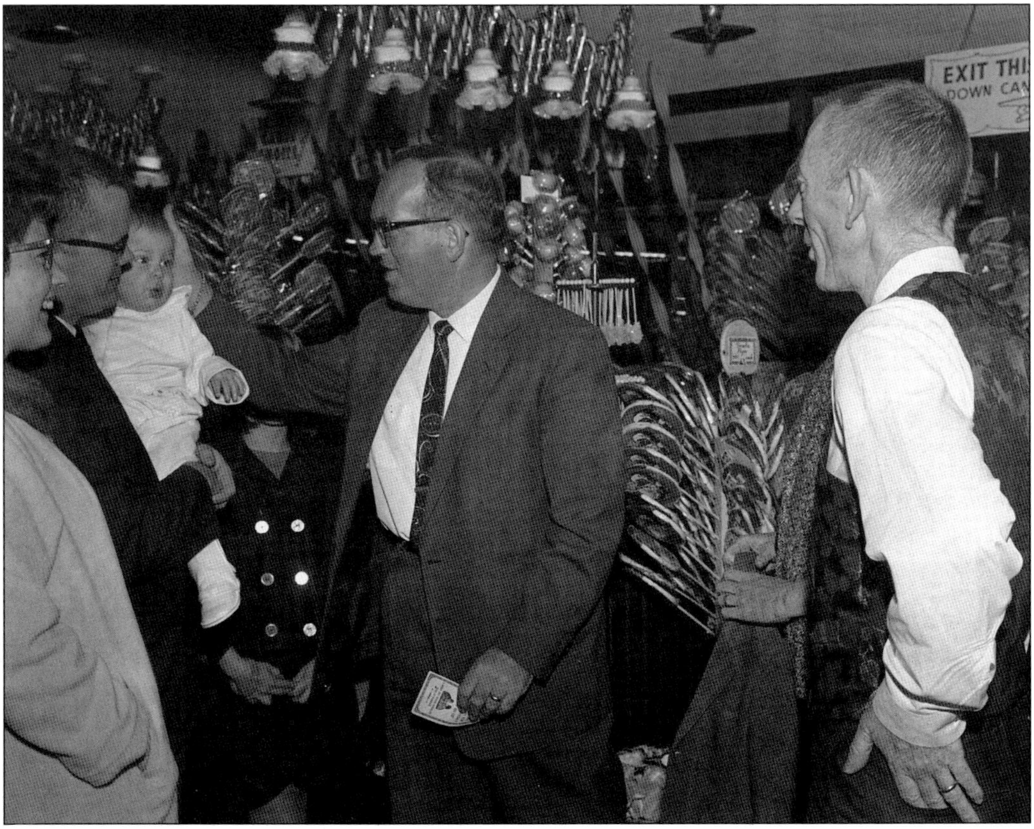

Ken McCarthy (right) is seen talking with invited guests at the preopening party. While Farrell's was better known by the time the Raleigh Hills location opened, the preopening party was still held to train the staff. Most locations hired more employees than needed, knowing that not all employees would make the cut after a couple of weeks of operations.

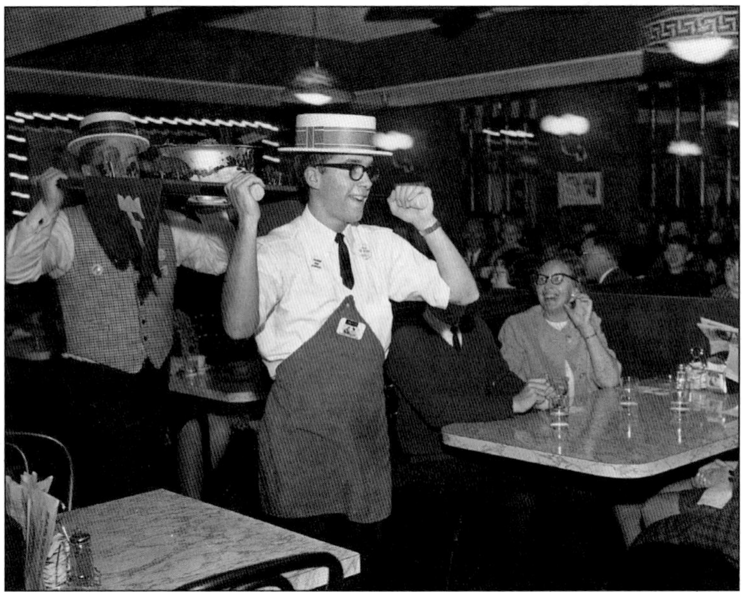

Two employees are shown running the Portland Zoo sundae to a table. The Zoo run was accompanied by the sound of a siren and the clanging of a bell from the fountain. The employees often ran the Zoo around the location a few times before delivering it to the destination.

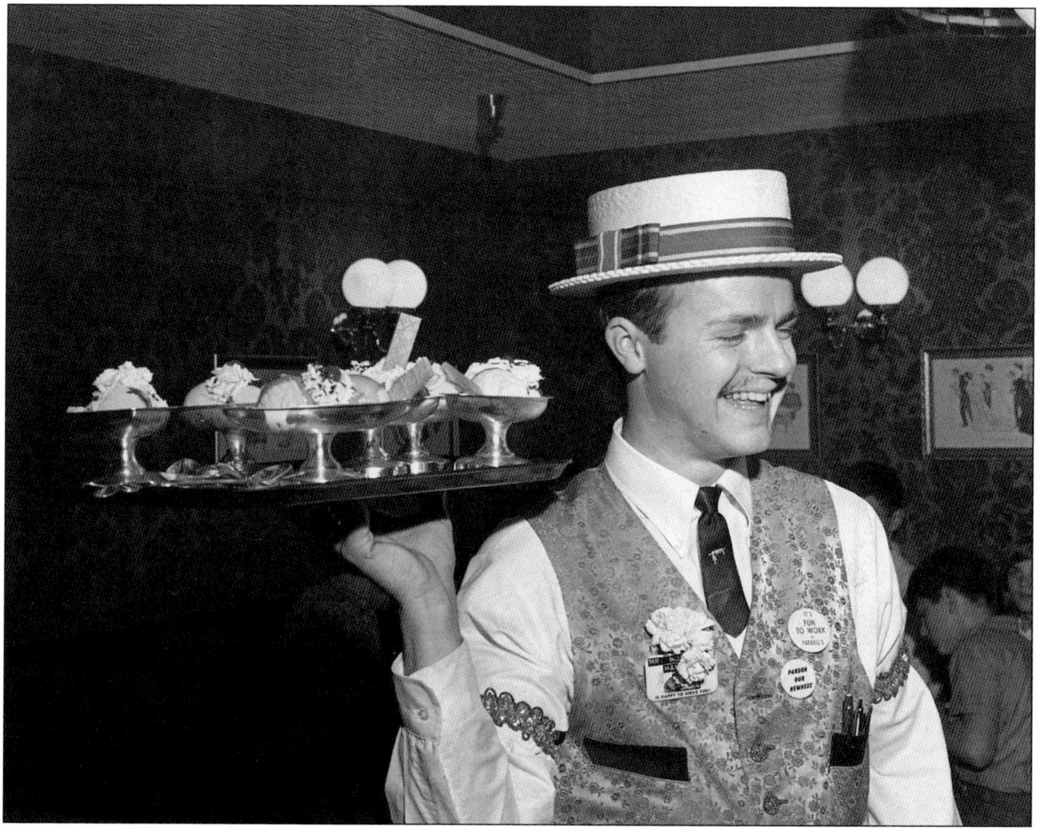

One of the new managers is seen delivering a tray of sundaes to waiting customers. The management training program at Farrell's required new managers to become proficient in all jobs.

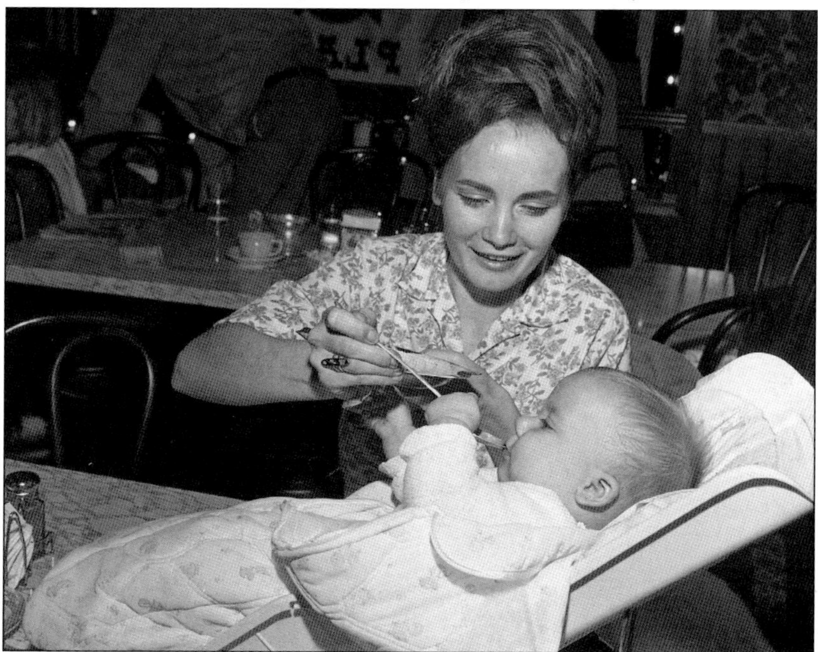

Even the youngest guests get to enjoy ice cream at the opening of a Farrell's. Here, a mother shares her ice cream with her young baby.

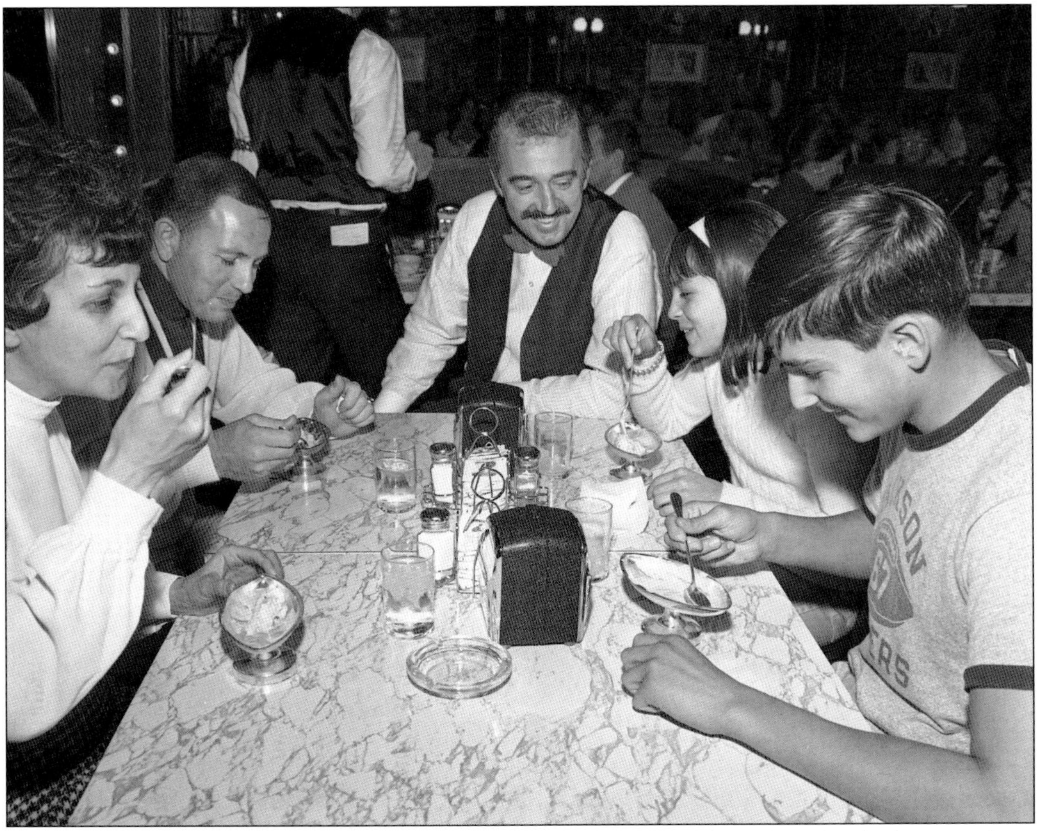

Bob Farrell (center) is shown taking the time to visit with a family as they finish their sundaes. During the early years of Farrell's, Farrell was often away from home for long stretches and did not get to see much of his own family. He made up for that later in his life, spending more time with his kids and grandkids.

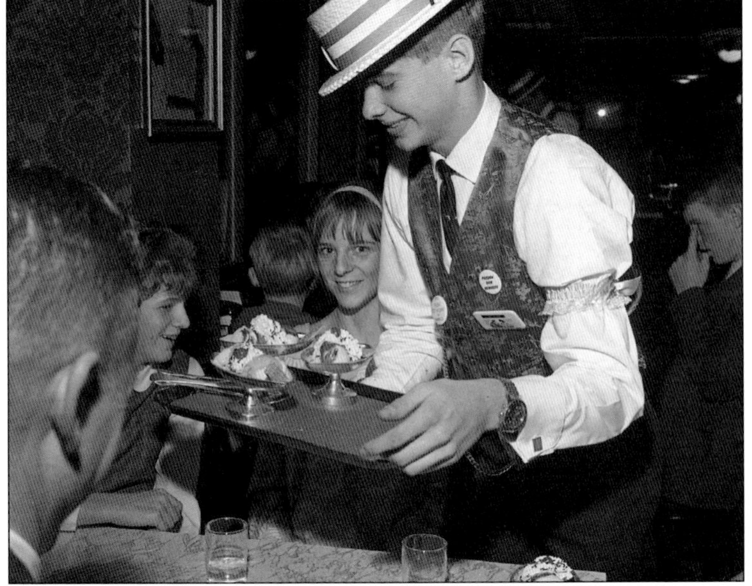

A young waiter is seen learning how to deliver sundaes to a table of customers. When Farrell's would open a new location, other restaurateurs would compliment them on the training program. During these years, a newly opened Farrell's was as efficient as a location that had been open for a couple of years.

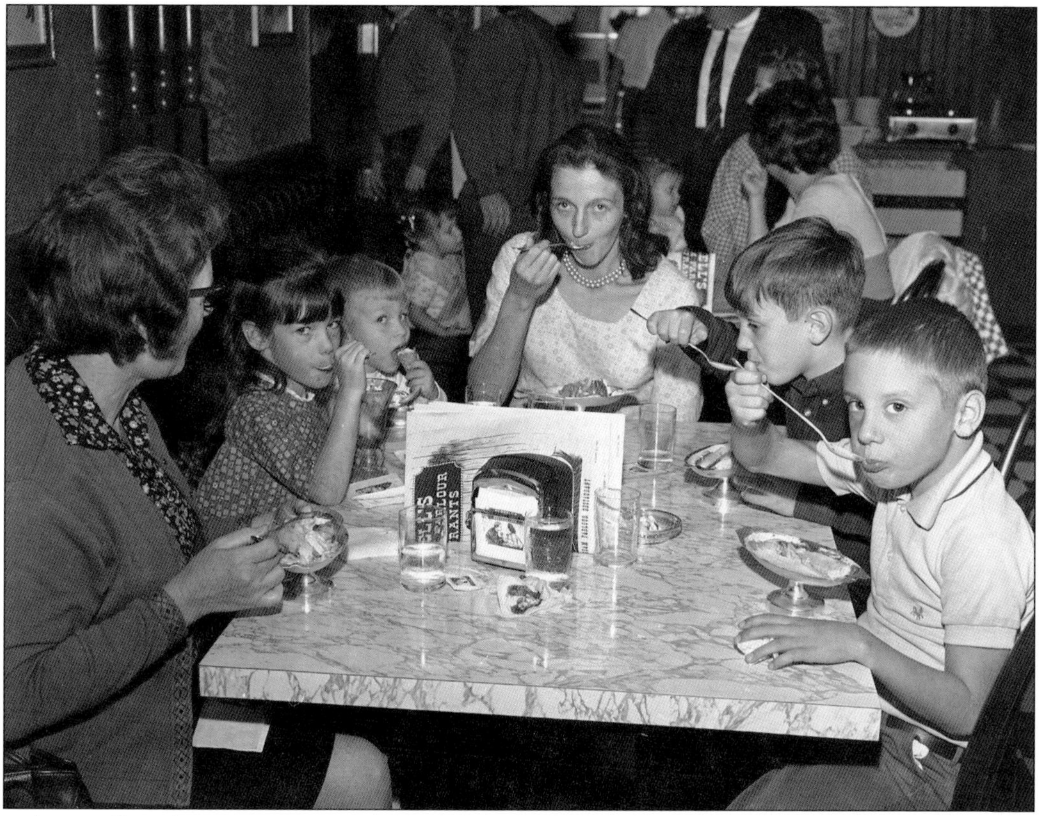

Bob Farrell and Ken McCarthy intended Farrell's to be a nonalcoholic nightclub. Their plan for Farrell's was to create a family-friendly atmosphere for children of all ages. Many guests who were children in the 1960s returned to Farrell's in the 1970s as teenagers and still enjoyed the Farrell's experience.

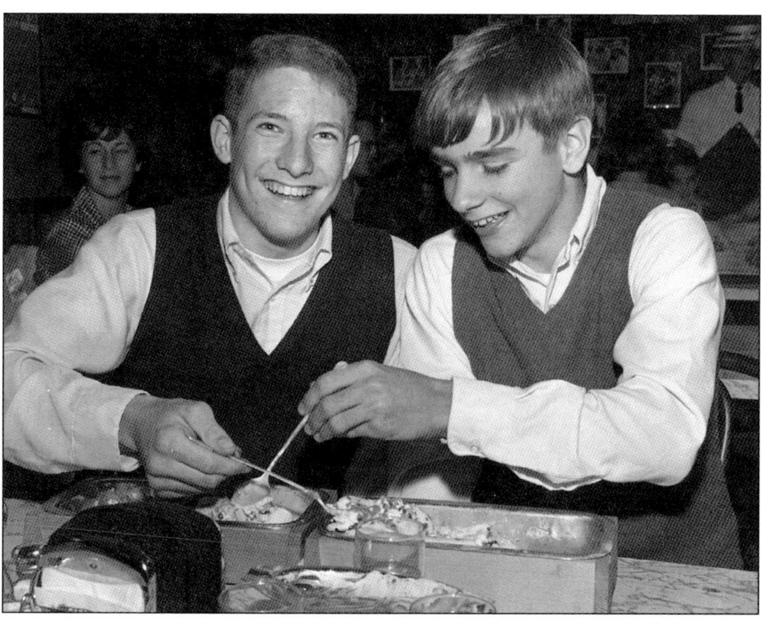

Farrell's became popular with teenagers. Bob Farrell and Ken McCarthy believed that a wholesome, family-friendly restaurant would create a good environment for teenage customers. Farrell's often became the place to go to after high school dances and other functions.

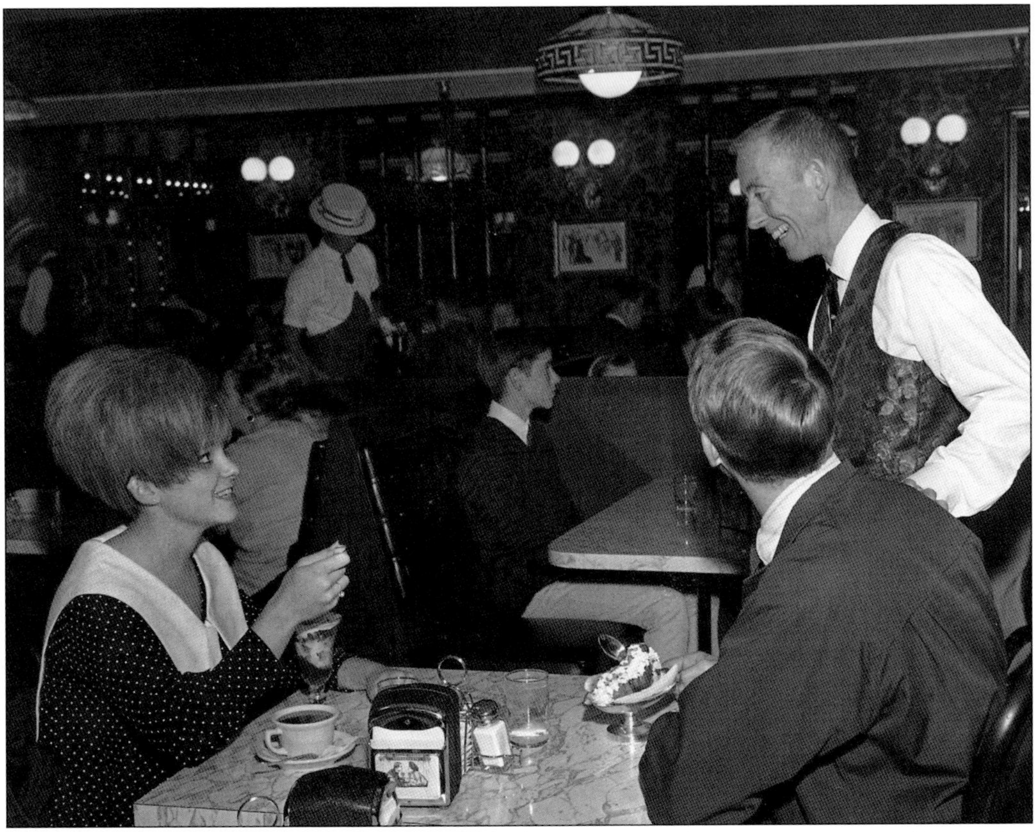

Ken McCarthy (standing right) is seen visiting with customers at the preopening party. For the first location, McCarthy would spend most of his time training the fountain men. As the chain grew, he was able to rely on his fountain training staff to handle this function so he could spend more time talking with the guests. McCarthy believed the systems he created and the training program he developed were key in turning Farrell's into a profitable company.

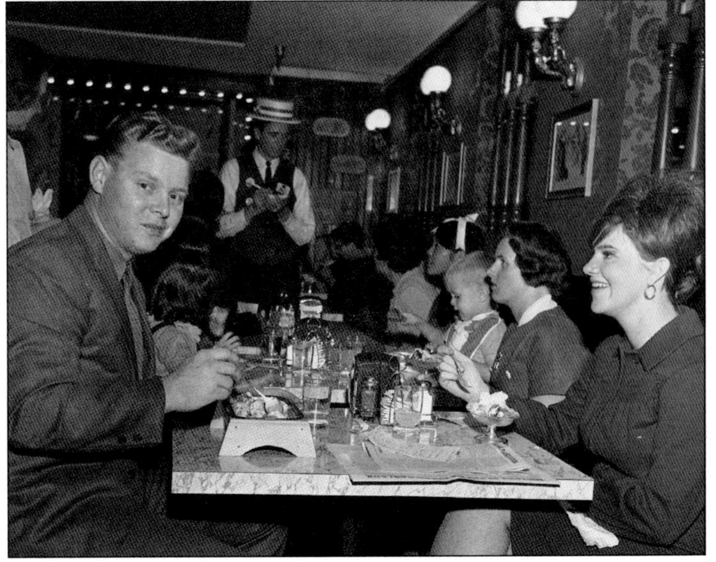

As they opened new locations, Bob Farrell and Ken McCarthy learned to have table sizes that could be moved around based on customer needs. This section was made up of two-top tables that could be pushed together for a larger group or separated for two customers.

A young customer enjoys his two-scoop sundae. As Farrell's became known as a place to celebrate birthdays, this sundae was given away as the free sundae for one's birthday. When Marriott took ownership of Farrell's in 1972, it reduced the size of the birthday sundae to one scoop to save money.

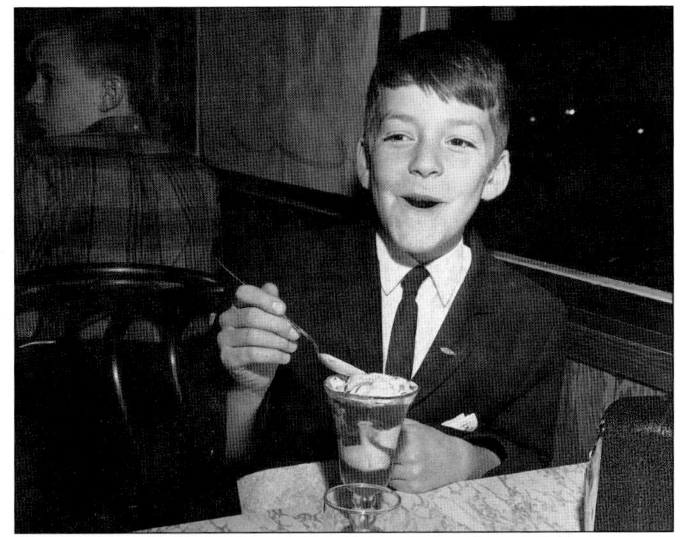

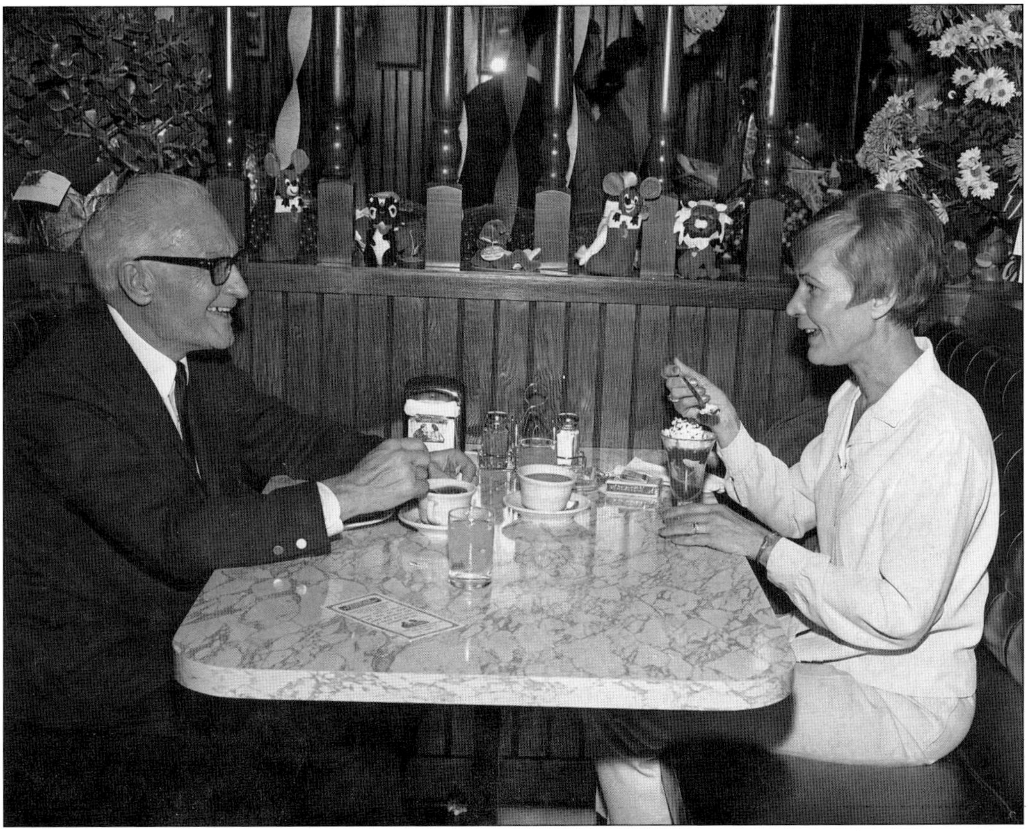

Farrell's partner and accountant Dale Belford (left) is seen enjoying a sundae with his wife, Audrey (right). Dale was responsible for putting Farrell's on a smooth financial track and making it possible to franchise the concept. As the franchise program grew, Farrell's provided accounting services for each location. These functions were originally provided out of Dale's accounting firm offices. When Farrell's outgrew its offices, it would rent space in the newly constructed Farley building in Portland, Oregon.

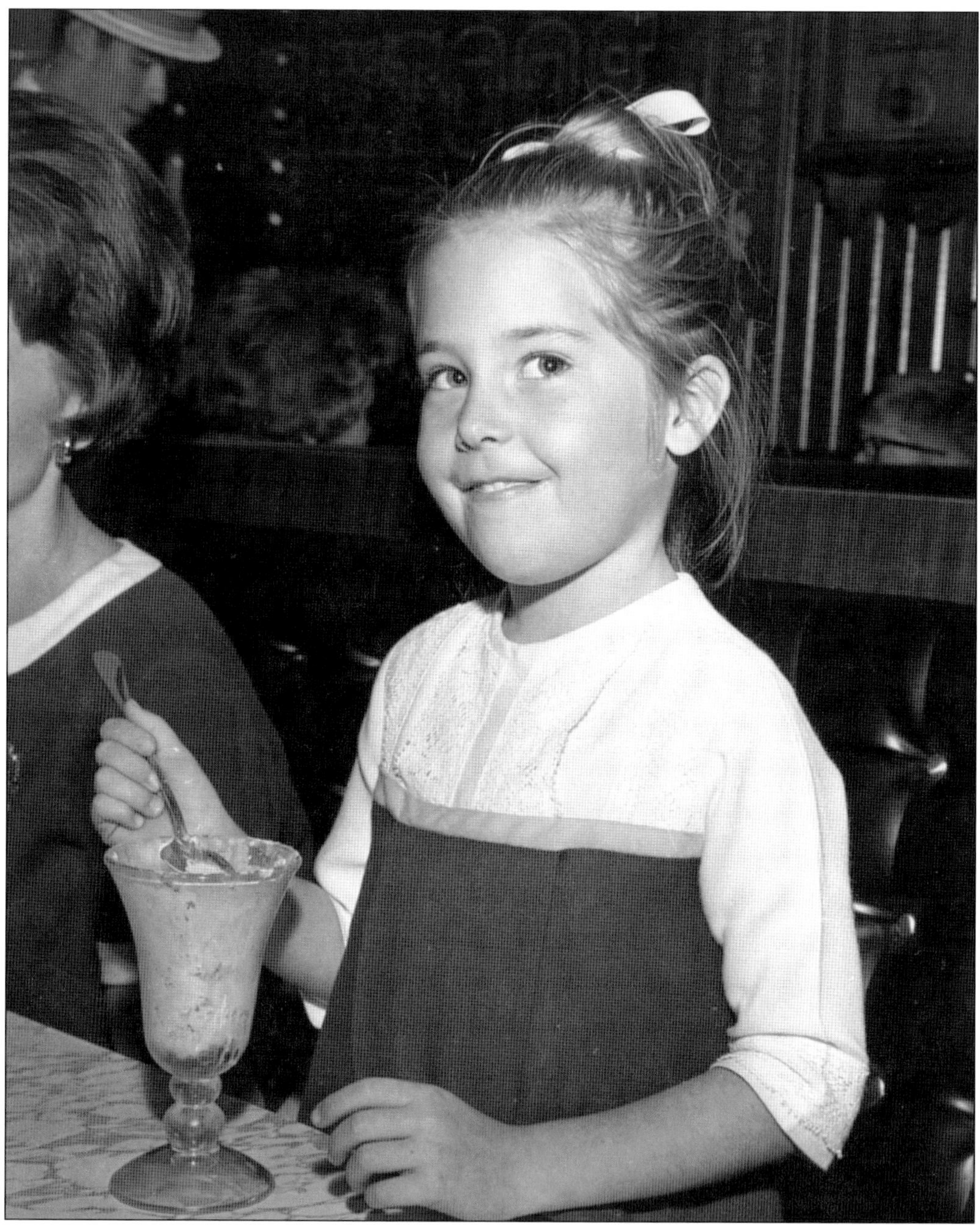

While soft serve was becoming popular in the 1960s, Bob Farrell and Ken McCarthy believed there was still a customer base for traditional ice cream sundaes served with hard-packed ice cream. Farrell's became an early entrant into the superpremium ice cream industry by first serving Carnation ice cream and then with its own proprietary formulas. By the time Marriott took ownership of Farrell's in 1972, the quality was reduced to supermarket quality with a lower butterfat content.

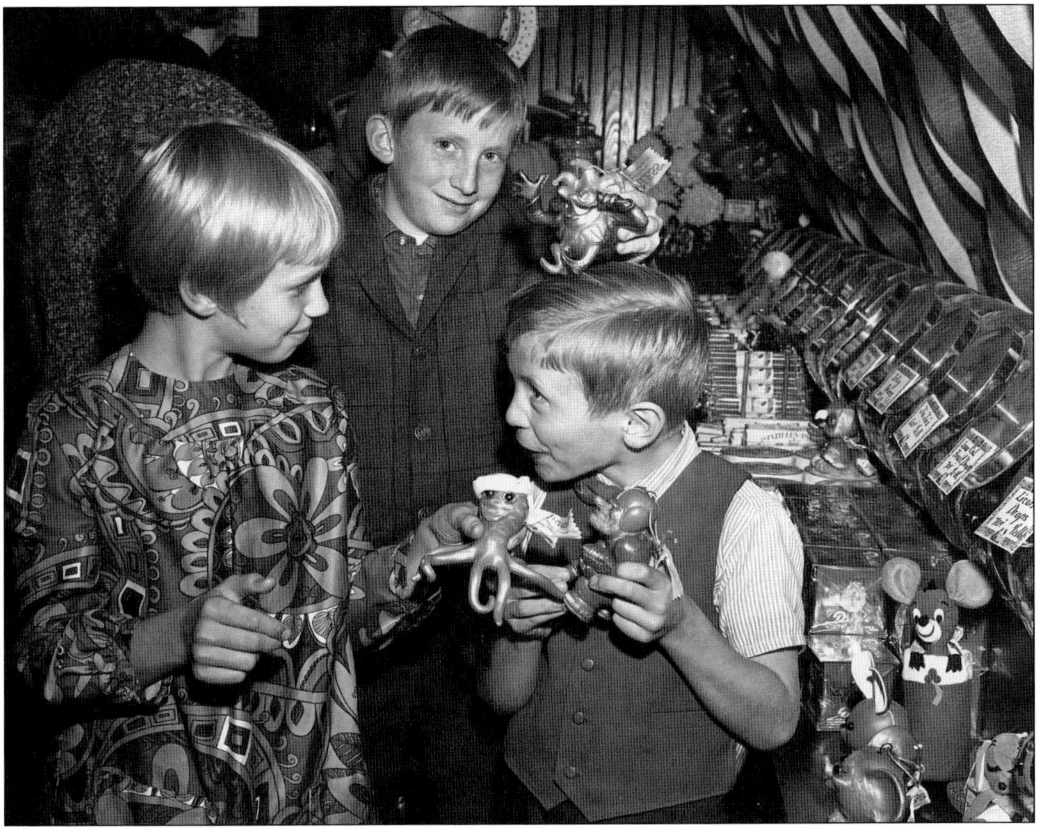

As each new location was developed, the candy section took up more room. Ken McCarthy's wife, Ruth, was originally responsible for purchasing candy for the stores by attending candy shows in San Francisco. She was also the first bookkeeper until accountant Dale Belford joined Farrell's and took over the accounting functions.

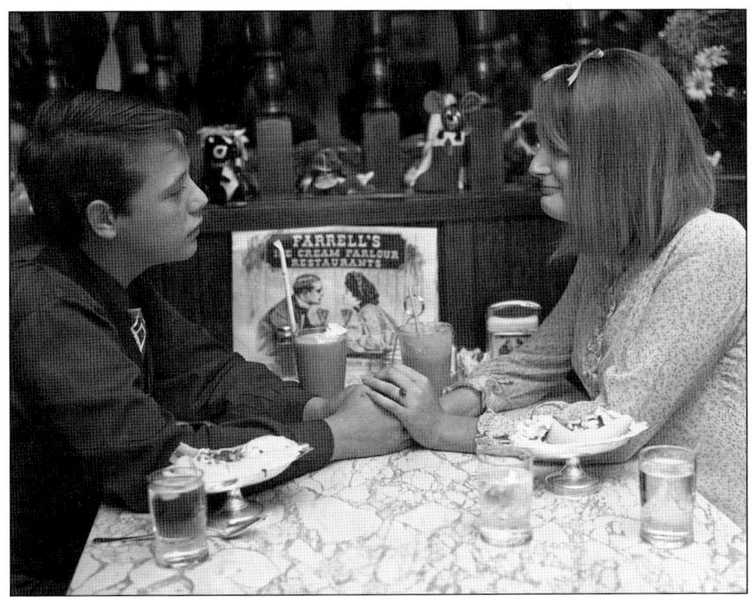

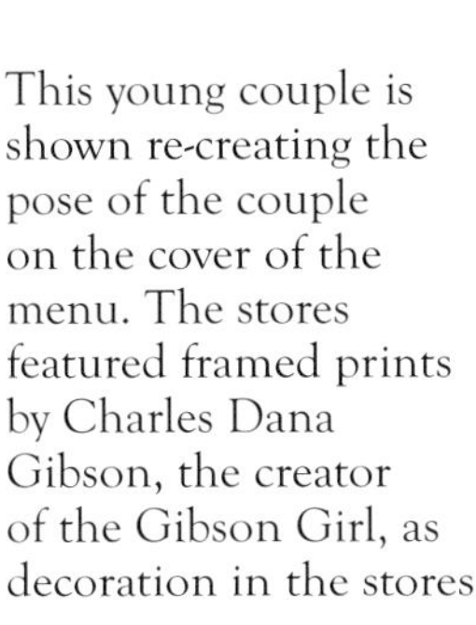
This young couple is shown re-creating the pose of the couple on the cover of the menu. The stores featured framed prints by Charles Dana Gibson, the creator of the Gibson Girl, as decoration in the stores.

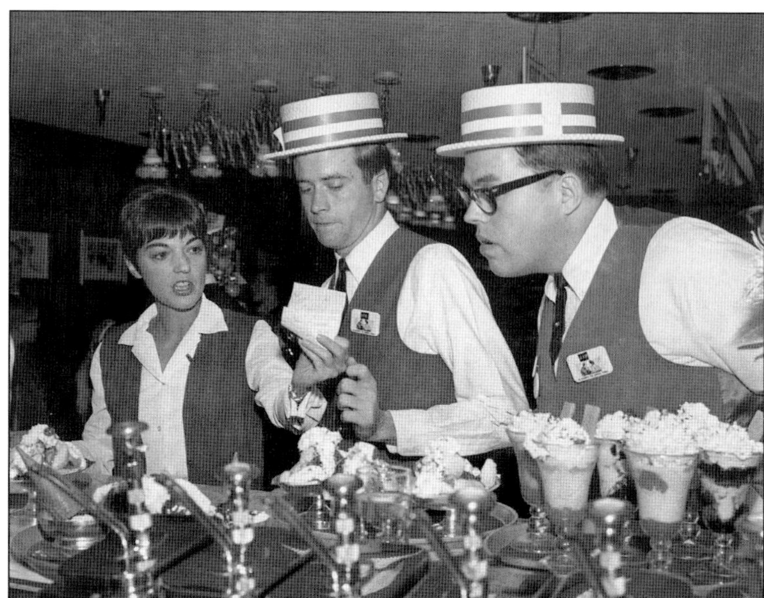

Training for waiters included learning how to identify sundaes and match them up with the guest check. On a busy night, the fountain counter would be filled with sundaes to be delivered. Knowing how to identify each sundae was an important skill.

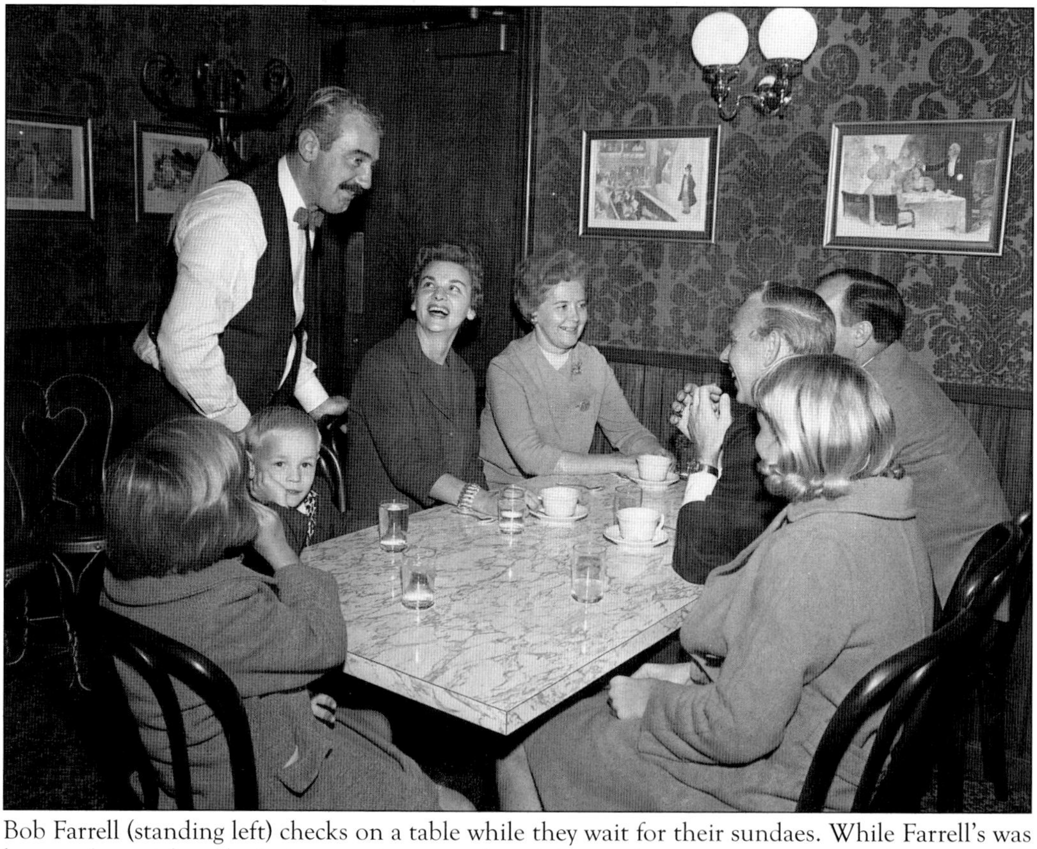

Bob Farrell (standing left) checks on a table while they wait for their sundaes. While Farrell's was known for quick and efficient service, it took training and experience to get to that point. As more locations opened, experienced restaurant operators were often amazed at how well the new employees were trained.

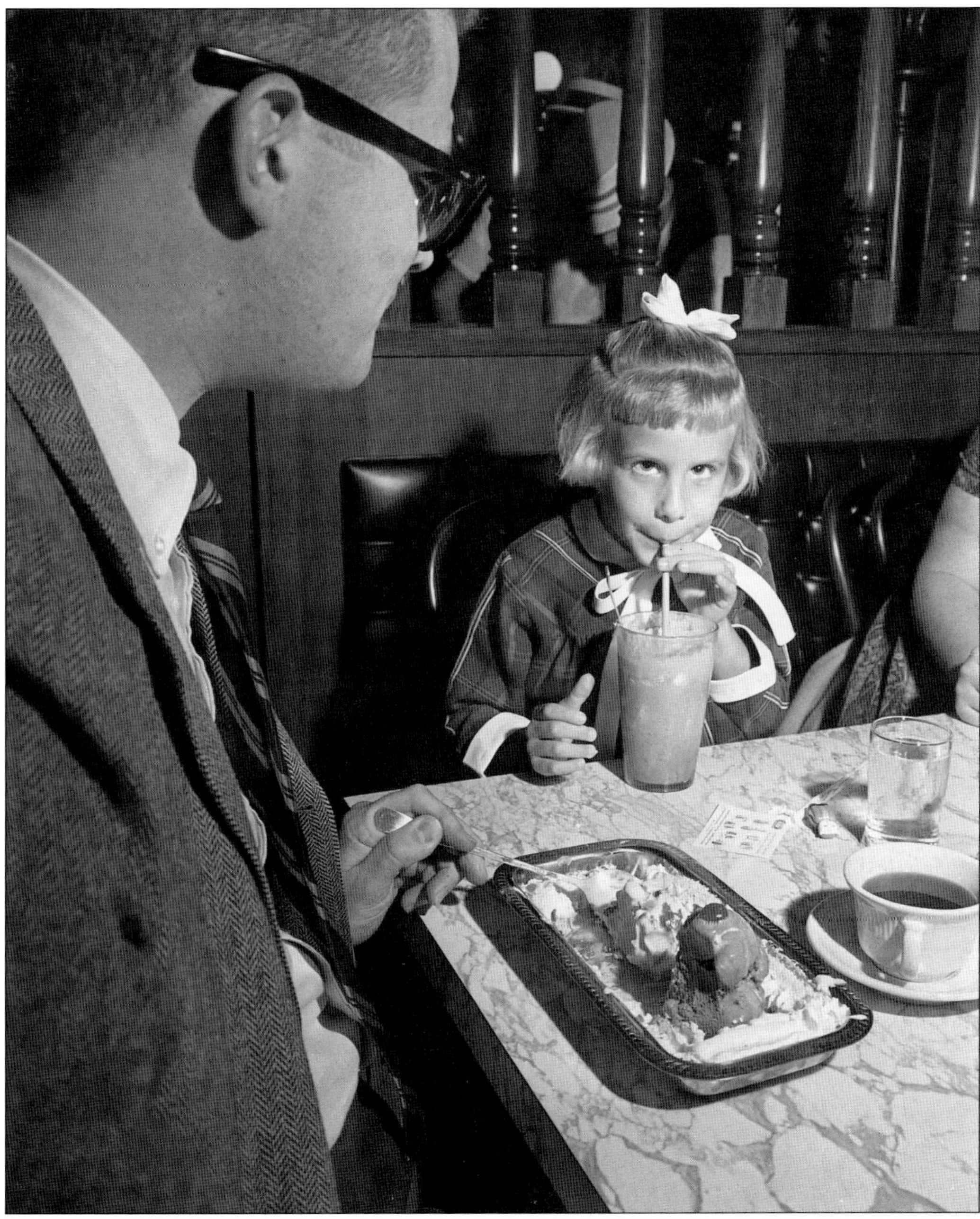

A young customer enjoys an ice cream soda. Farrell's was known for their old-fashioned treats, and the ice cream soda was a throwback to the early days of soda fountains. Bob Farrell grew up in Brooklyn, New York, and had fond memories of old-fashioned soda fountains.

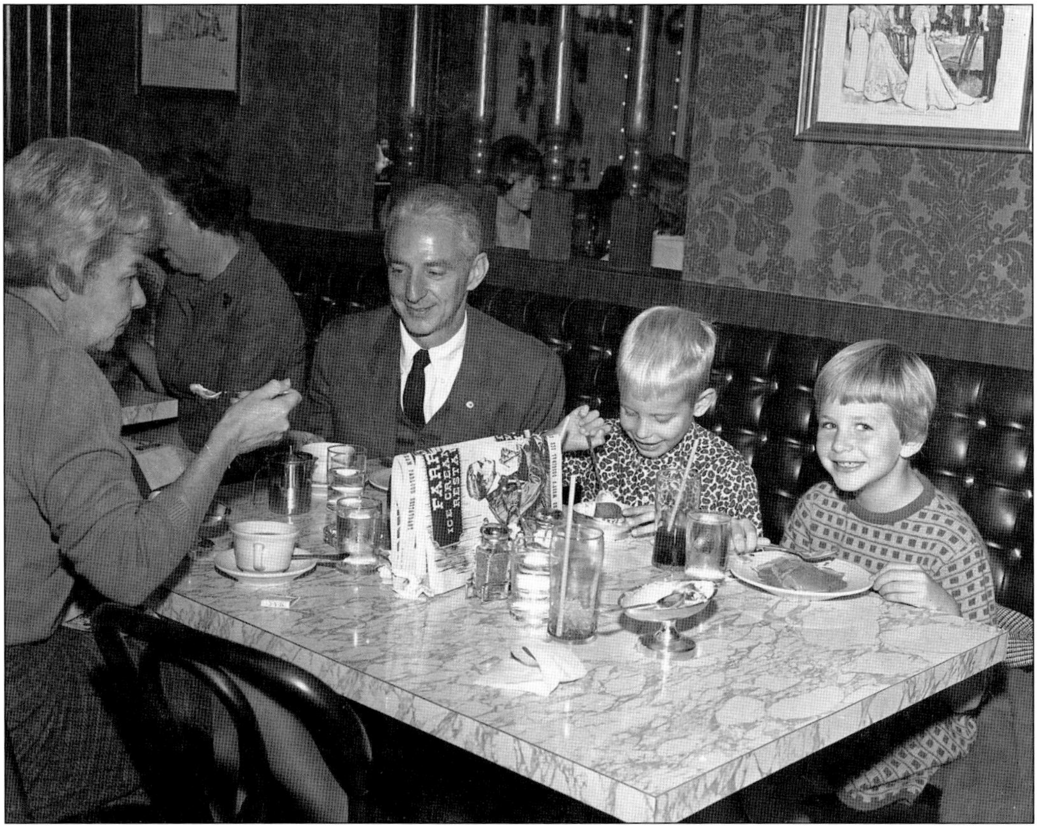

Bob Farrell took his family to the restaurant at the Olympic Hotel in Seattle for hot fudge sundaes. When the waiter treated his family poorly because they were not having dinner, Farrell decided he wanted to open a restaurant that treated everyone with respect.

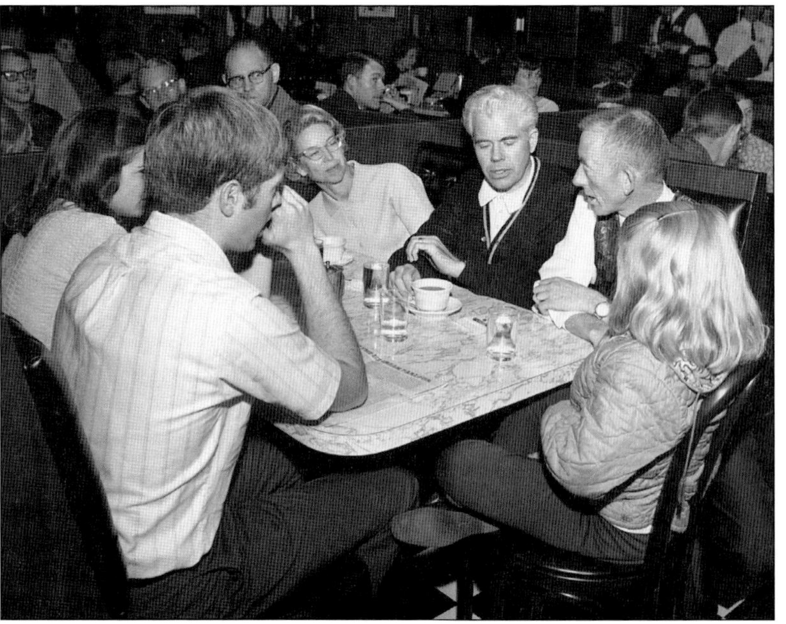

Ken McCarthy (seated top right) visits with another family as they wait for their sundaes. It was McCarthy's belief that a restaurant owner should always be learning and improving based on the input learned from the customers.

A trio of customers is seen enjoying Farrell's Old Fashion sundaes. This sundae was comprised of vanilla ice cream topped with the topping of the customers' choice, whipped cream, sprinkles, and a cherry.

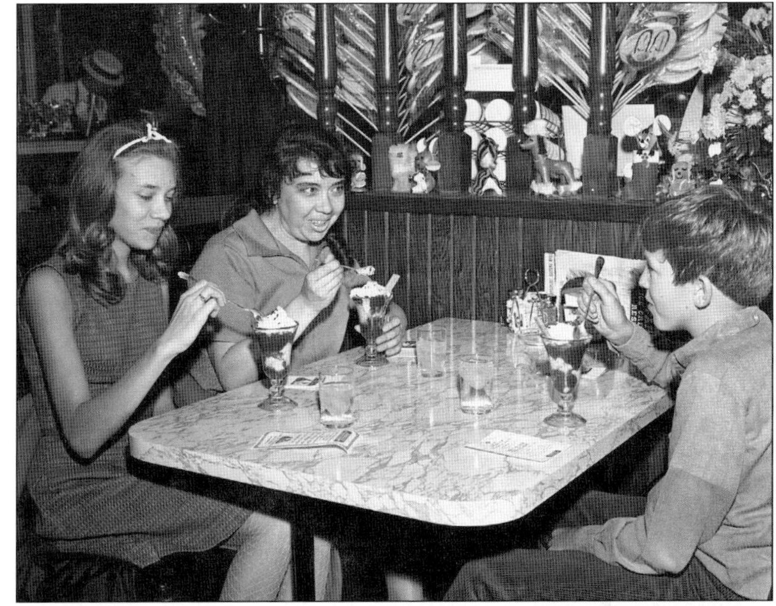

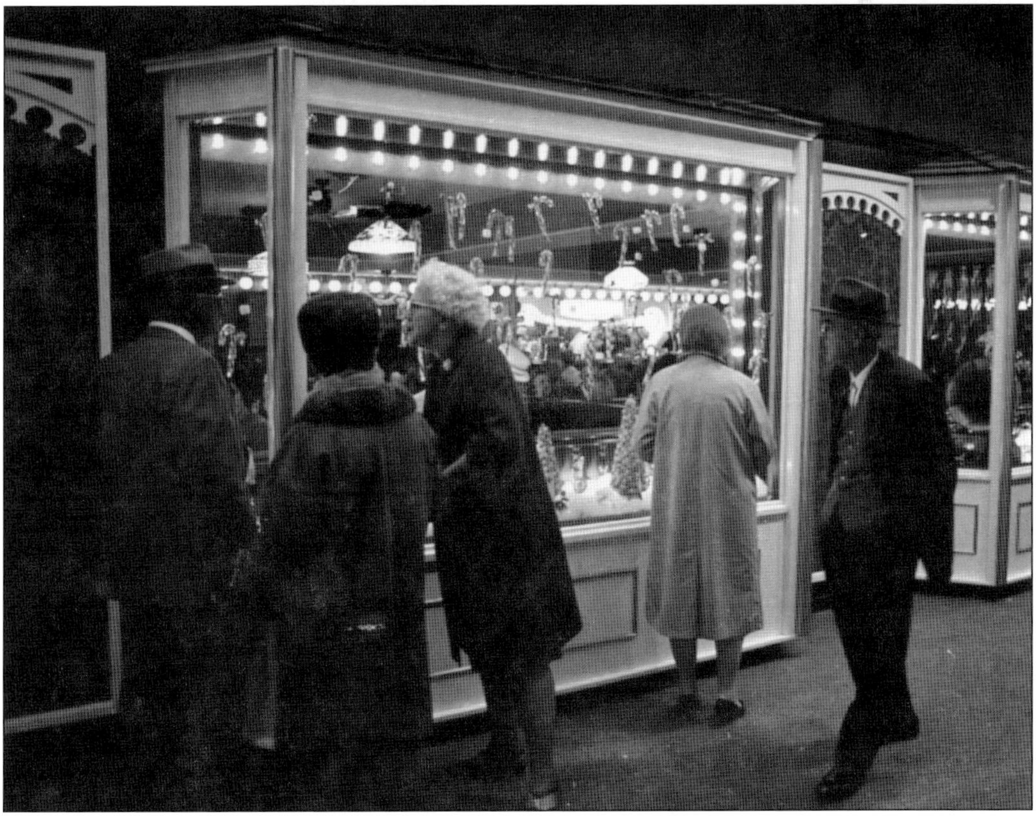

As the Raleigh Hills location opened in November, the window displays were already decorated for Christmas. Farrell's became known for the bay windows that could be decorated for holidays and local events. Bob Farrell later stated that the window decorations ended up taking more effort than they were worth.

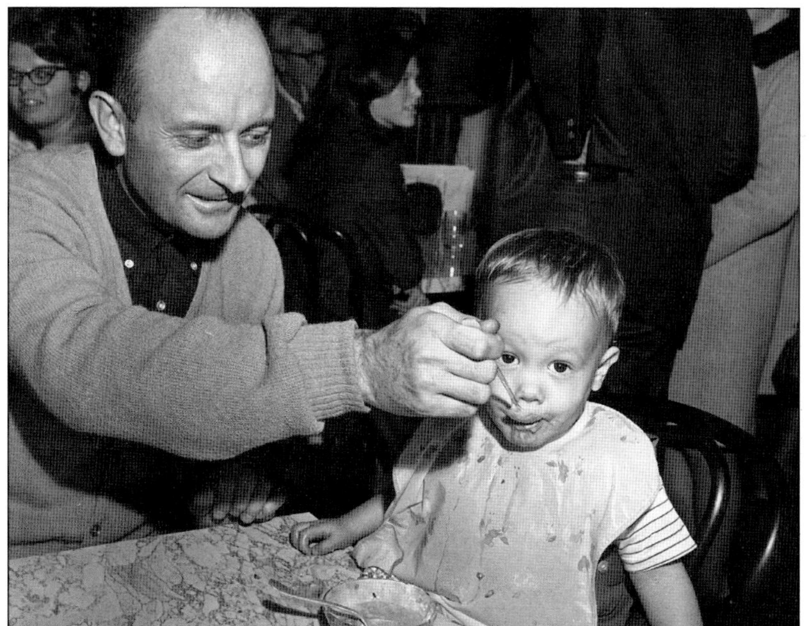

The Clown sundae was on the Farrell's menu from the very beginning. The kiddie menu also featured Little Malts and Little Sodas for guests under the age of 10. The kitchen menu featured a variety of kiddie sandwiches.

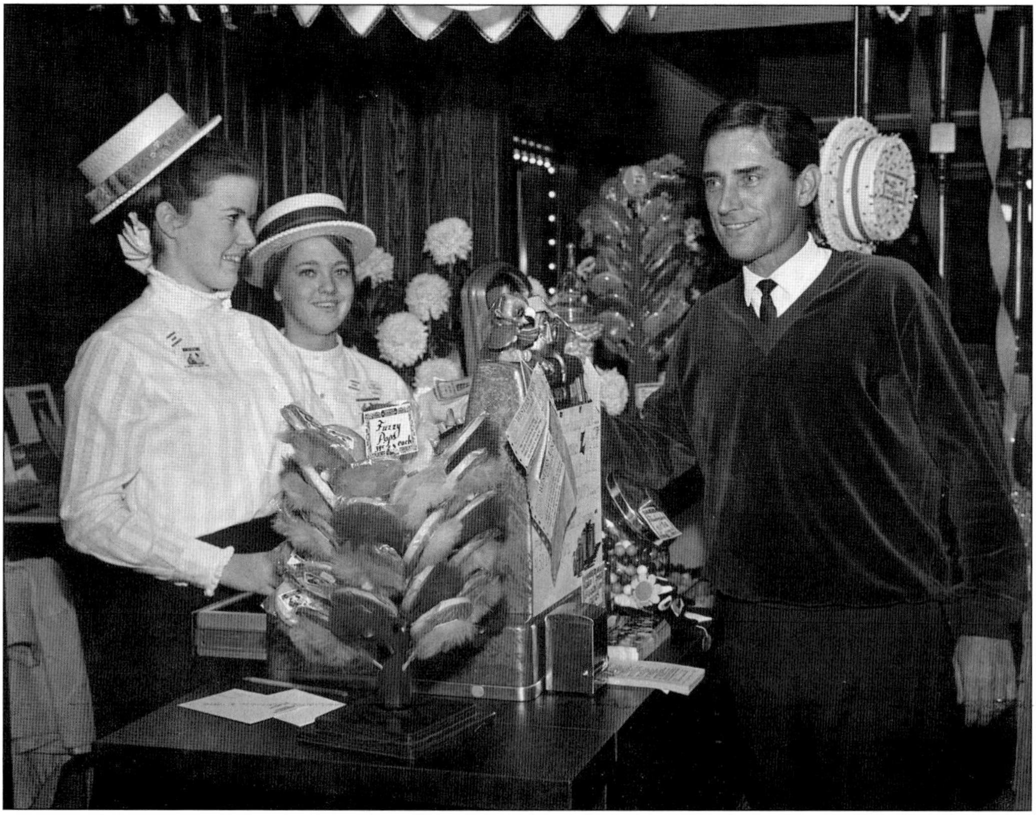

By placing the cashier in the candy section, Bob Farrell knew that customers would have to navigate through the displays with their children. The idea came from theme parks that have guests exit a ride through a gift shop. This layout increased the impulse purchase of candy.

A young guest enjoys her Clown sundae. This sundae proved to be so popular that other ice cream chains featured their own versions.

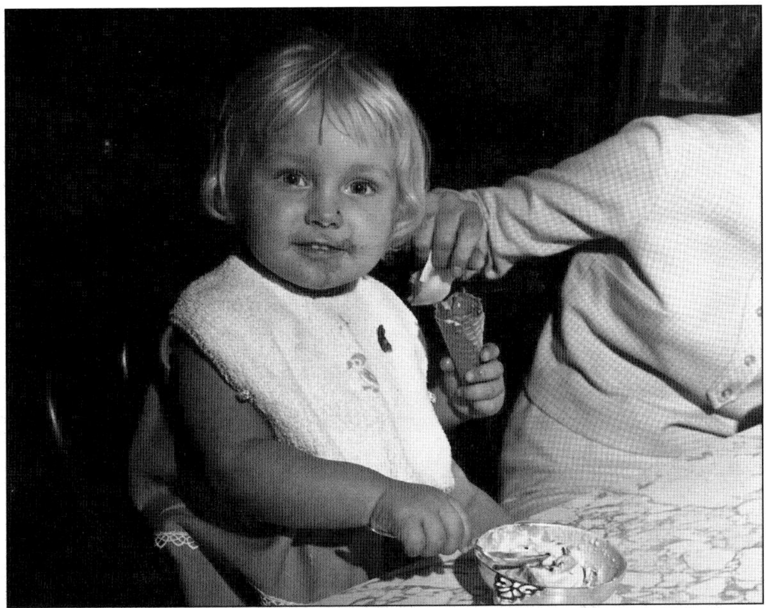

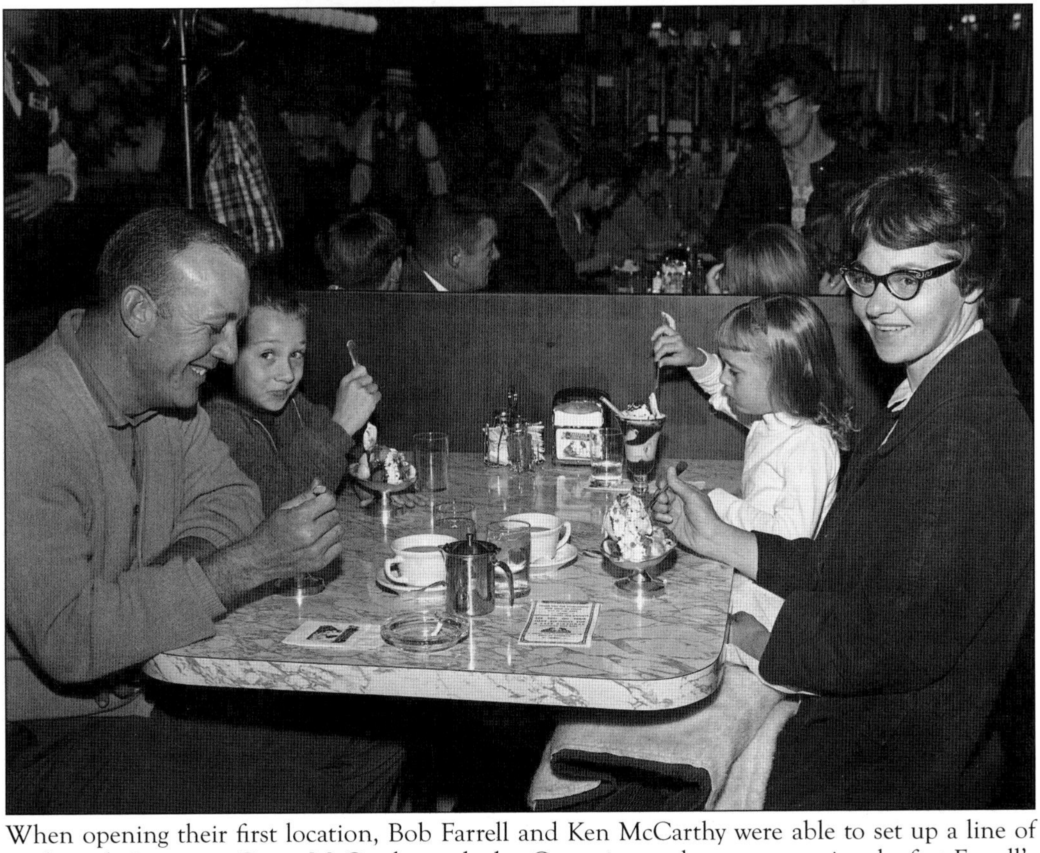

When opening their first location, Bob Farrell and Ken McCarthy were able to set up a line of credit with Carnation Dairy. McCarthy worked at Carnation as they were opening the first Farrell's and was able to use that relationship to secure financing. As new locations were opened, they established 10-year leases based on the available credit.

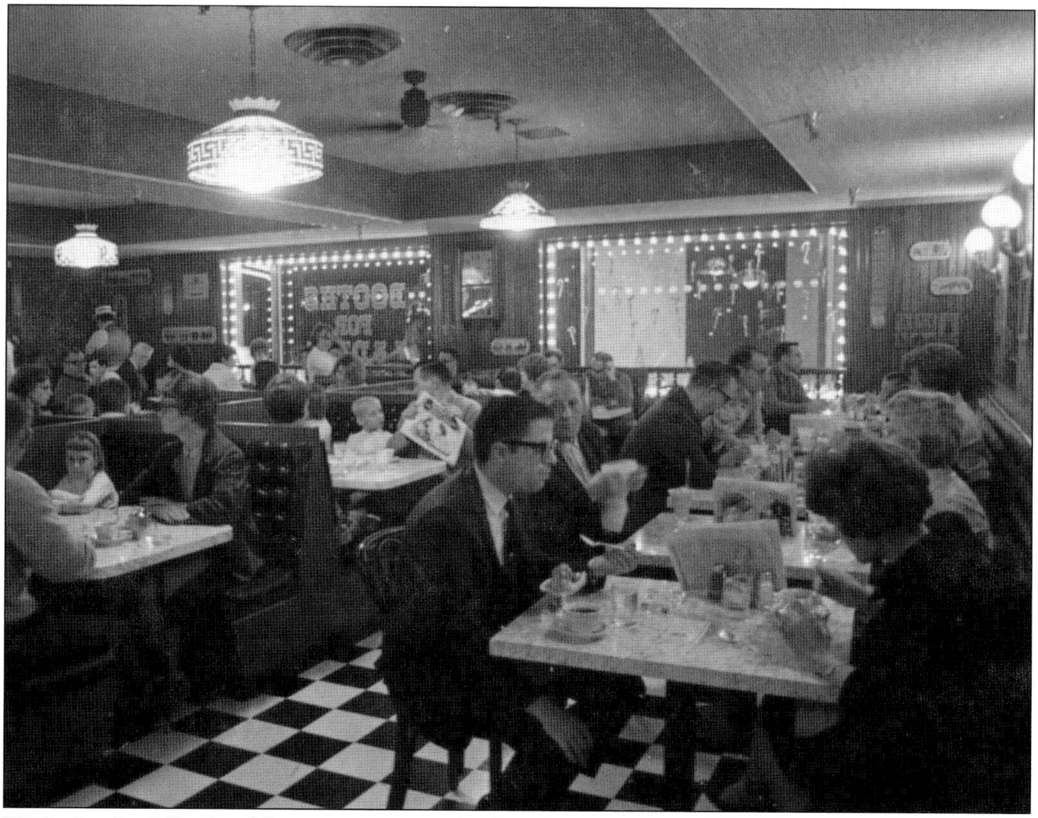

With the third Portland location open and a fourth one in the planning stage, Carnation Dairy rescinded its line of credit for Farrell's, as the operation had become too large for them. Ken McCarthy reached out to a friend who was the general manager of Darigold Dairies in Seattle, Washington, and was able to set up a $250,000 revolving line of credit to fund the expansion.

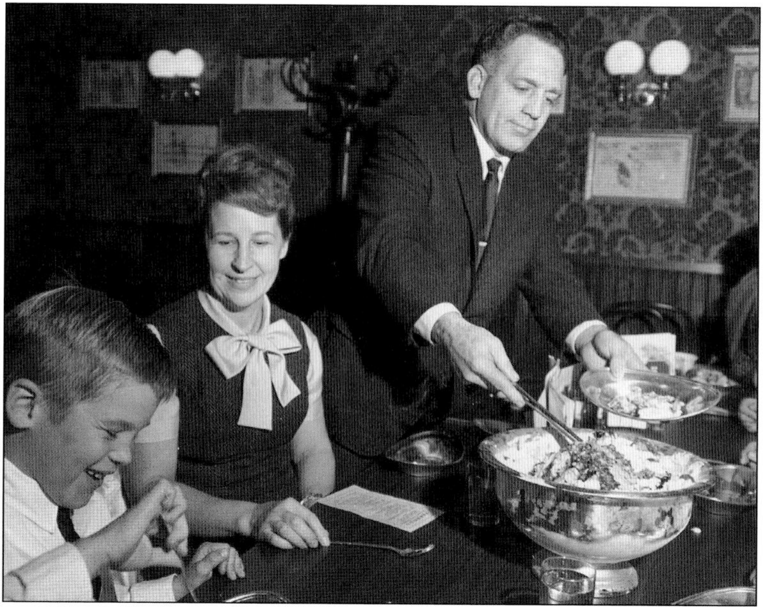

As Farrell's grew, it began to develop proprietary sundae toppings at Richardson & Holland Topping Company in Seattle, Washington. Ken McCarthy would spend a great deal of time there working on topping and ice cream formulations.

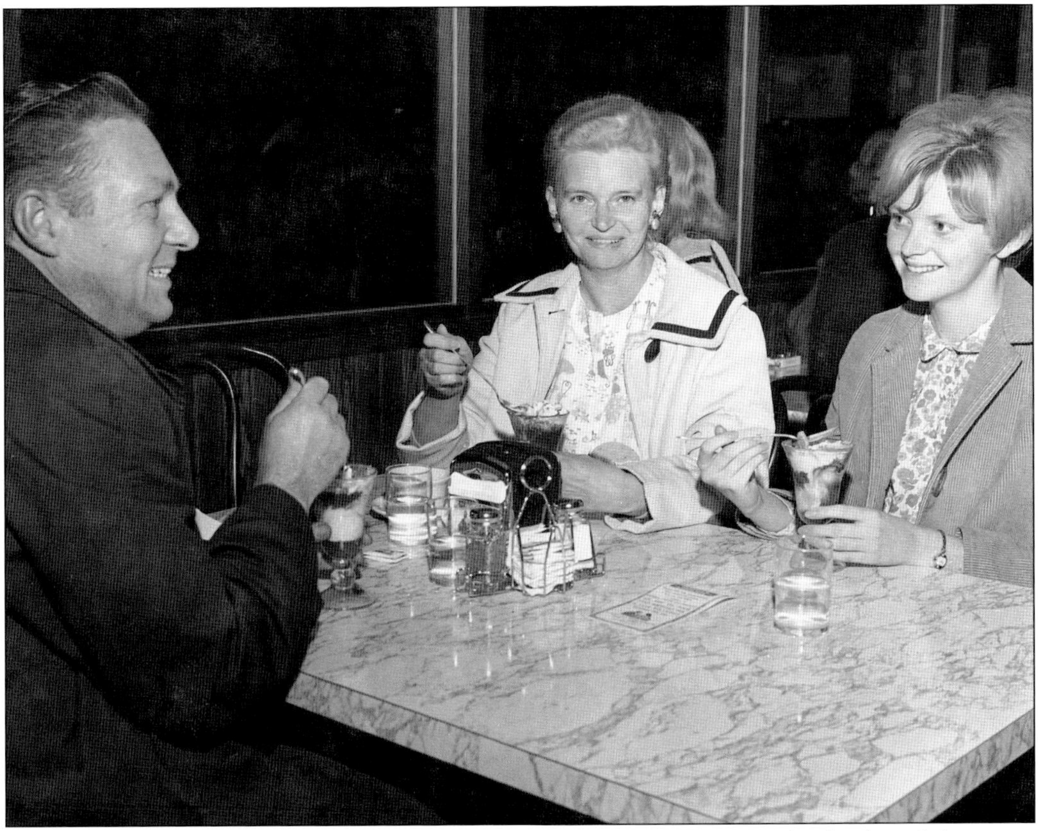

While Farrell's originally served Carnation-brand ice cream, Ken McCarthy developed their own formulas for ice cream using a 16 percent butterfat content. At the time, most supermarket-quality ice cream had only 10 percent butterfat. Farrell's was an early entrant into the superpremium ice cream market.

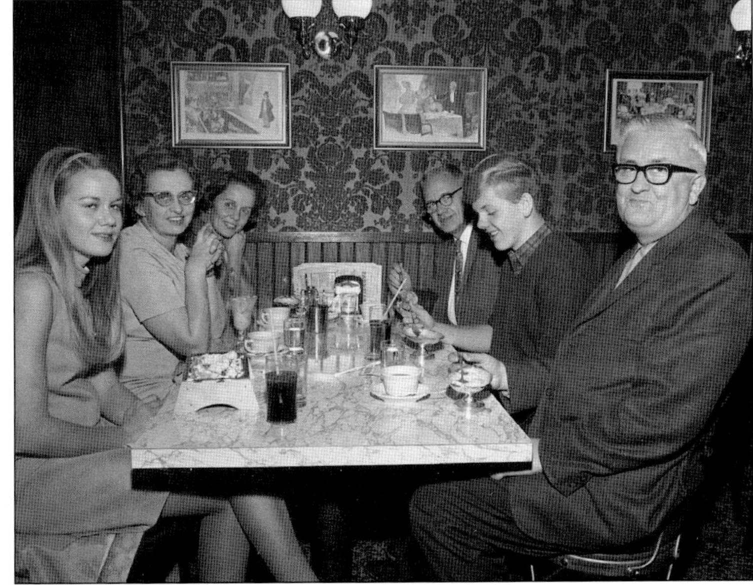

In the 1960s, Farrell's would introduce a flavor of the month into its ice cream menu, including seasonal flavors such as eggnog-flavored ice cream and pumpkin ice cream.

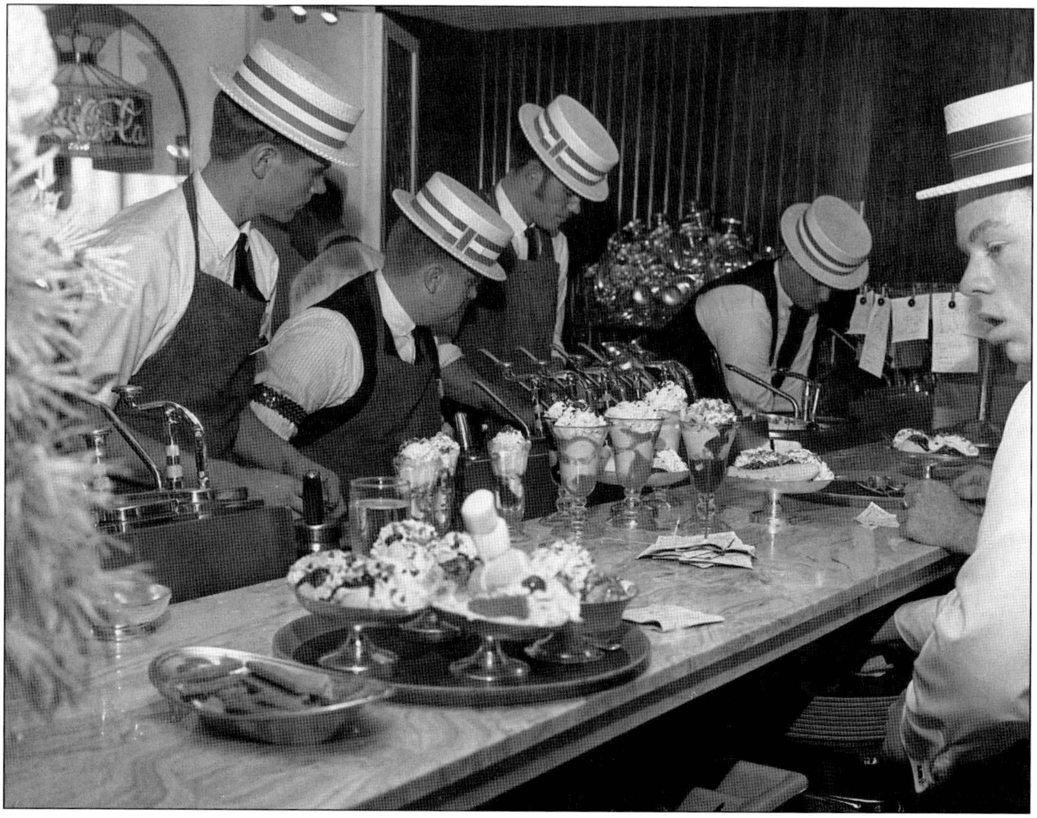

Fountain men were trained in proper ice cream scooping. Gouging of the ice cream tubs resulted in compression of air in the product and reduced the yield. To properly scoop ice cream, the scoop was used to cut into the ice cream in a motion that follows the contour of the tub. A properly scooped tub resulted in a flat top on the remaining ice cream.

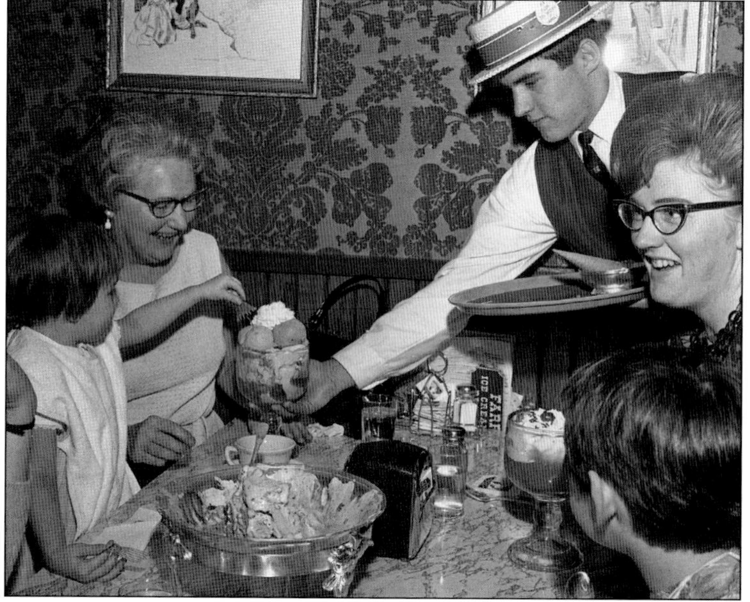

A waiter is shown serving a Gibson Girl sundae to a guest. The Gibson Girl was vanilla ice cream topped with grenadine syrup and banana syrup topped with scoops of lime sherbet, orange sherbet, and raspberry sherbet topped with whipped cream, nuts, and a cherry.

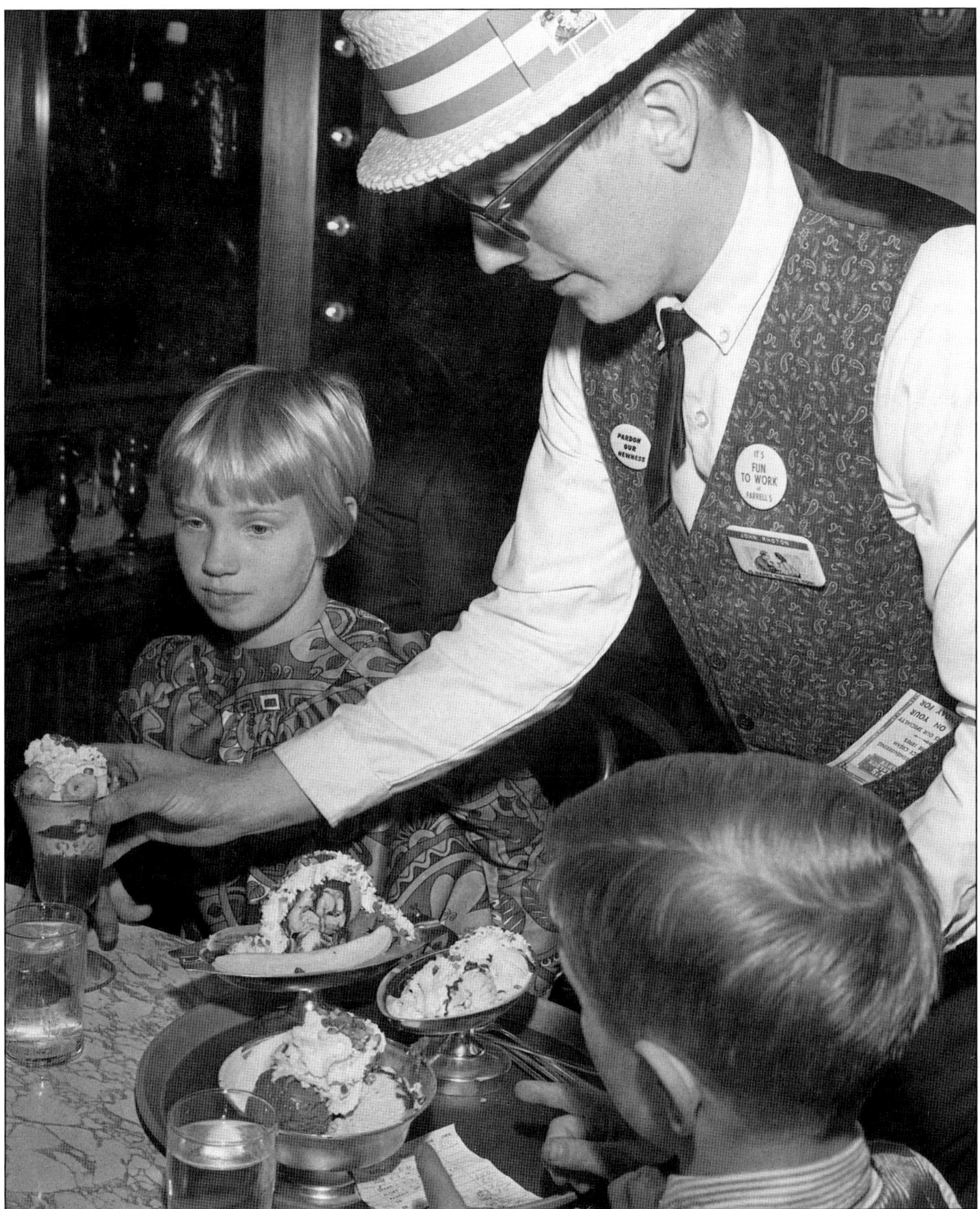

Here, a waiter is seen serving a Straw-Ana sundae at the preopening party. Served in a tulip dish, this sundae was made with vanilla ice cream, strawberry topping, bananas, almonds, and whipped cream.

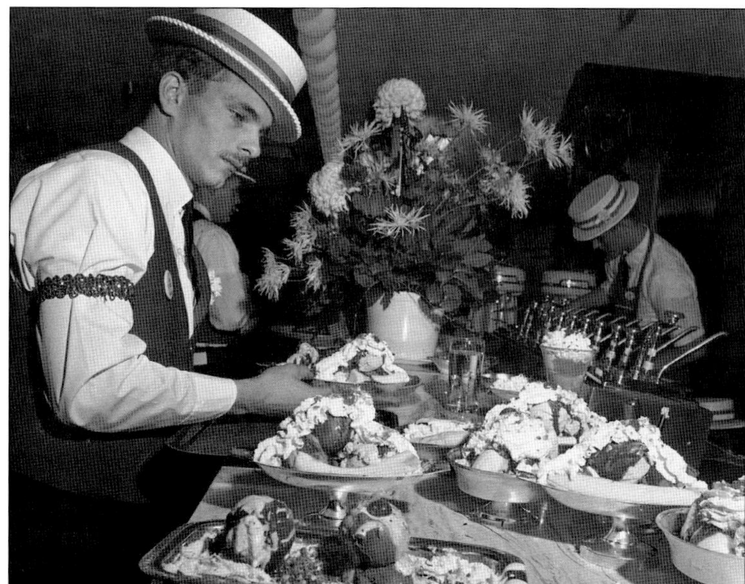

A waiter is seen organizing sundaes on a tray for delivery. With an initial menu of three dozen sundaes, the serving staff needed to know the difference between the sundaes.

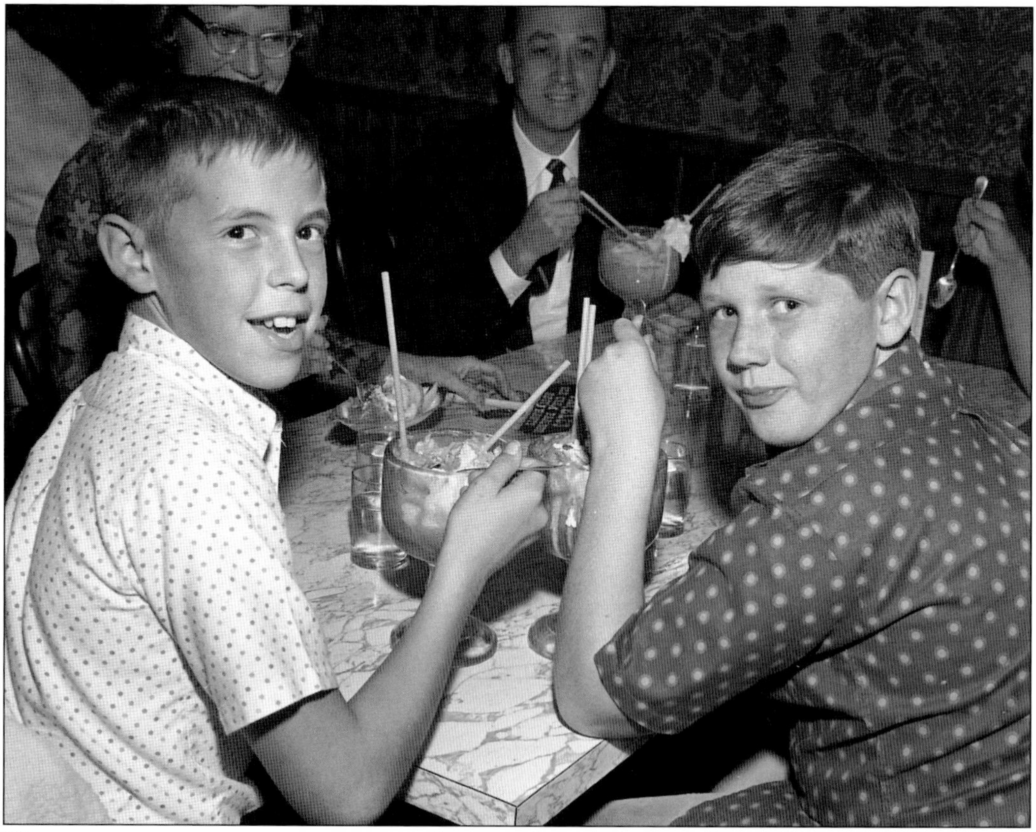

These two young customers are enjoying their root beer floats. Ken McCarthy trained the fountain workers to drop the ice cream into the root beer moments before delivery. A waiter would yell out "float it" when they were ready to pick up the float. Putting the ice cream in before the root beer resulted in too much foaming.

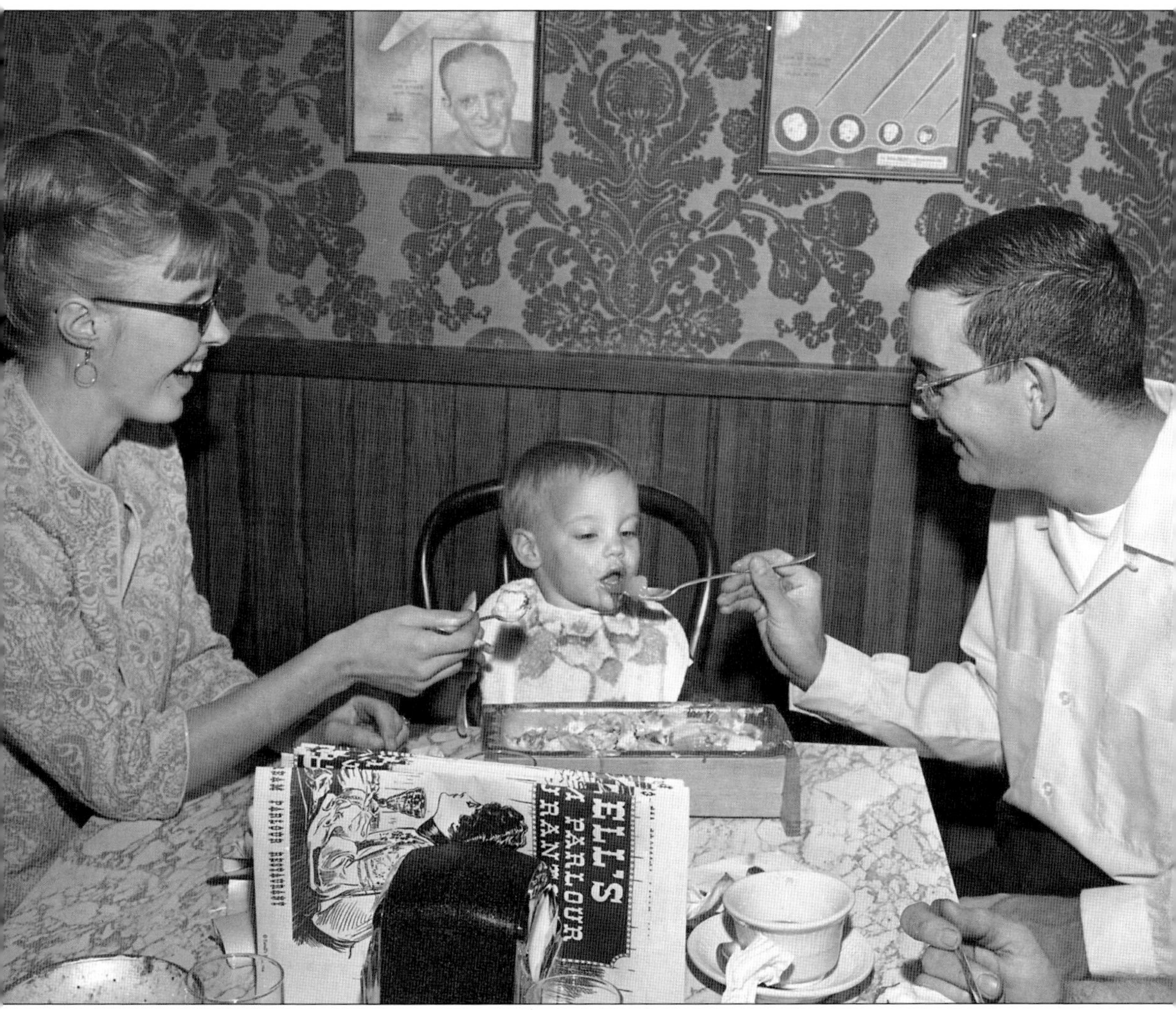

While the Trough was essentially a double banana split, the scoops of ice cream were a little smaller. The presentation in a trough was more for entertainment purposes than anything else. Later versions increased the size of the scoops and the number of scoops. At one point during the early 1980s, the sundae was prepared with 12 scoops of ice cream.

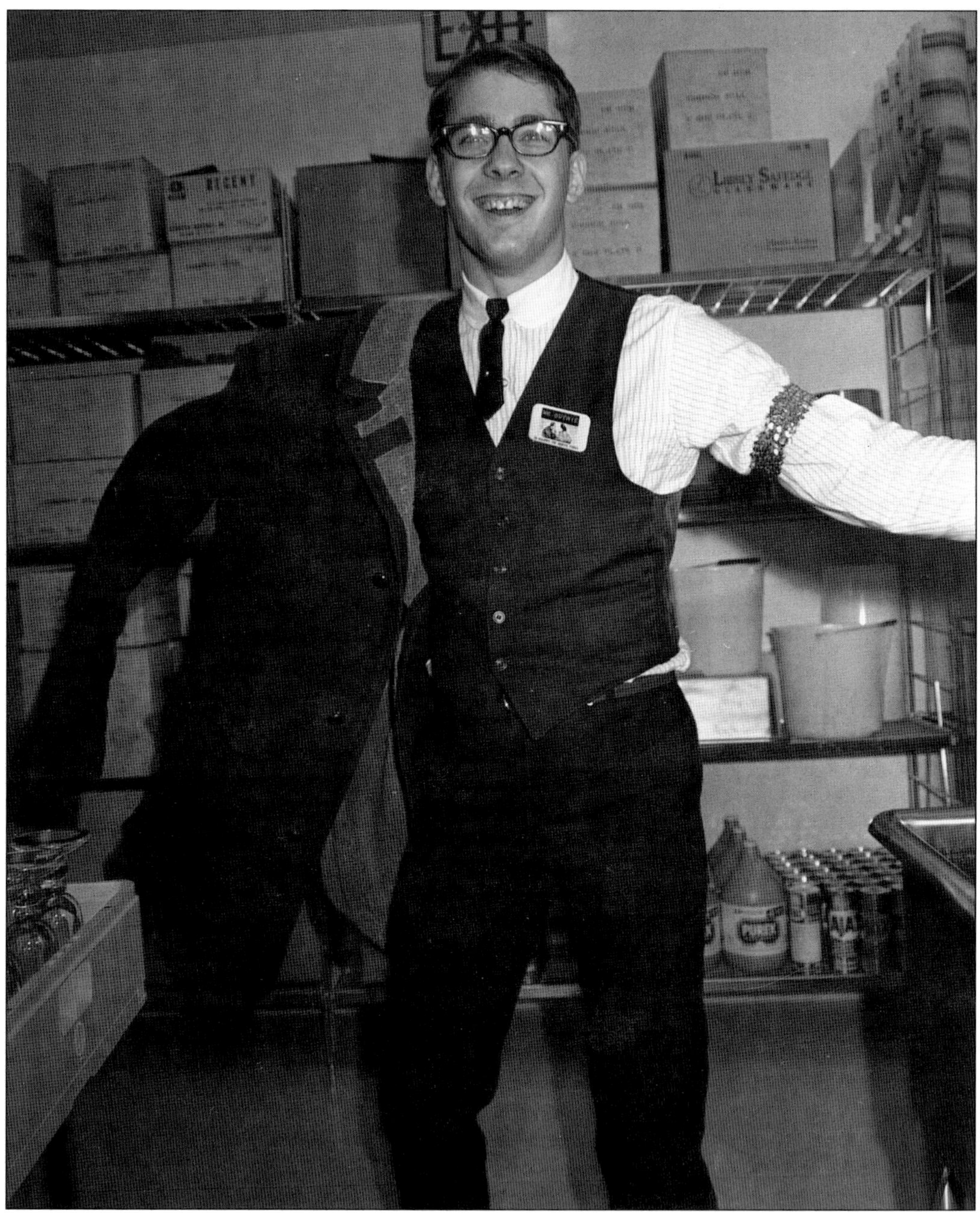

For the first location, Bob Farrell and Ken McCarthy took turns as managers. Both were putting in 100 hours per week as they ramped up operations. By the time they opened their third Portland location, they were able to hire and train qualified men to be managers and assistant managers. As the chain grew in popularity, recruiting new managers became much easier.

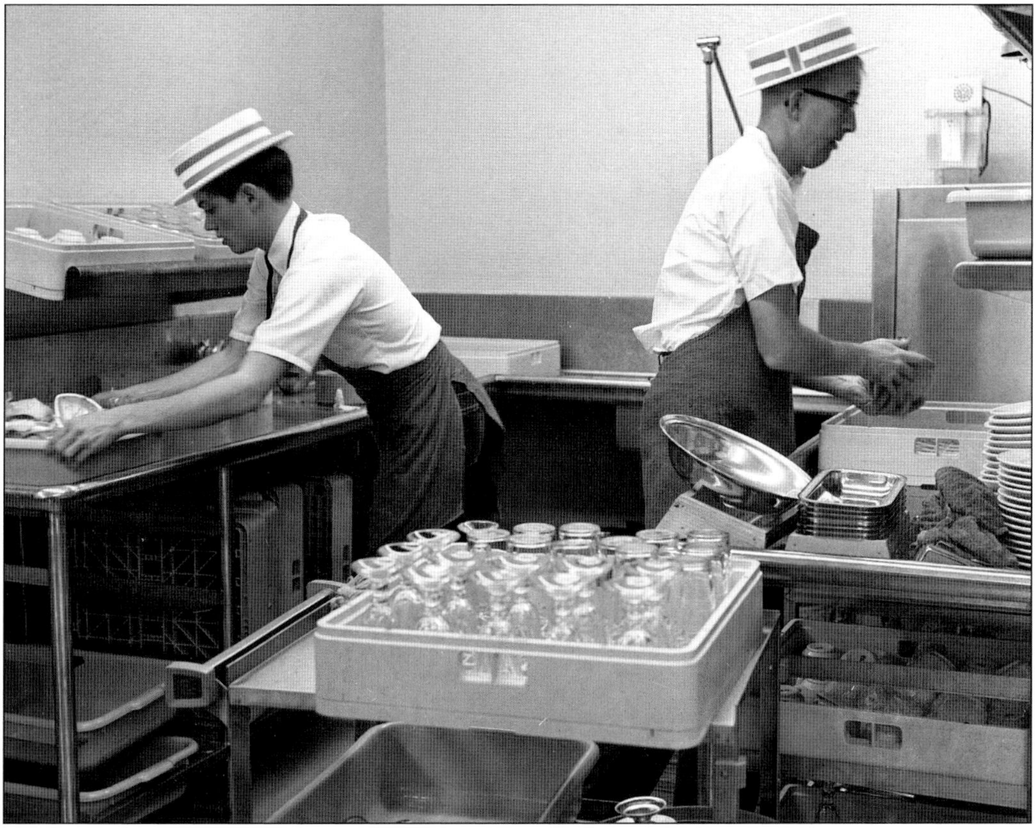

A dishwasher at Farrell's had a thankless job. Ken McCarthy learned that a dishwasher could better diagnose kitchen problems than any other employee based on what kitchen items remained uneaten. One dishwasher showed McCarthy that the burgers were undercooked, leading him to learn that the griddle was not holding the proper temperature.

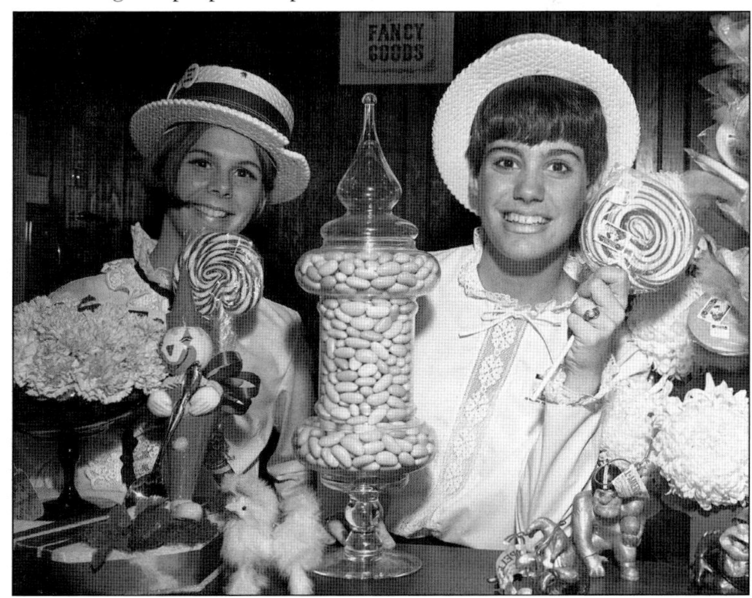

These two cashiers are showing off their smiles at the opening. Rather than have the waiter or waitress take the payment, Farrell's used cashiers. This sped up the process of turning a table over, and it forced the guests to exit through the candy section, increasing the impulse purchase of candy.

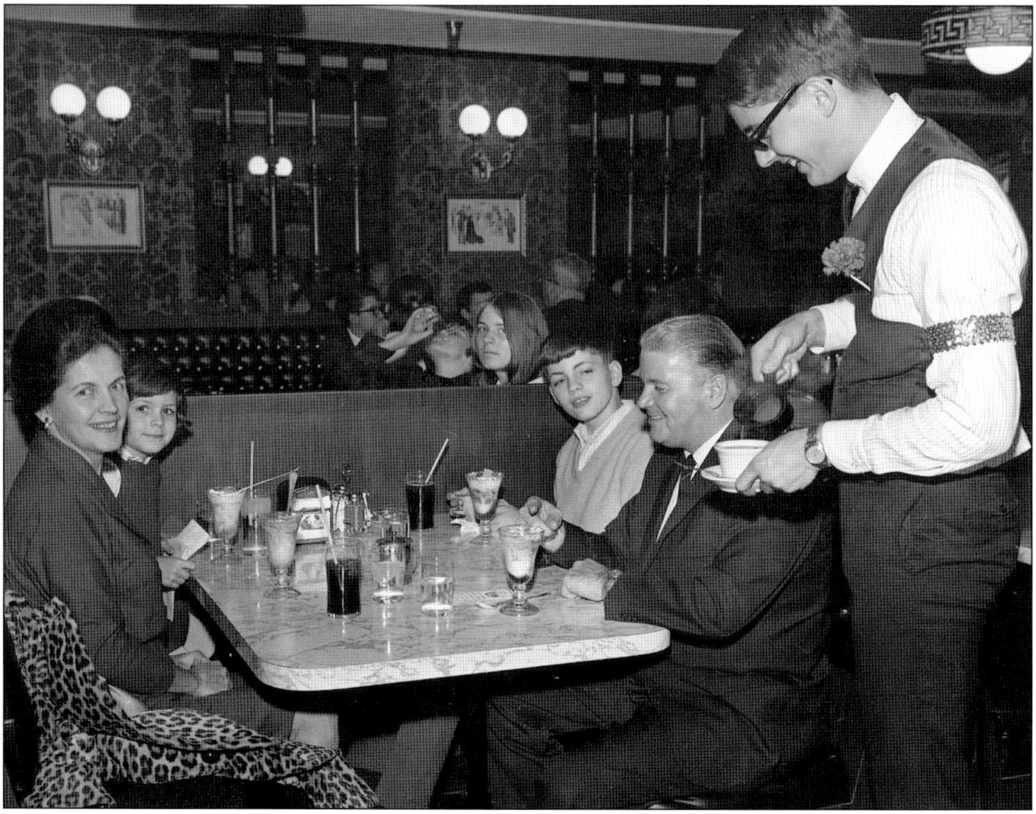

A manager refills the coffee cups of guests. Known as a "coffee skate," this was an important task, as it gave the shift manager the opportunity to survey the dining room and check with customers on service and food quality.

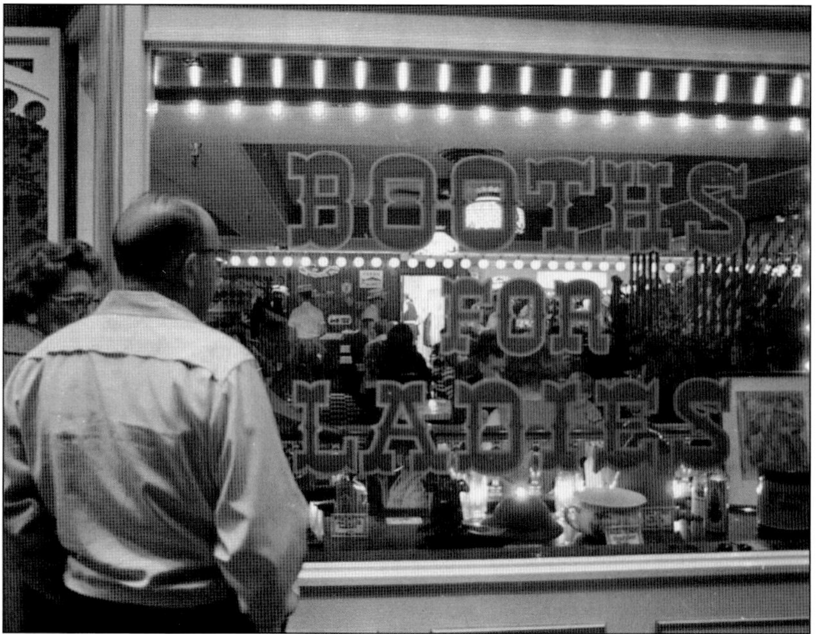

Two guests are seen looking into the main dining room of the Raleigh Hills location. The painted "Booths For Ladies" sign became a staple for Farrell's, providing an old-time flair to the stores.

Four

Lloyd Center

Ken McCarthy finally was able to open a freestanding location in Portland. A new building was constructed near Lloyd Center Mall for the newest and largest Portland location. The landlord for the very first location was upset that the partners did not choose one of his properties near the mall. But the Farrell's partners still had bad memories of the problems he created after they opened the original location at Twenty-first Avenue and Burnside Street.

A new franchised location was opened in La Mesa, California, in February 1968 by John Ortman. Ortman would go on to own eight Farrell's in the San Diego area; his final location closed in 2006. This was followed by a franchised location in Woodland Hills, California, in March 1968. This location would be owned by Bruce Pelton and Dallas Ivey.

The Lloyd Center store followed the layout used in the La Mesa and Woodland Hills locations and included two party rooms. Both party rooms could be closed off on a quiet weekday evening, giving the appearance of a full dining room. Like the Eugene location, the Lloyd Center store lasted longer than most other locations, finally closing in 2001. As new locations were built larger than the early locations, it became clear that a slow weekday evening would never seem as exciting as a busy Saturday night. Farrell's became the place where customers went mostly on weekends.

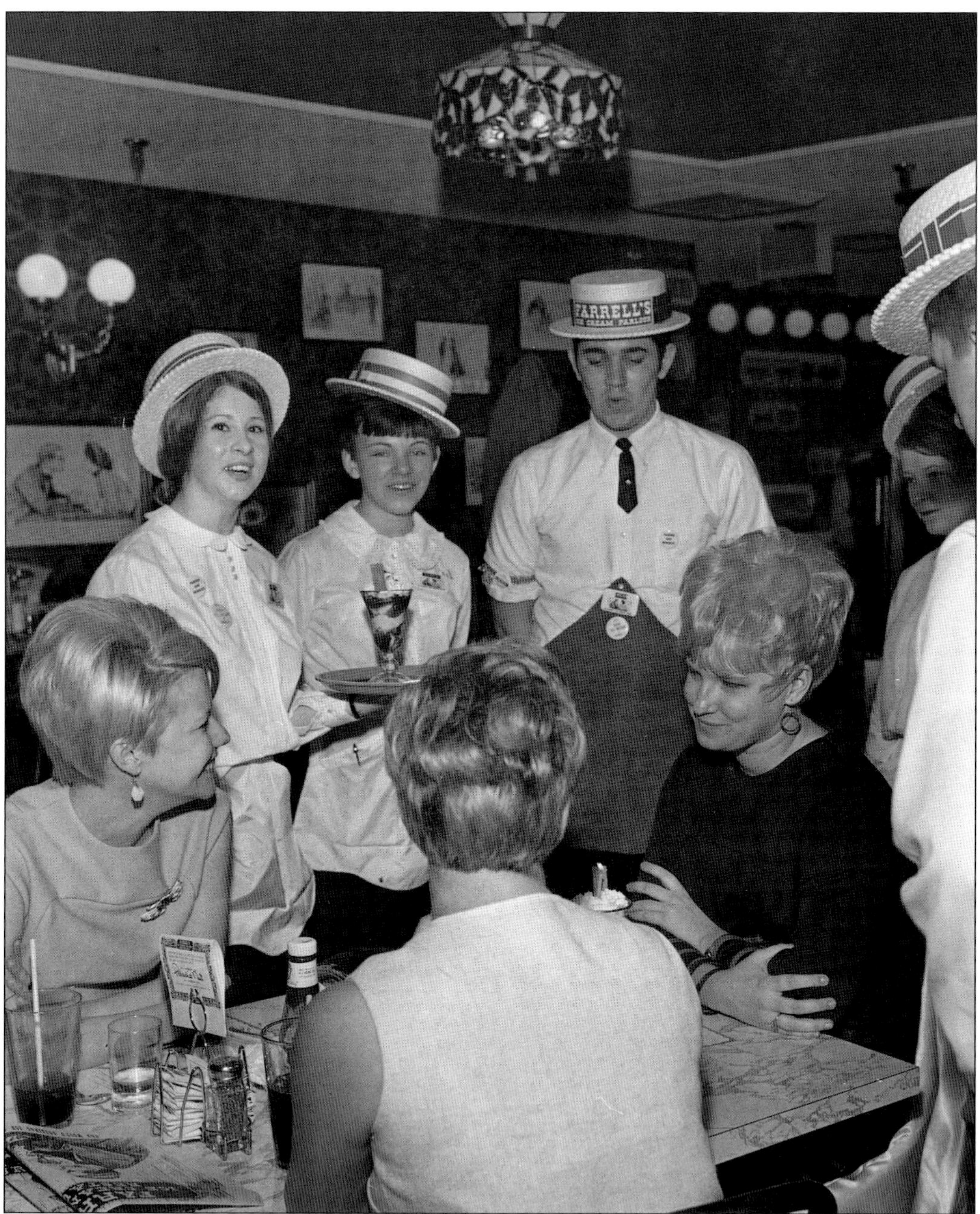

In 1968, a group of Farrell's employees sing "Happy Birthday" to a customer while serving the birthday sundae. While the tradition of singing "Happy Birthday" was in place at the opening of the very first location, it became more popular as the chain grew. The birthday song was accompanied by the pounding of Farrell's bass drum, the clanging of the bell, and a siren.

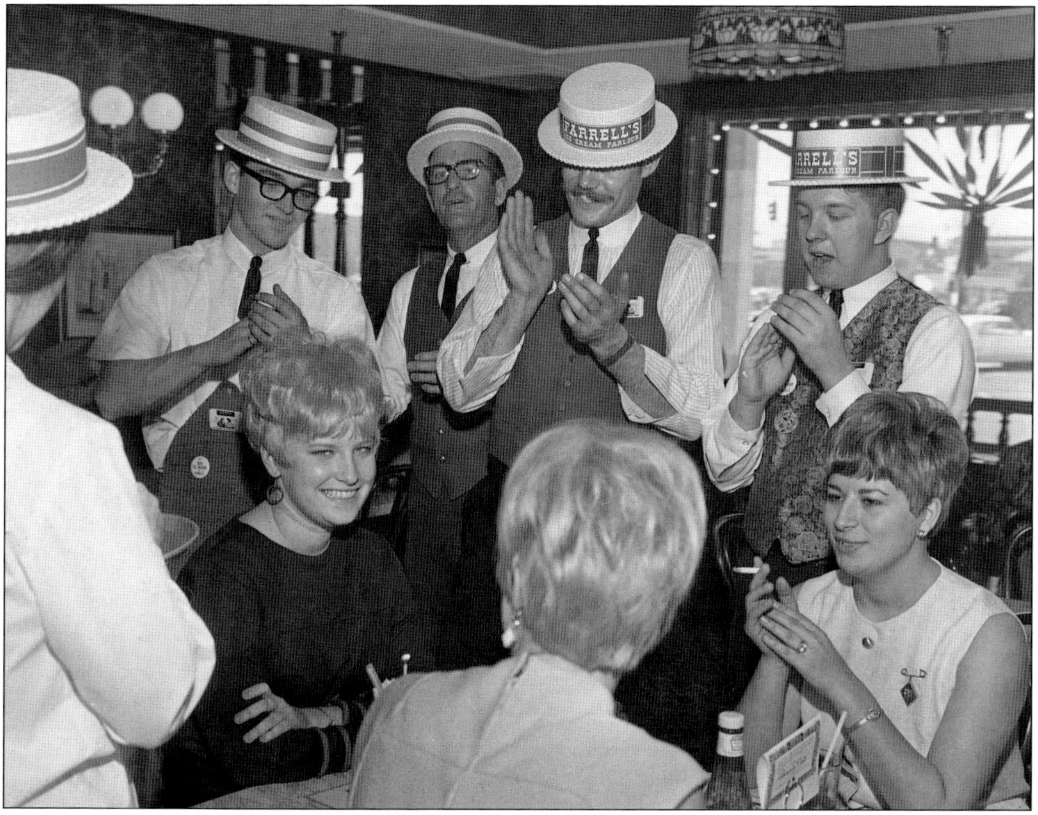

The advantage of singing "Happy Birthday" was that everyone knew the lyrics. A dining room full of customers meant that Farrell's employees would have a large accompaniment of singers joining in. The free birthday sundae often resulted in the birthday guest bringing in friends or family who would purchase more ice cream. Eventually, Farrell's was primarily known as a place to celebrate birthdays.

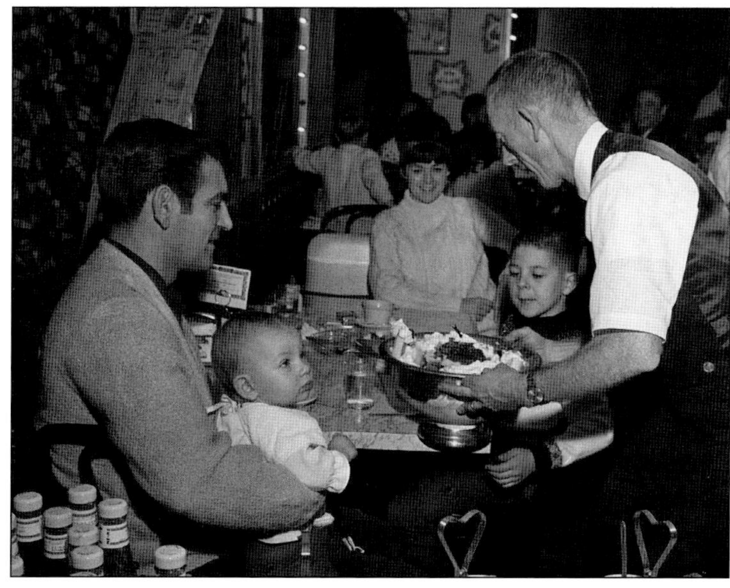

Ken McCarthy is seen hand-delivering a Portland Zoo sundae to a family. When large groups had more than one Portland Zoo, the first sundae was delivered on a stretcher to generate excitement in the dining room while the remaining sundaes were simply brought out by hand.

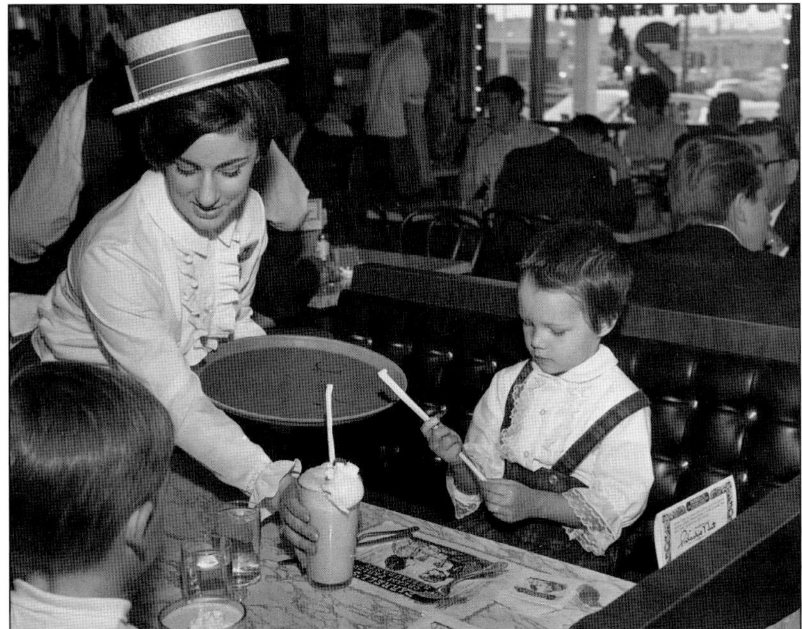

A waitress is seen delivering an ice cream soda to a young customer. The ice cream soda recipe started with a pump of flavoring syrup, melted ice cream, soda water, and a scoop of ice cream on the lip of the glass.

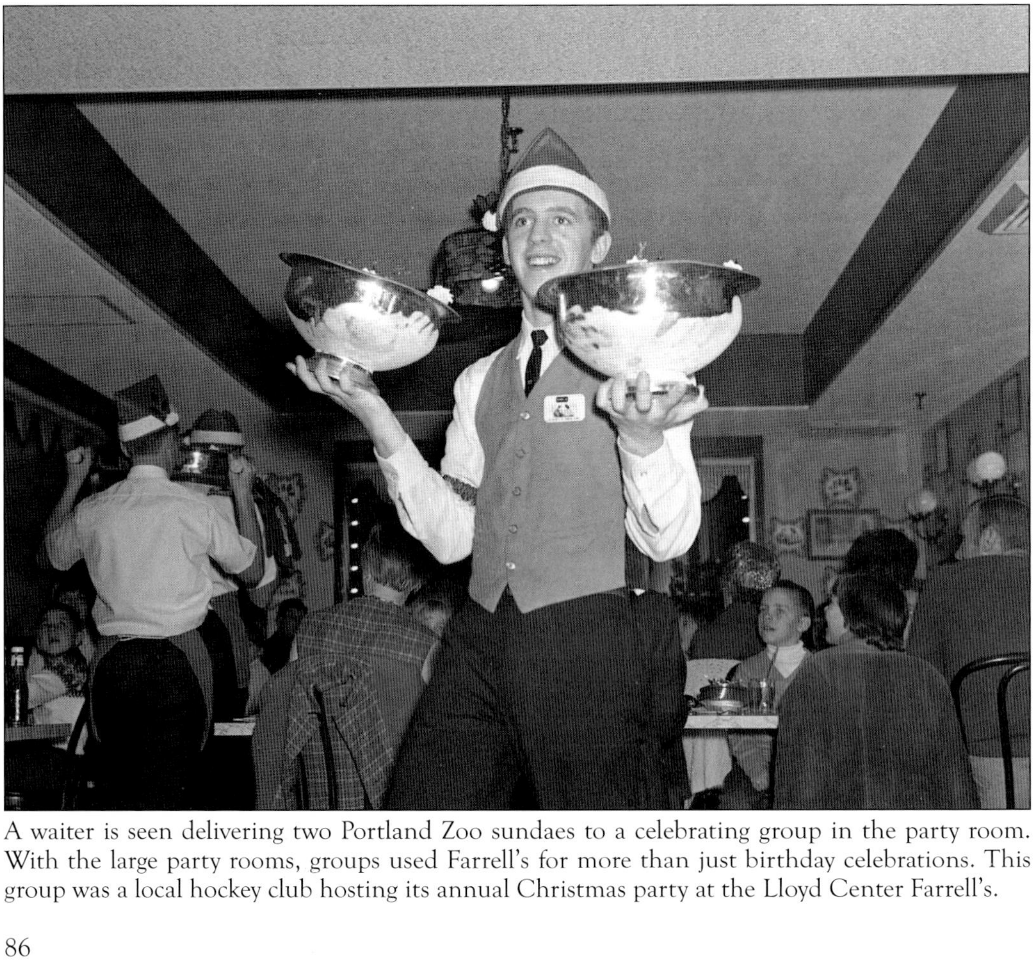

A waiter is seen delivering two Portland Zoo sundaes to a celebrating group in the party room. With the large party rooms, groups used Farrell's for more than just birthday celebrations. This group was a local hockey club hosting its annual Christmas party at the Lloyd Center Farrell's.

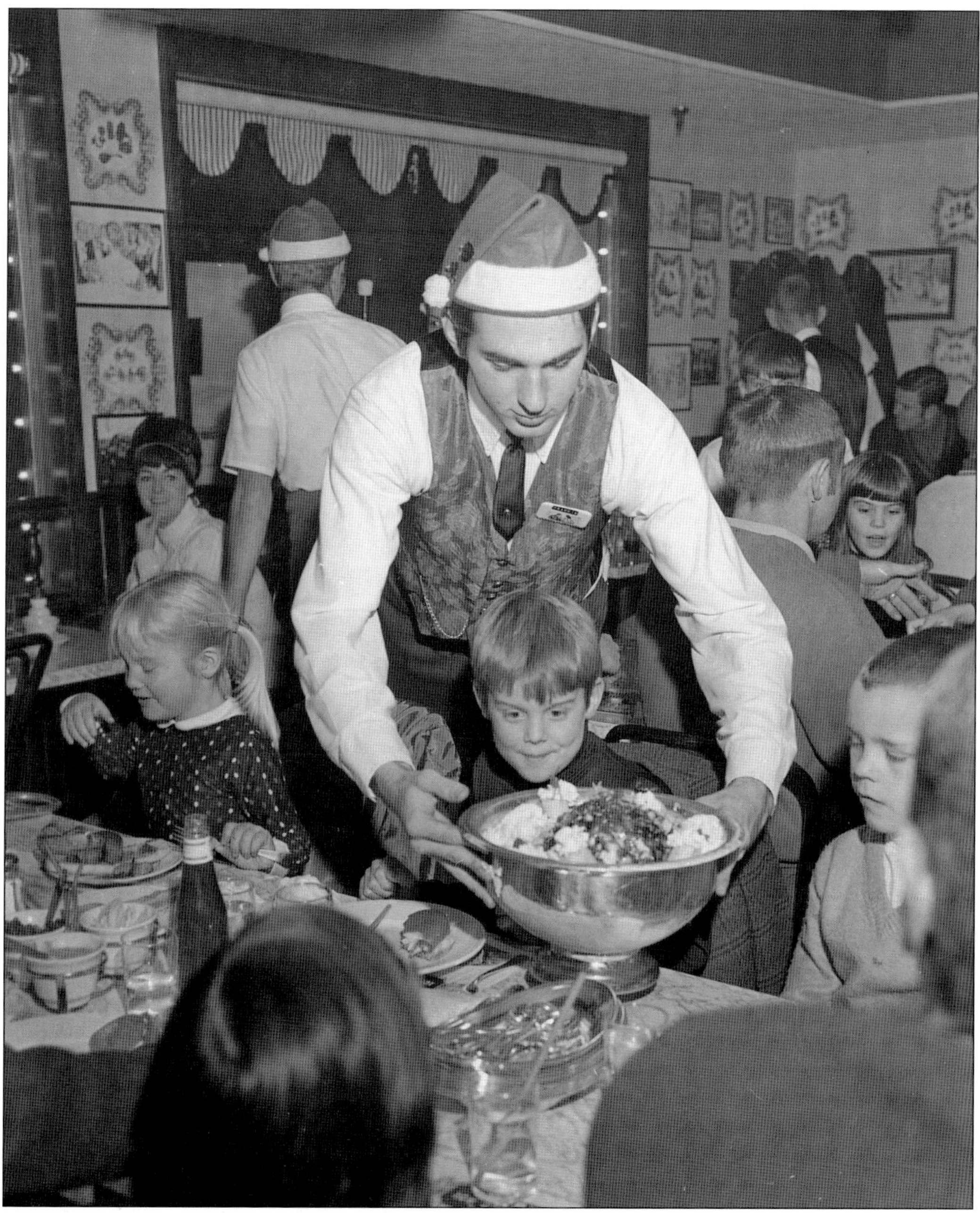

This young guest is very happy to have the Portland Zoo sundae placed in front of him. It is very difficult to be sad with a very large ice cream sundae on one's table.

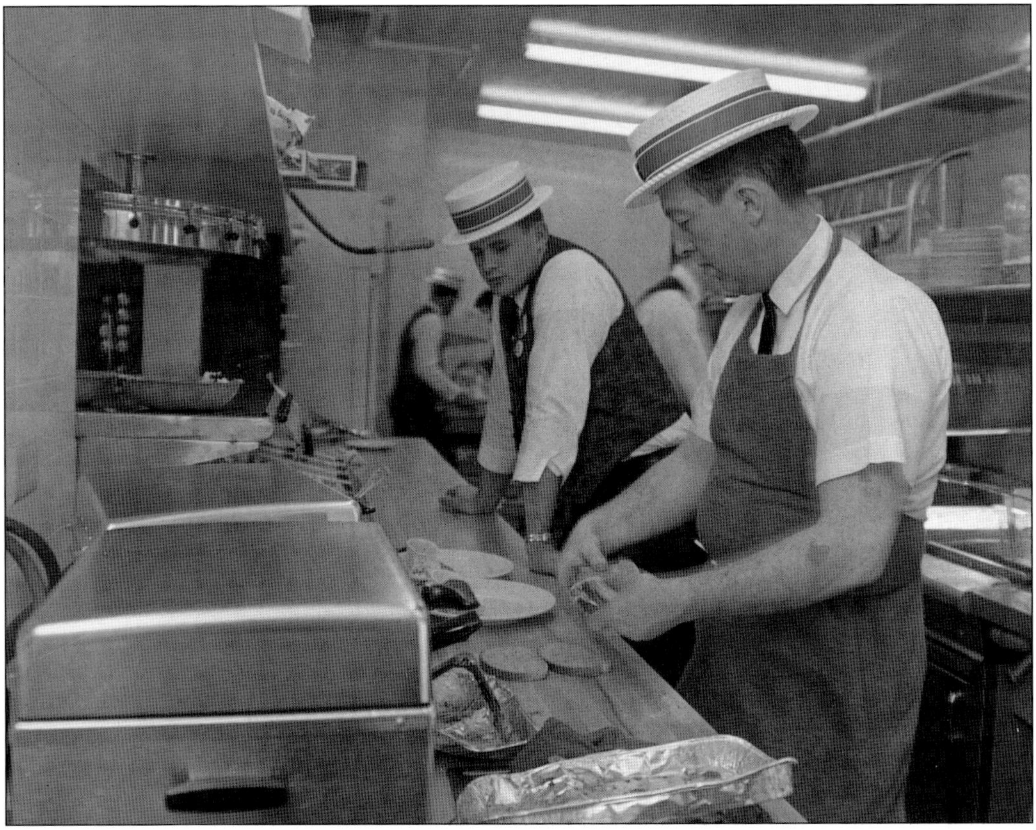

A cook is seen preparing a deli sandwich in the kitchen. Farrell's became known for hamburgers from fresh beef and deli-style sandwiches. Kitchen menus at this time were mostly hamburgers, corned beef sandwiches, turkey sandwiches, and hot dogs. The original menu also included waffles and eggs, but the breakfast items were soon discarded.

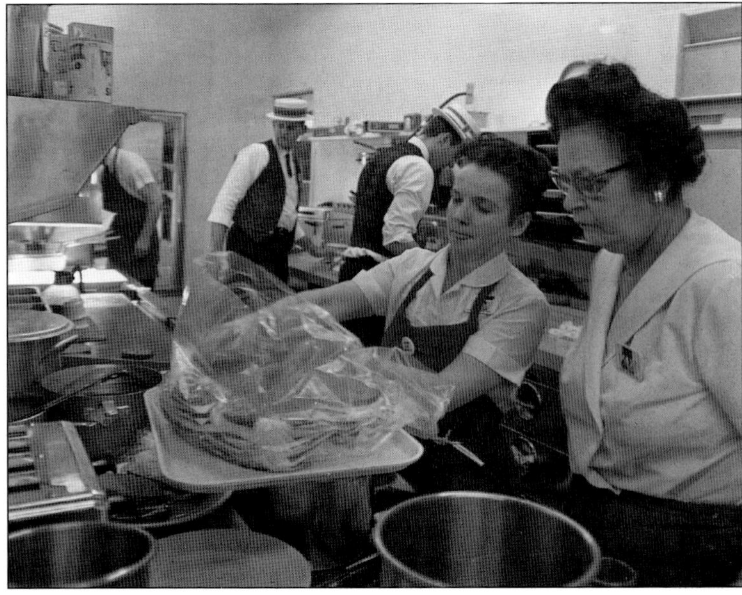

Two women are unpacking pre-formed hamburgers for preparation. Farrell's used locally ground fresh beef for its hamburgers. Later, under Marriott's ownership, Farrell's switched over to frozen beef patties to save costs.

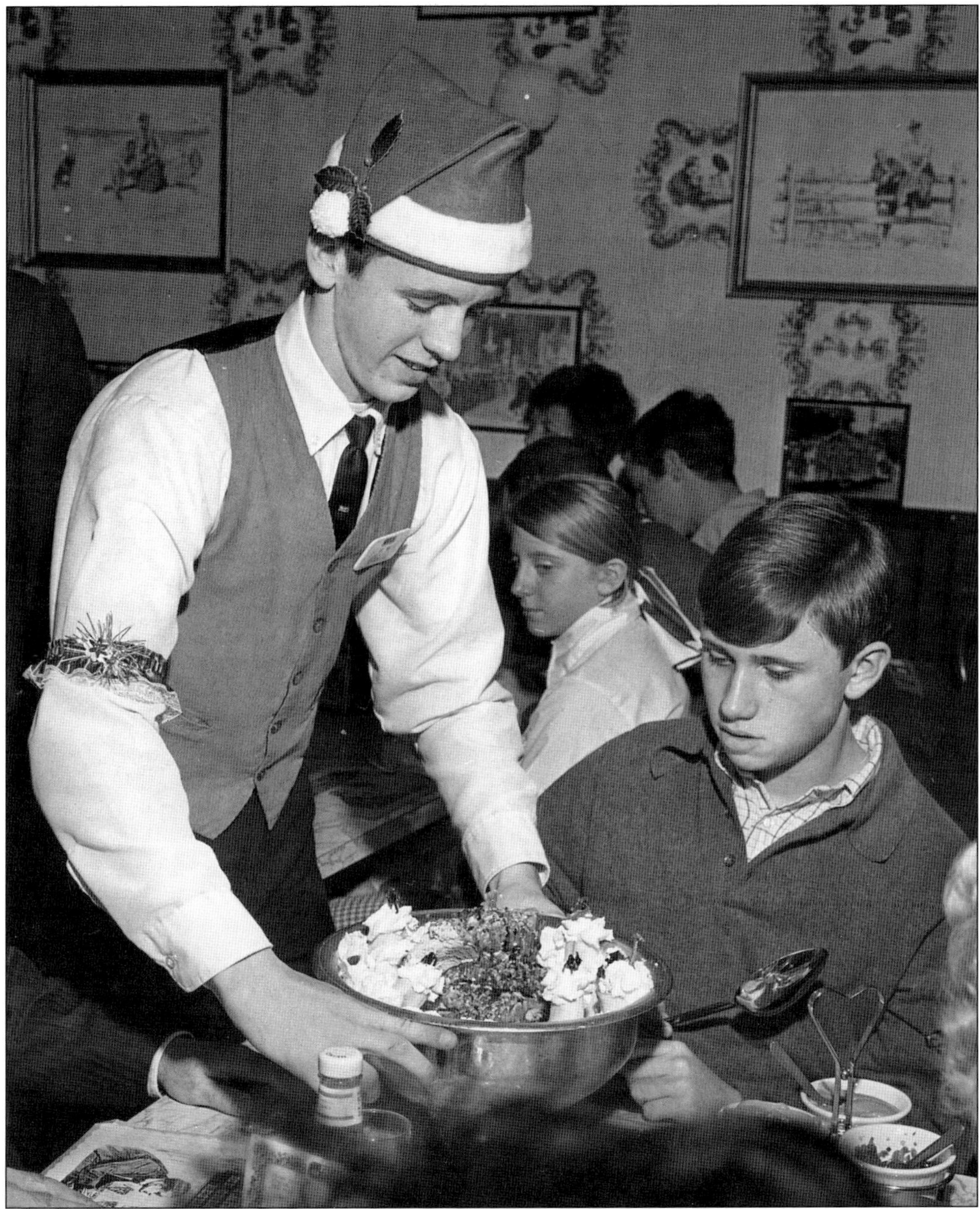

At the hockey club Christmas party, a Farrell's waiter is seen delivering the Portland Zoo to a young gentleman who appears willing to eat the entire sundae himself. Over the years, Farrell's often had guests attempt to eat an entire Zoo sundae themselves. Some were successful.

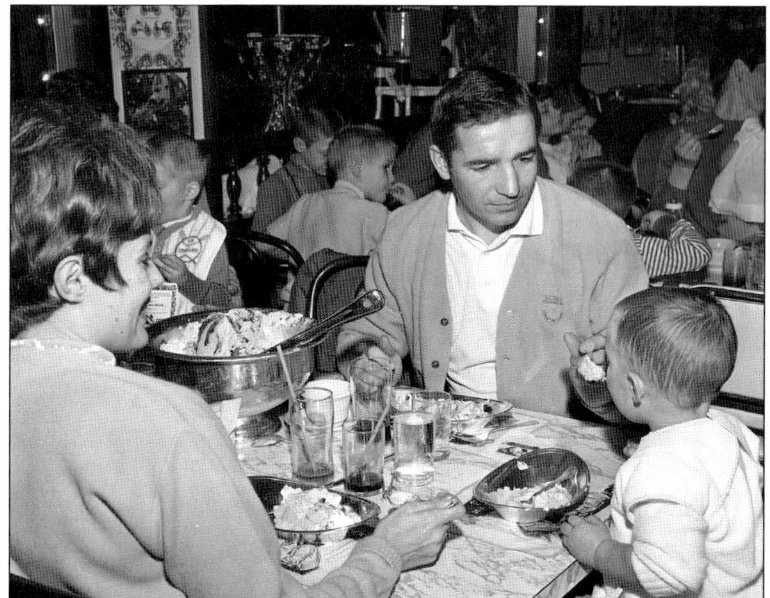

The Portland Zoo became the most popular sundae for large group celebrations. It was easier to prepare one big sundae than 10 small ones. If the party made a reservation in advance, the fountain men could scoop the ice cream portion of the sundae in advance and freeze it until it was ready for toppings.

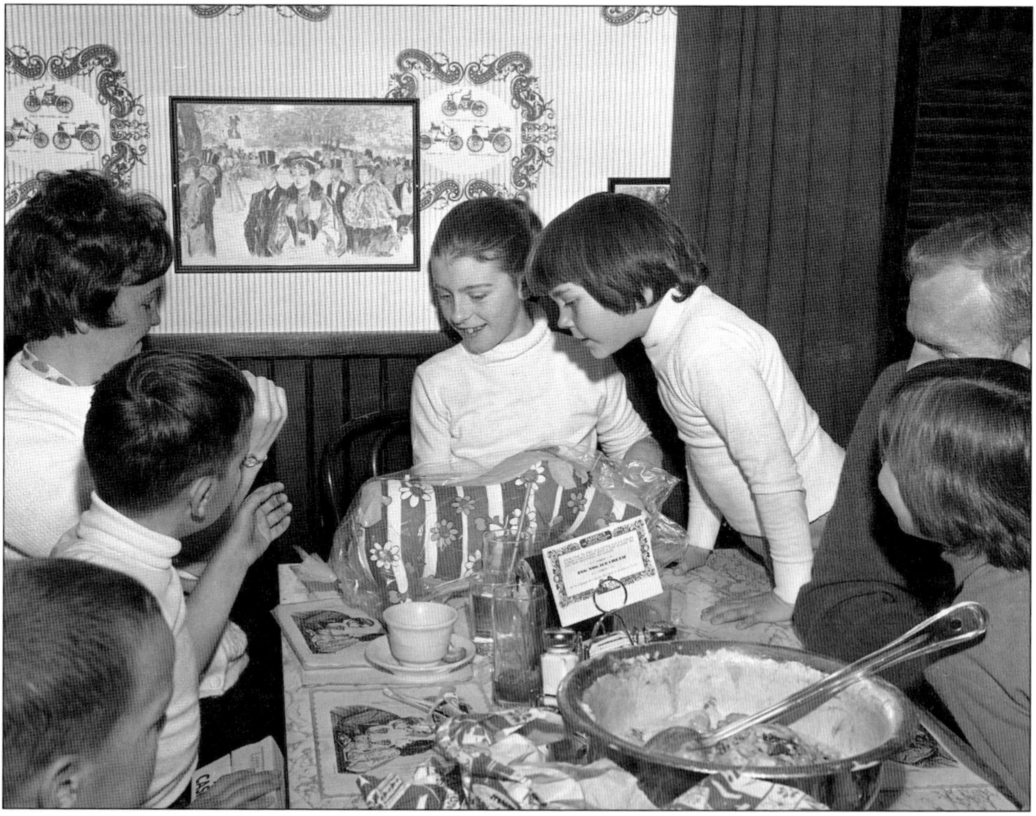

After finishing off a Portland Zoo sundae, a family starts to open Christmas gifts. Parents soon realized the advantage of having parties at Farrell's meant not only would they not have to cleanup the dishes after the food and ice cream were served, but Farrell's employees would also cleanup the wrapping paper and any other mess created by gift openings.

The kitchen workers are busy preparing the food orders at the Lloyd Center location. Farrell's installed microphones so the workers in the kitchen could use the PA system in the store to call for the waiters and waitresses to pick up their food orders.

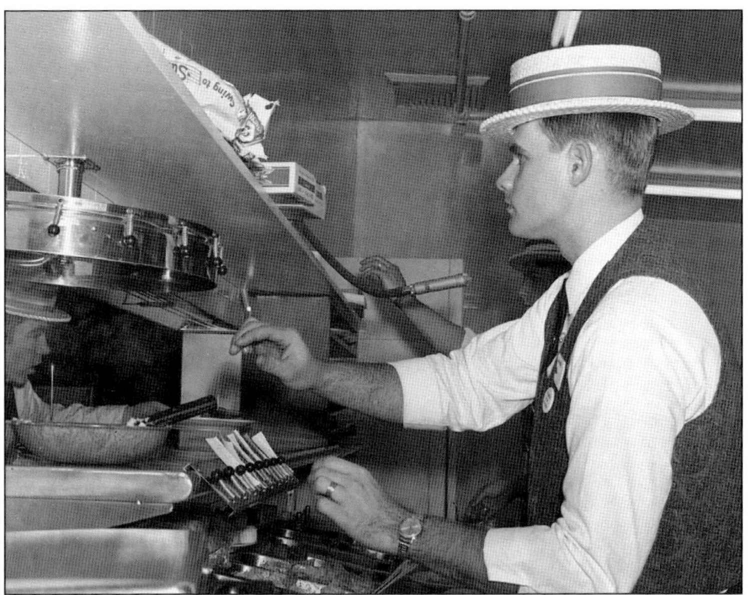

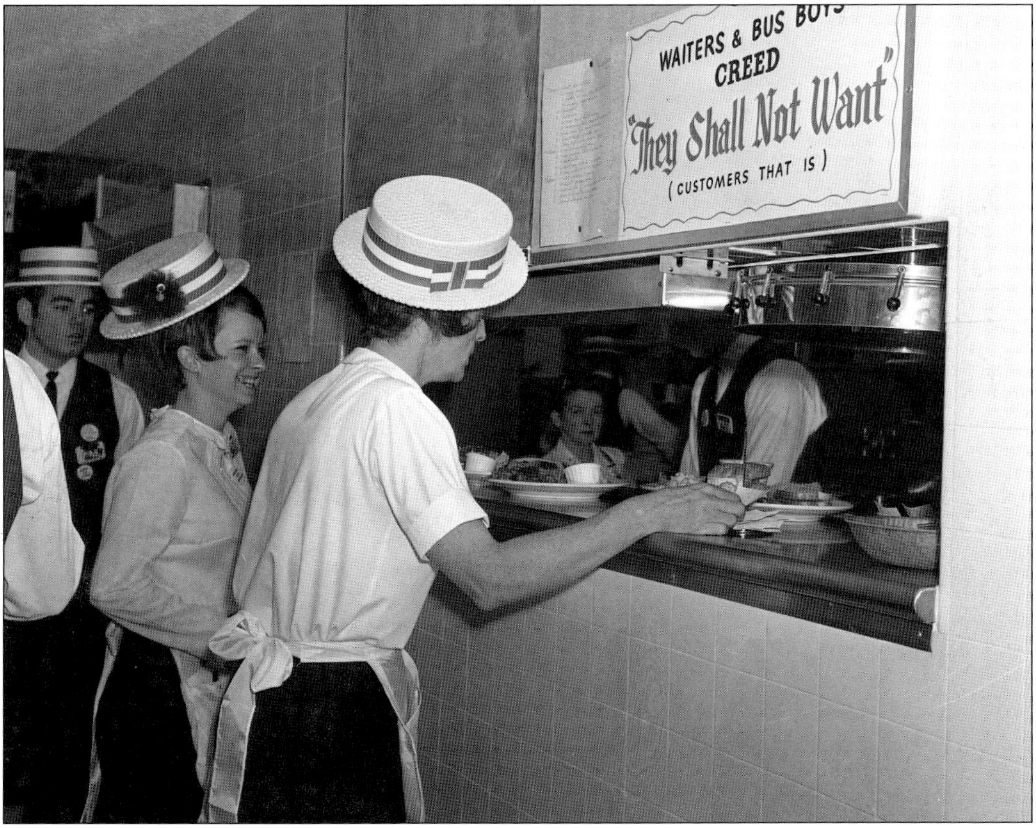

Waiters and waitresses wait at the kitchen window in the server area as orders back up in the kitchen. As the food business grew with the introduction of mall-based locations, the kitchen window would become larger at later stores. Most kitchen sales at the early locations happened at lunchtime.

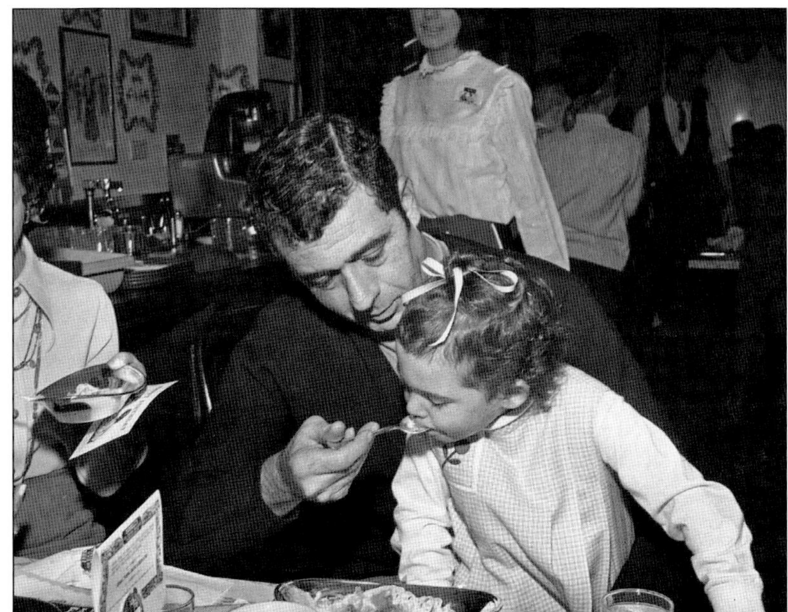

A father and daughter sharing ice cream is shown here. Many customers would go on to have fond memories of Farrell's experiences with their families. Farrell's would be the place to celebrate family birthdays and first dates.

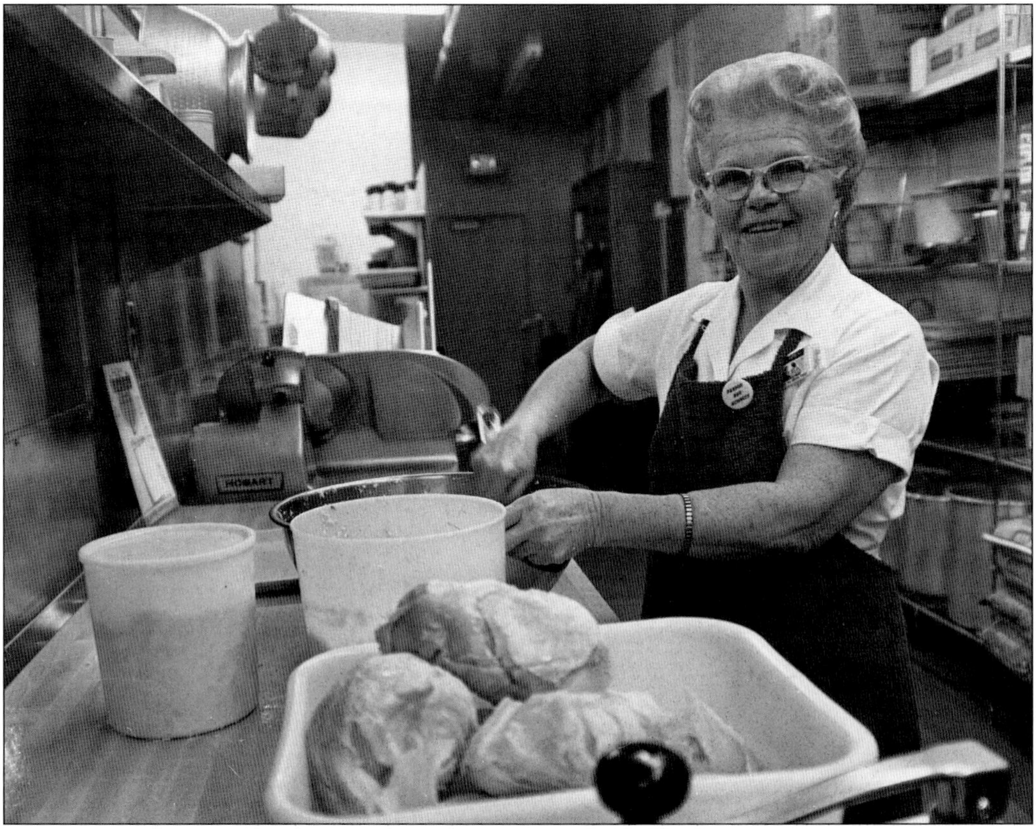

A kitchen worker preps items for the kitchen. The prep area was often behind or adjacent to the kitchen and was where vegetables were cleaned and chopped, meats were sliced, and other kitchen ingredients were prepared for use.

Two young girls are seen sharing their Christmas gift experiences with each other at the hockey club Christmas party in 1968.

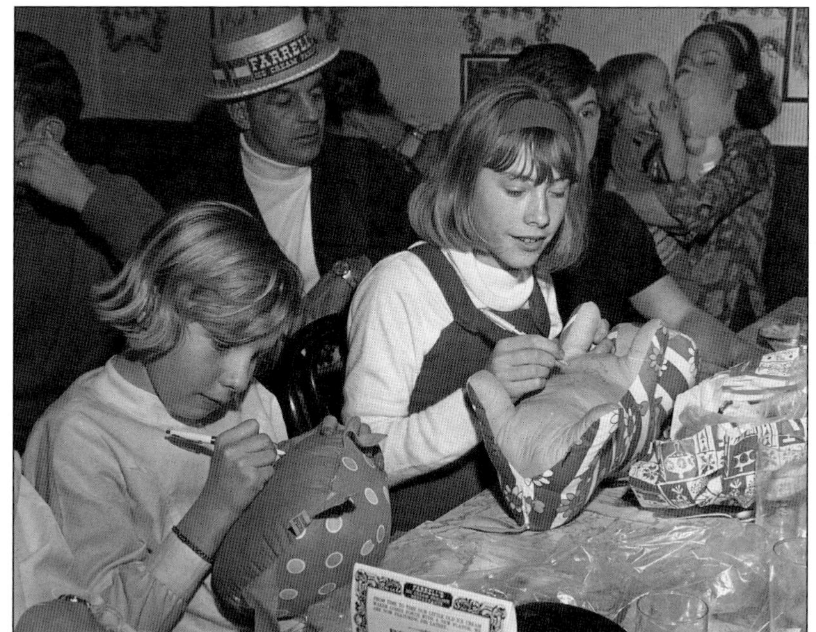

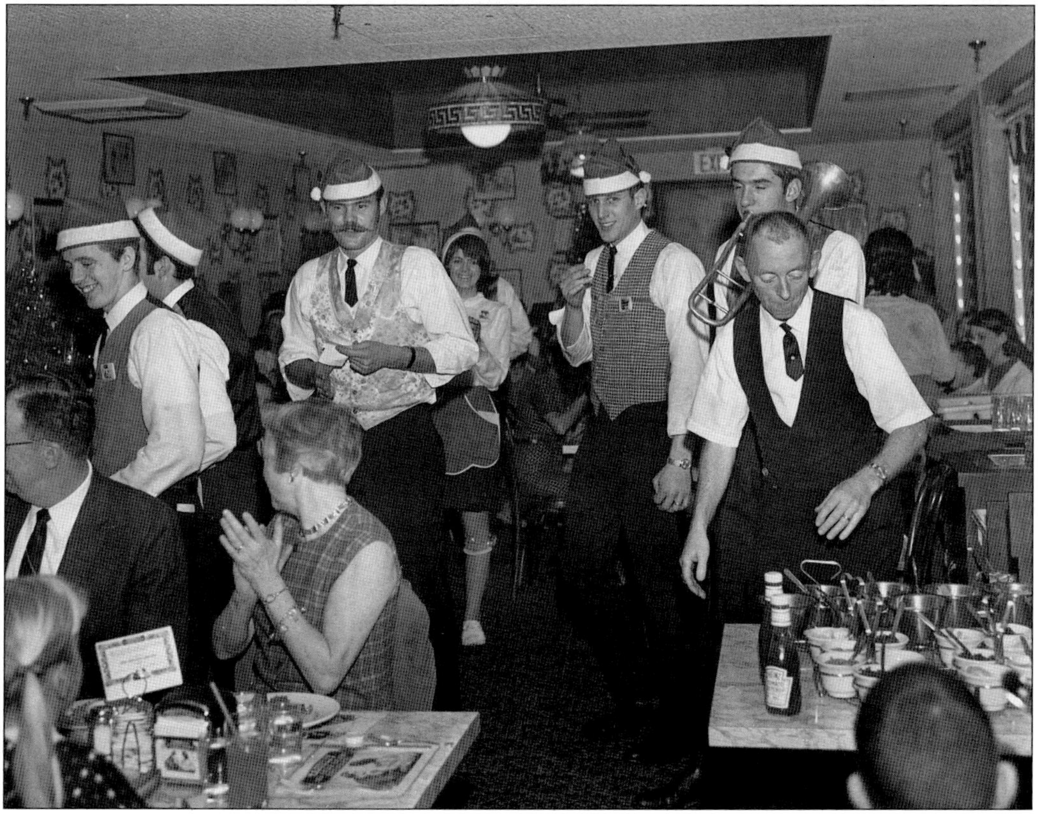

Managers and waiters are surveying the mess in one of the party rooms as the hockey club Christmas party starts to wind down. Co-owner Ken McCarthy (right) is seen helping assess the cleanup needs.

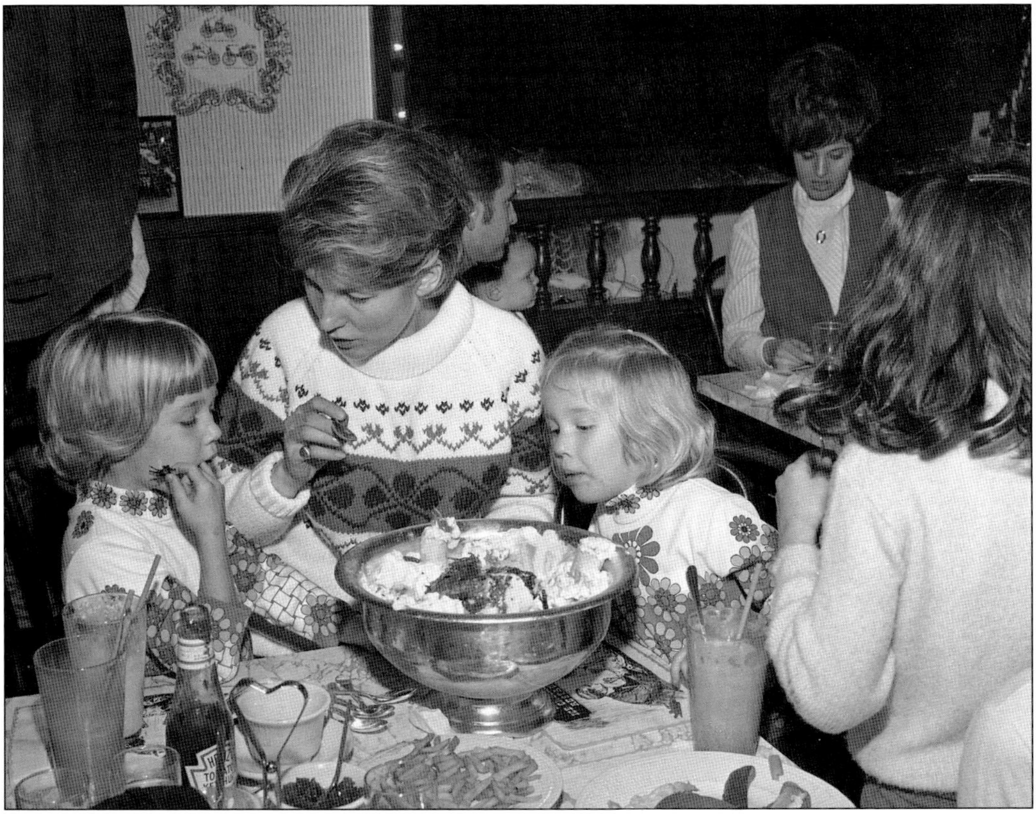

A mother and her daughters are evaluating the best attack on their Portland Zoo sundae. As this sundae contained all the flavors of ice cream carried by Farrell's, children would often have favorite parts of the Zoo sundae.

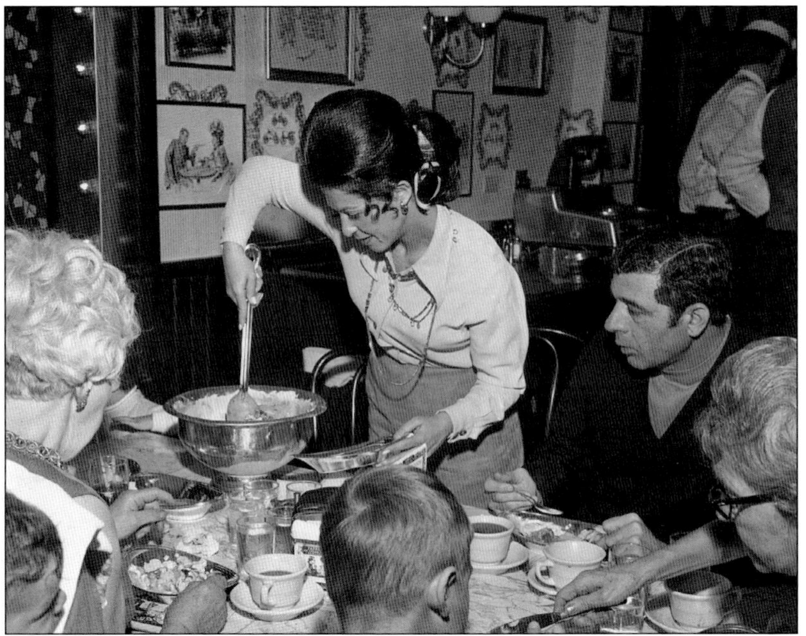

A family is shown sharing a Portland Zoo sundae at the hockey club Christmas party.

A mom and her child show off a couple of gifts distributed by Santa Claus at the 1968 hockey club Christmas party.

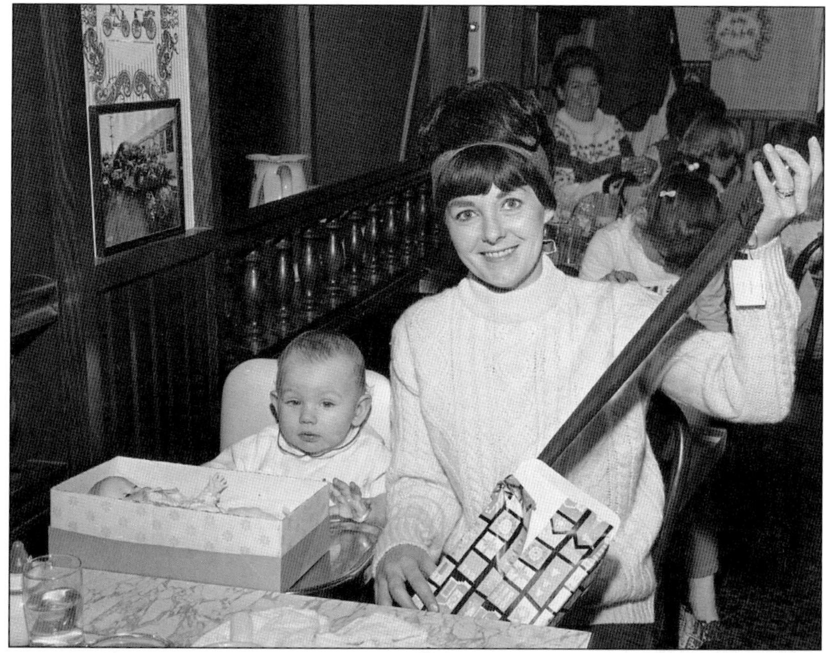

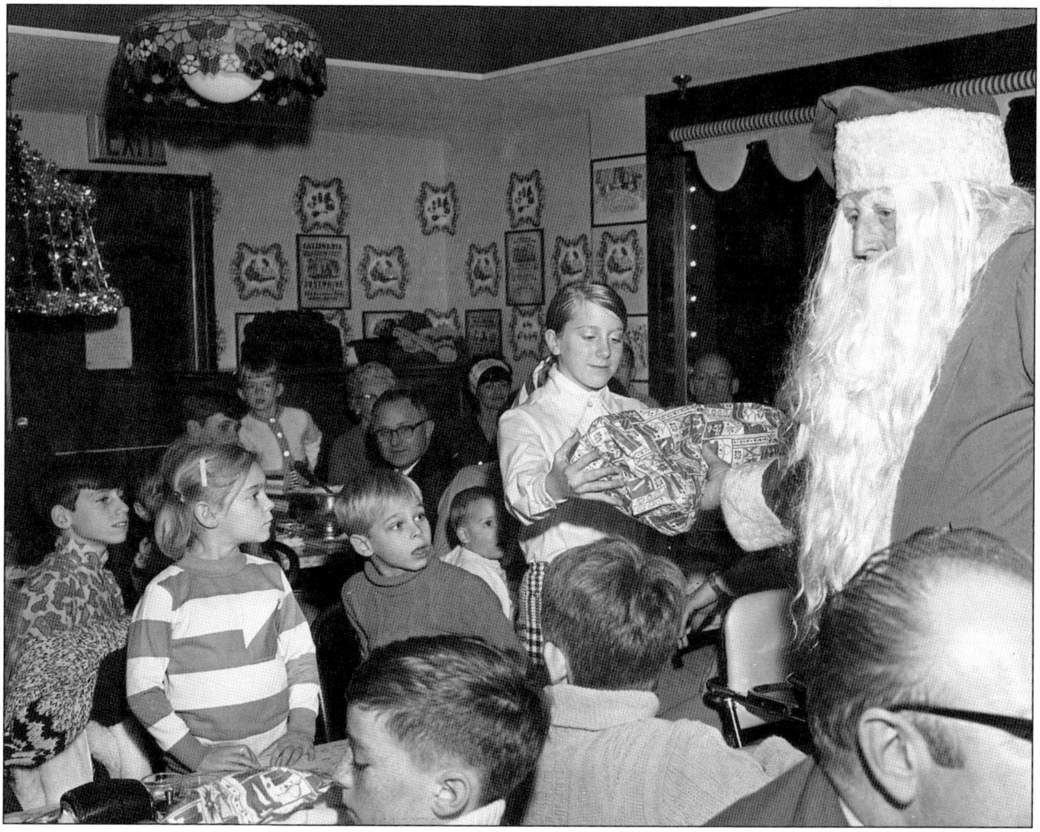

The children are all waiting for their Christmas gifts distributed by Santa Claus at the hockey club Christmas party.

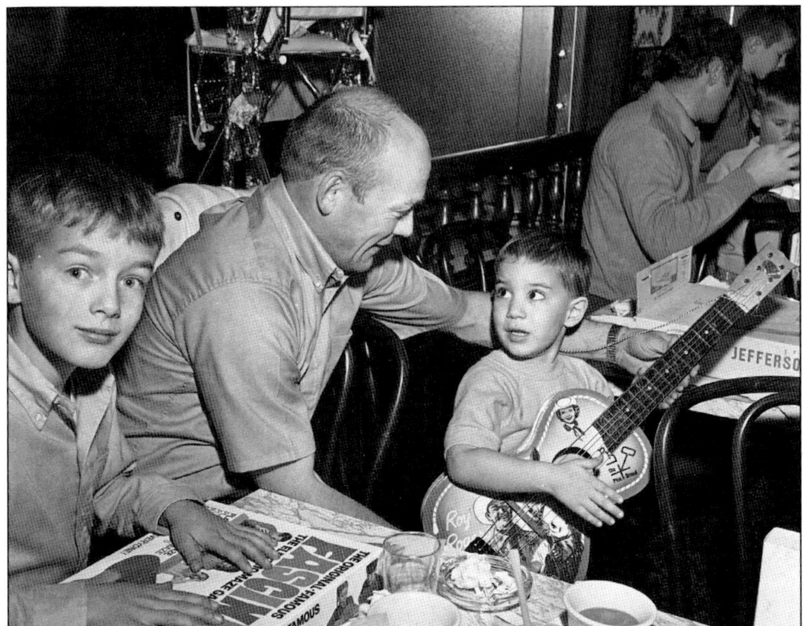

This father is trying to teach his son how to play the Roy Roger's guitar he received as a Christmas present.

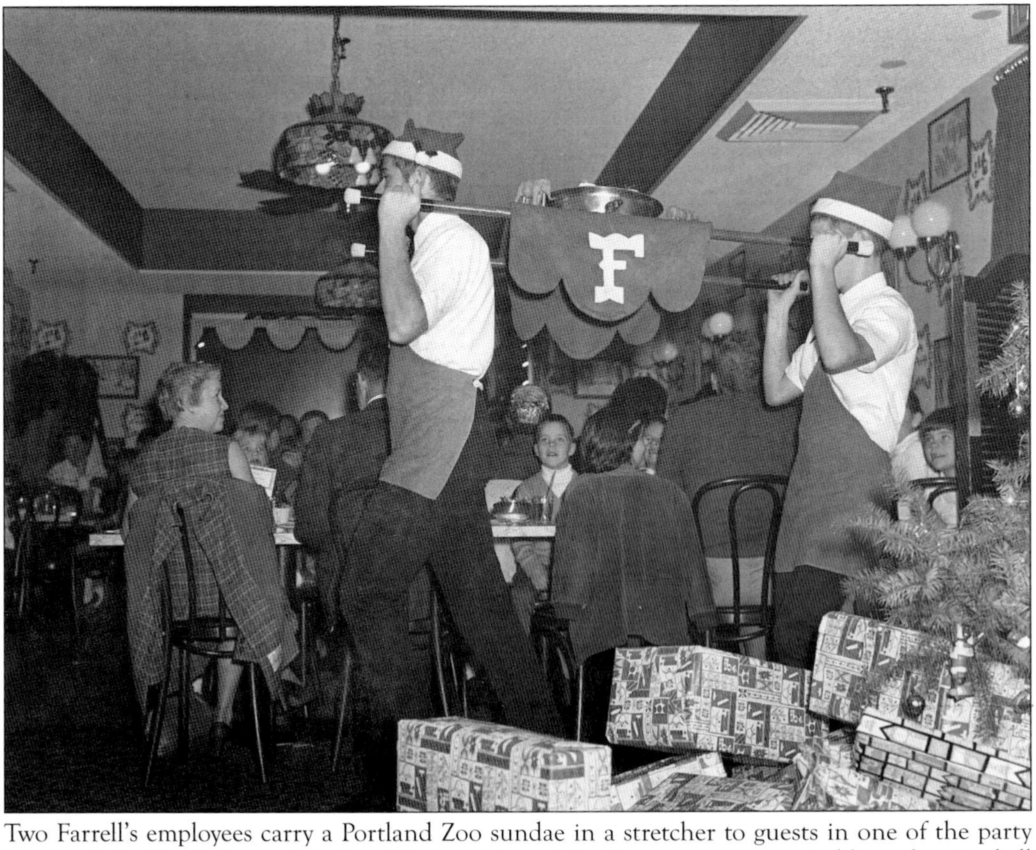

Two Farrell's employees carry a Portland Zoo sundae in a stretcher to guests in one of the party rooms of the Lloyd Center location. The running of the Zoo was accompanied by a clanging bell and siren.

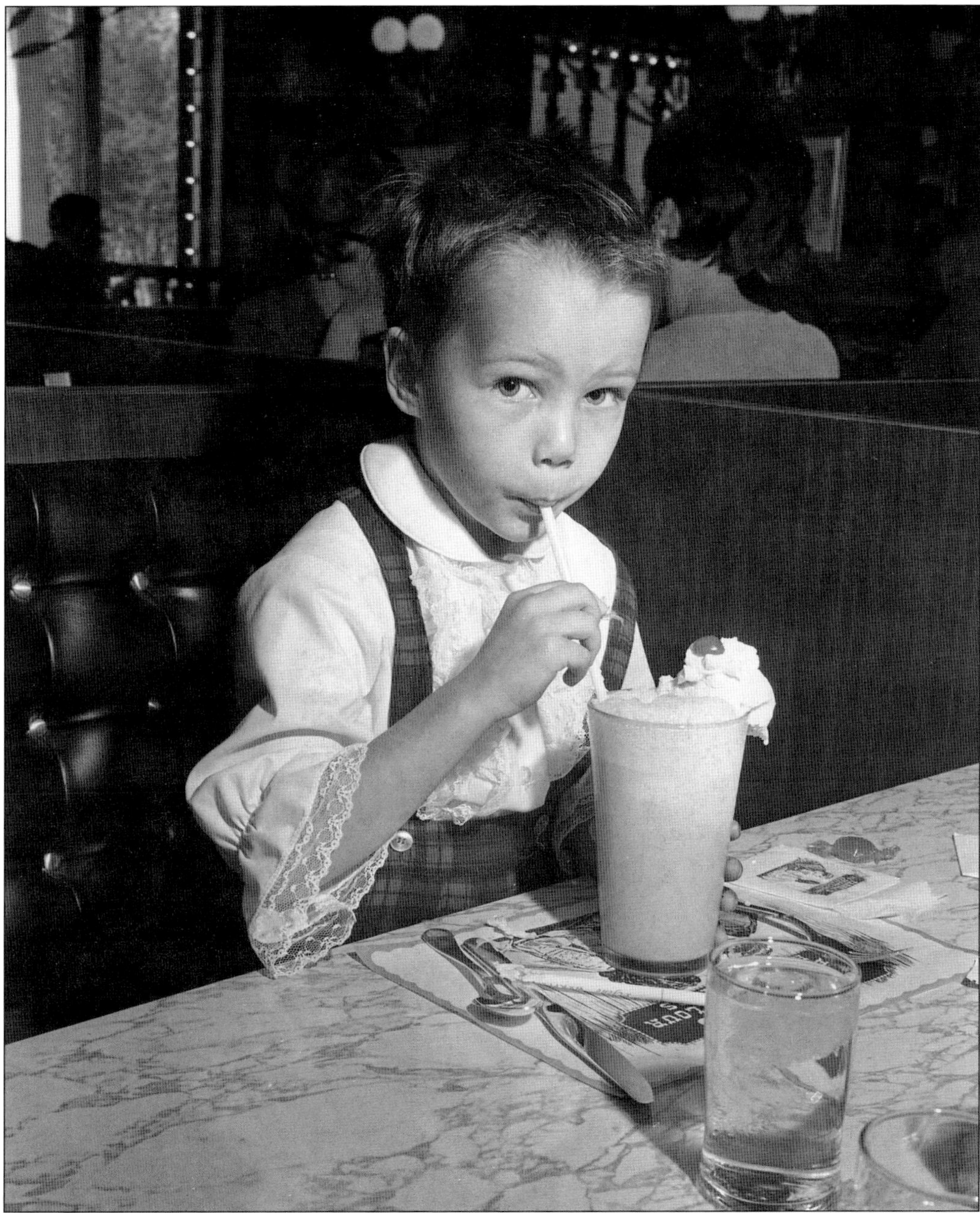

A young customer enjoys an ice cream soda in the main dining room at the Lloyd Center location. While this is the full-size serving, a kiddie-size soda was available for smaller appetites.

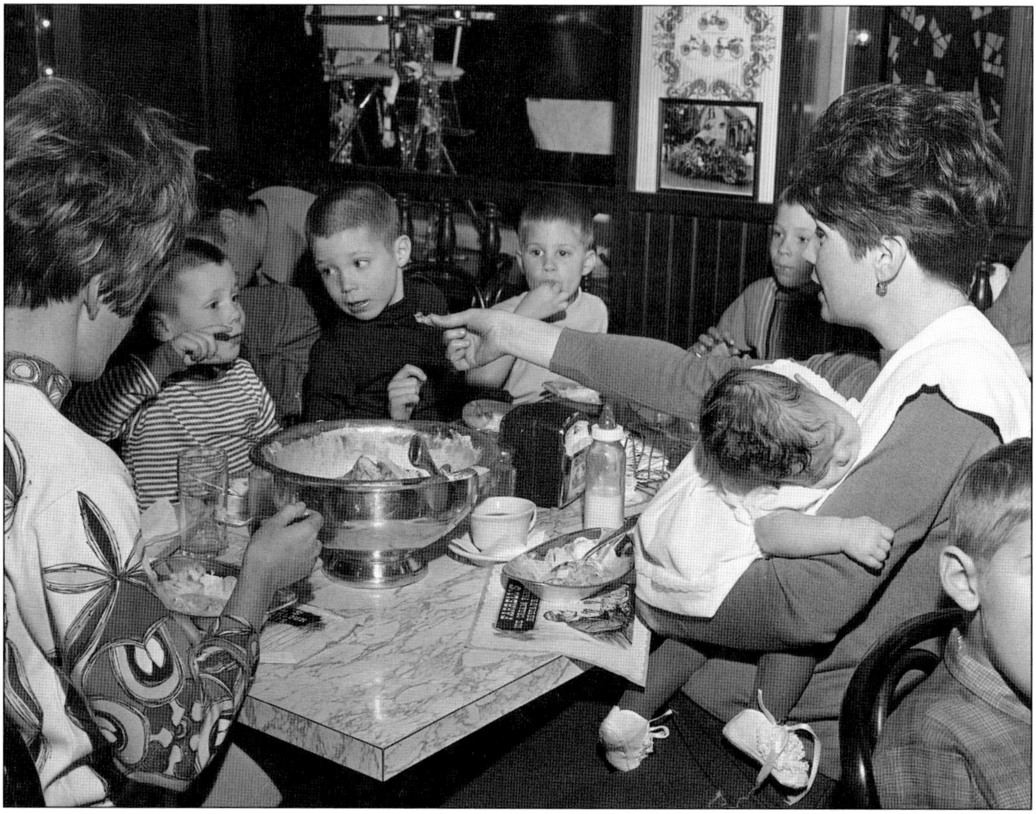

A mother is seen handing a small plastic animal pick pulled from the Portland Zoo sundae to a young boy. Amazingly, her young baby can sleep through all the noise from the hockey club Christmas party.

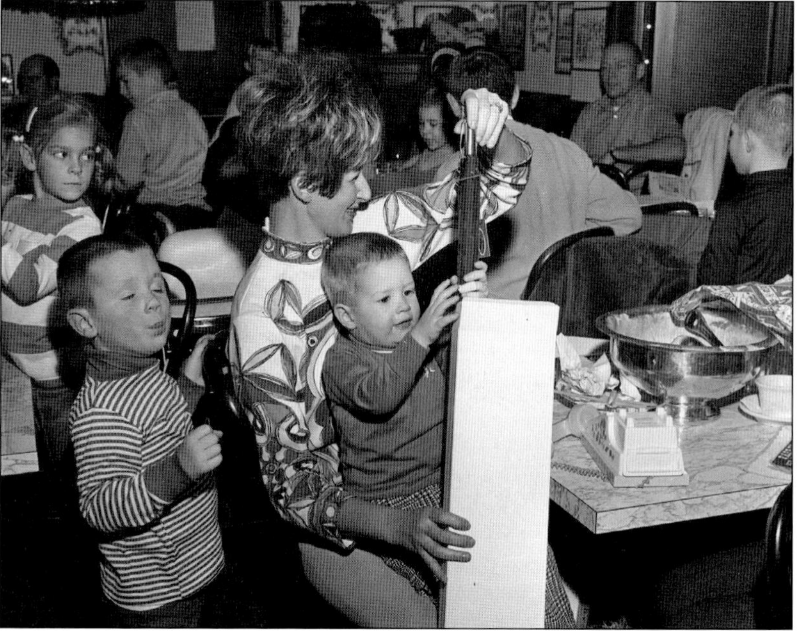

A young boy is shown checking out a toy rifle given as a gift from Santa Claus at the hockey club Christmas party.

A father happily spoons up helpings of the Portland Zoo sundae for his family. As this sundae was meant to serve 10 people, there was more than enough to share at this table.

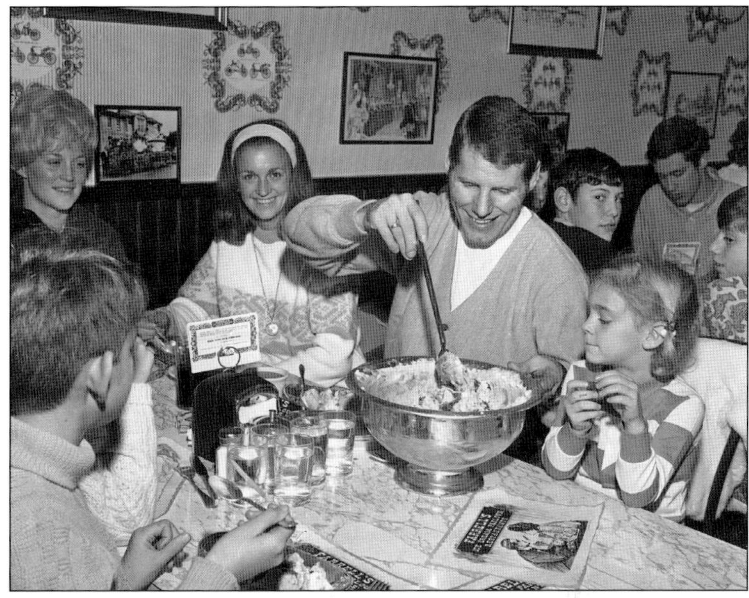

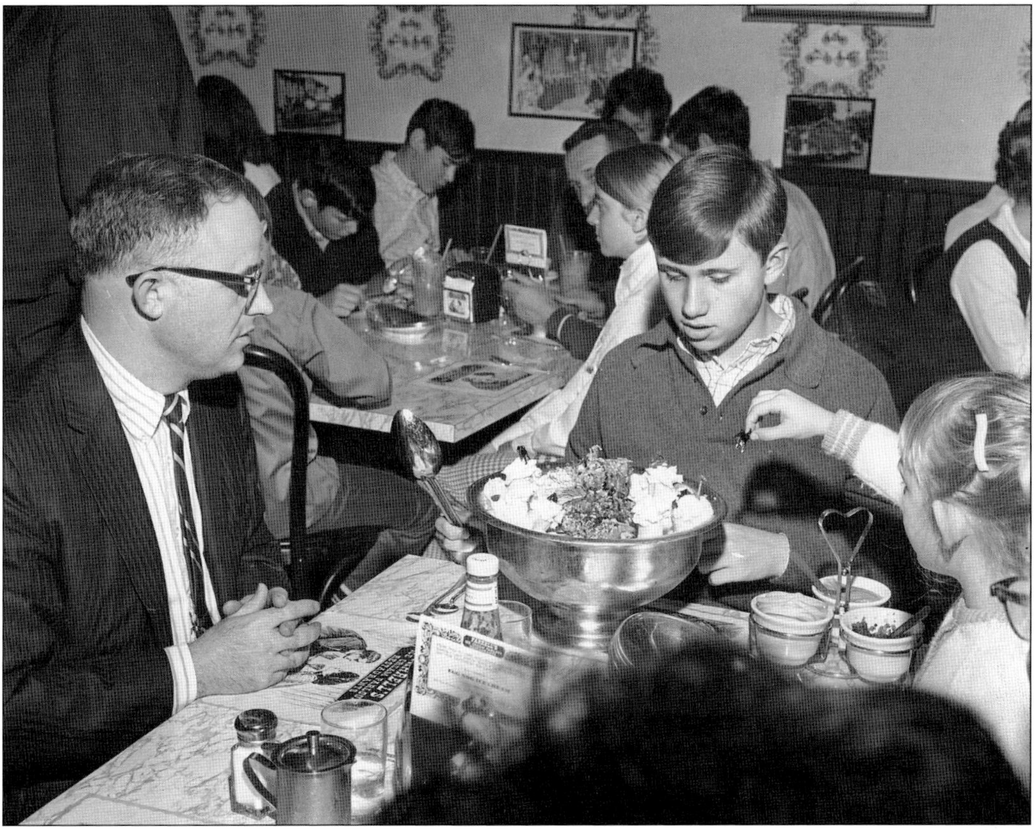

A young customer is deciding if he should try to eat the entire Portland Zoo sundae himself while his sister pulls out one of the plastic animal picks from the sundae. Later, Farrell's replaced the small plastic picks with animal cracker cookies for safety, as the plastic animal picks were a choking hazard.

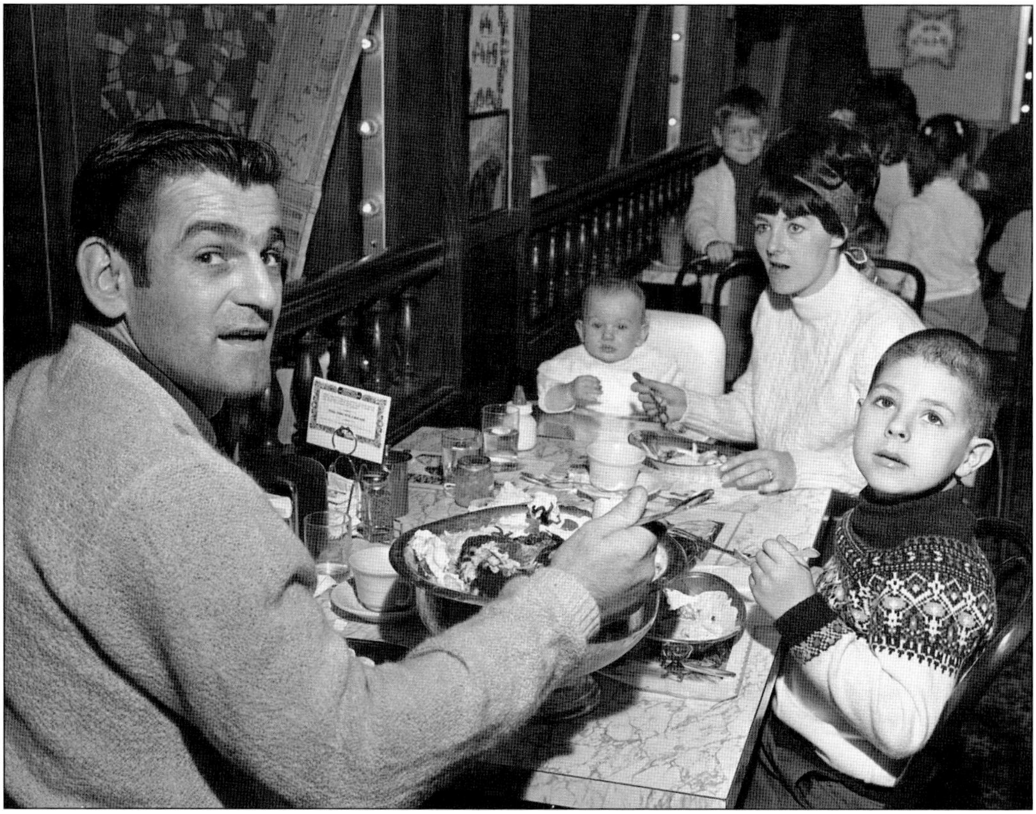

With the popularity of the Portland Zoo sundae, Farrell's later added the Hot Fudge Volcano sundae. This sundae was 30 scoops of vanilla ice cream served flaming, thanks to a couple of ice cubes soaked in lemon extract. The lava for this sundae was a super soda glass filled with hot fudge.

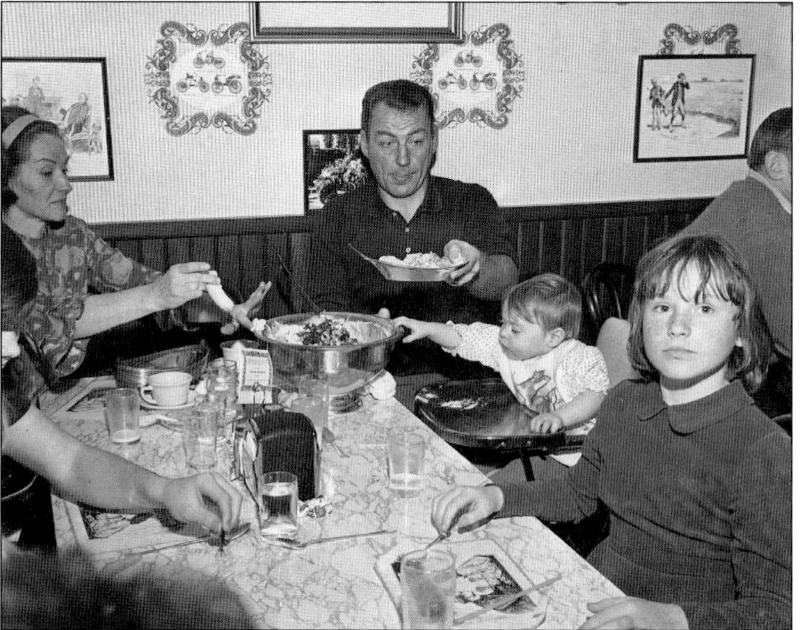

As parties at Farrell's grew in popularity, packages were added, including a Keystone Cop's–themed Police Farce party. A volcano party included Hawaiian grass skirts and leis.

A trio of customers check out the Christmas presents distributed at the hockey club Christmas party.

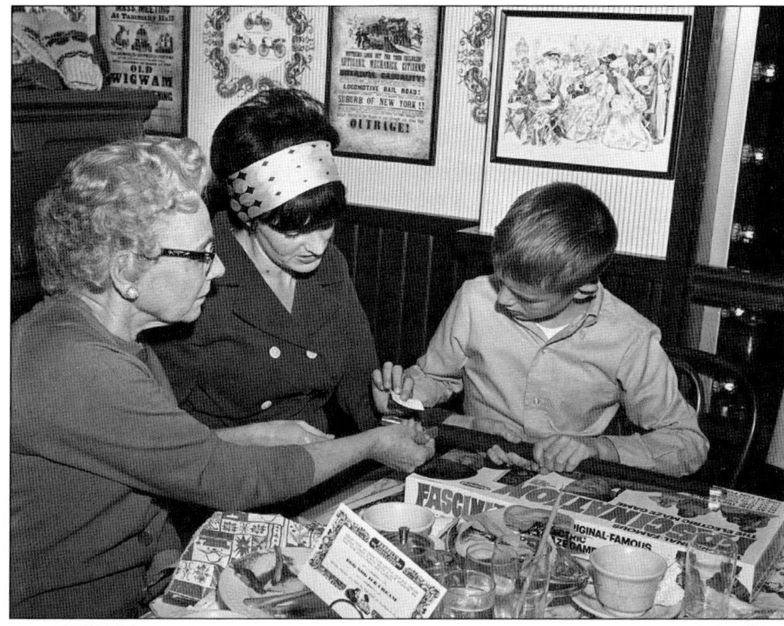

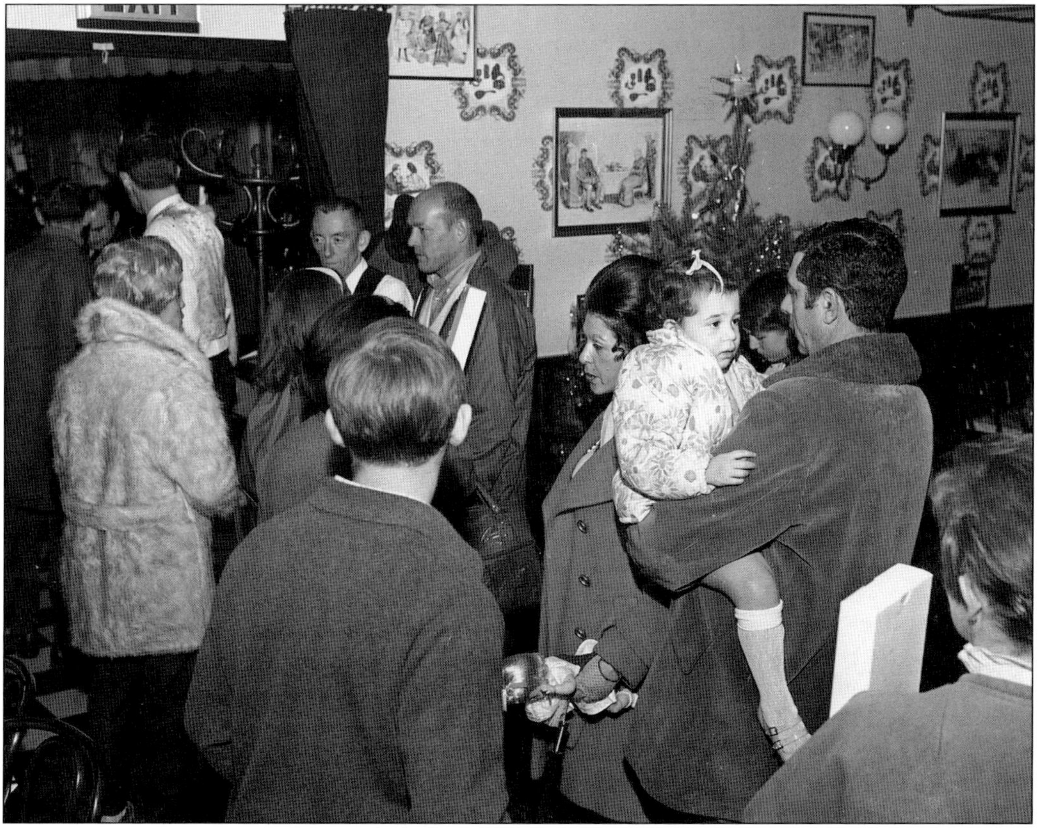

Hockey club guests leave behind a mess for the Farrell's staff to cleanup after their Christmas party. With multiple party rooms, large groups often held parties at Farrell's to avoid having to cleanup the mess at home.

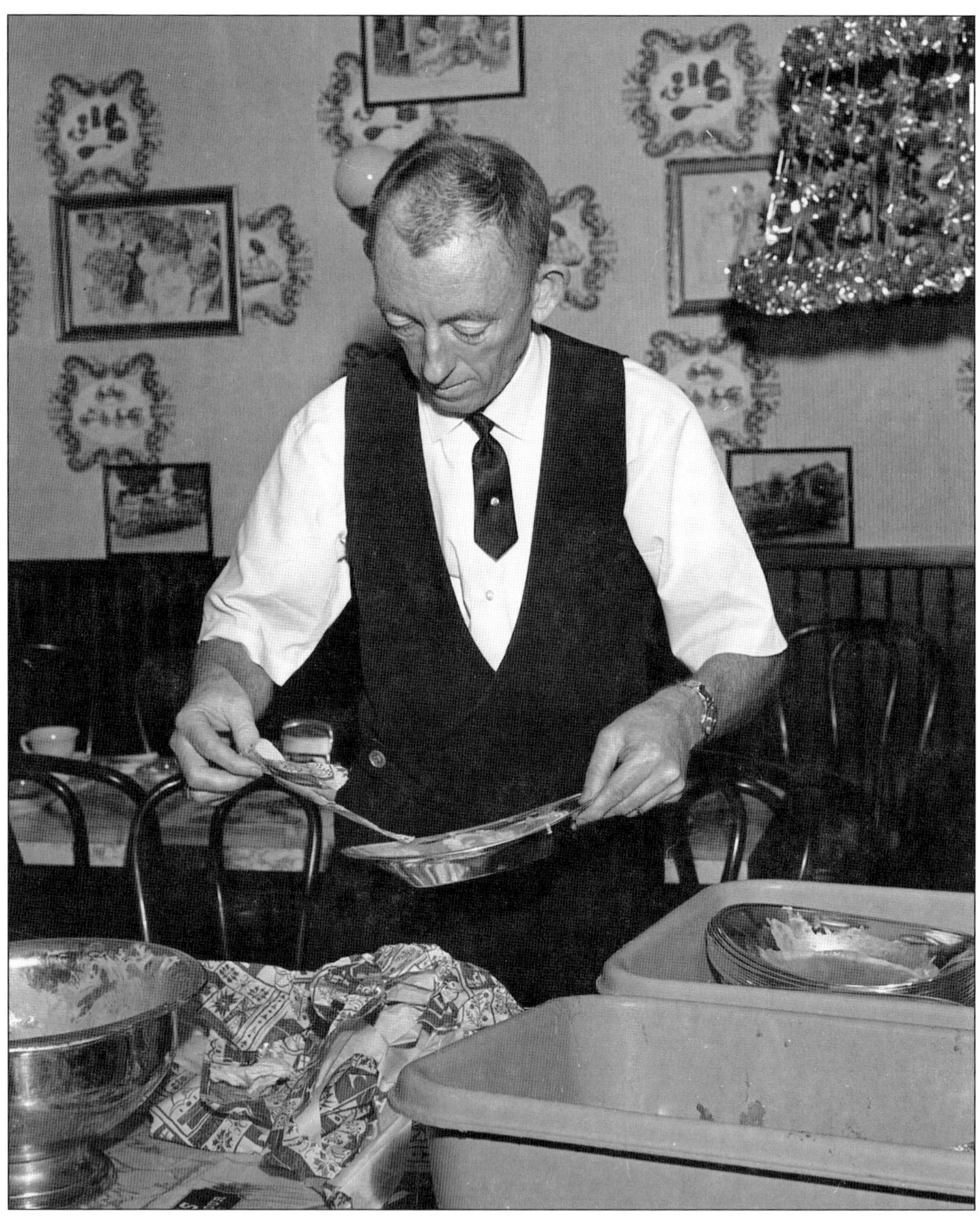

Ken McCarthy works on bussing a table following the hockey club party. After five years of ownership with Bob Farrell, McCarthy was starting to feel as though his contributions were not acknowledged.

Five

Sixth Anniversary and Beyond

On September 13, 1969, Farrell's Ice Cream Parlours celebrated its sixth anniversary. The chain was growing and successful, but cracks were showing up in the relationship between Bob Farrell and Ken McCarthy. When the two partners opened their first location, the plan was to build the chain up and sell it after 10 years. But, in 1969, the stress of running a successful and growing restaurant empire forced the partners to reevaluate their plans. After McCarthy's retirement from the company in 1970, profitability declined, and McCarthy was unhappy with the changes that were made. As an owner, McCarthy was still receiving financial reports for each Farrell's location.

They sold their chain after nine years. Bob Farrell went on to be involved in other restaurant brands with some of his former Farrell's managers. In 1976, he received the Horatio Alger Award for his "rags to riches" success. He also became a motivational speaker based on his "Give 'em the pickle" speech on customer service. Farrell remained as president of Farrell's under the ownership of Marriott Corporation. He continued in that role until 1975, when he retired from Farrell's.

Ken McCarthy pursued secondary education in biblical principles and Christian leadership, earned a doctorate of laws from the Judson Baptist College, and taught Bible study.

Ken McCarthy died in 2013, and Bob Farrell died in 2015.

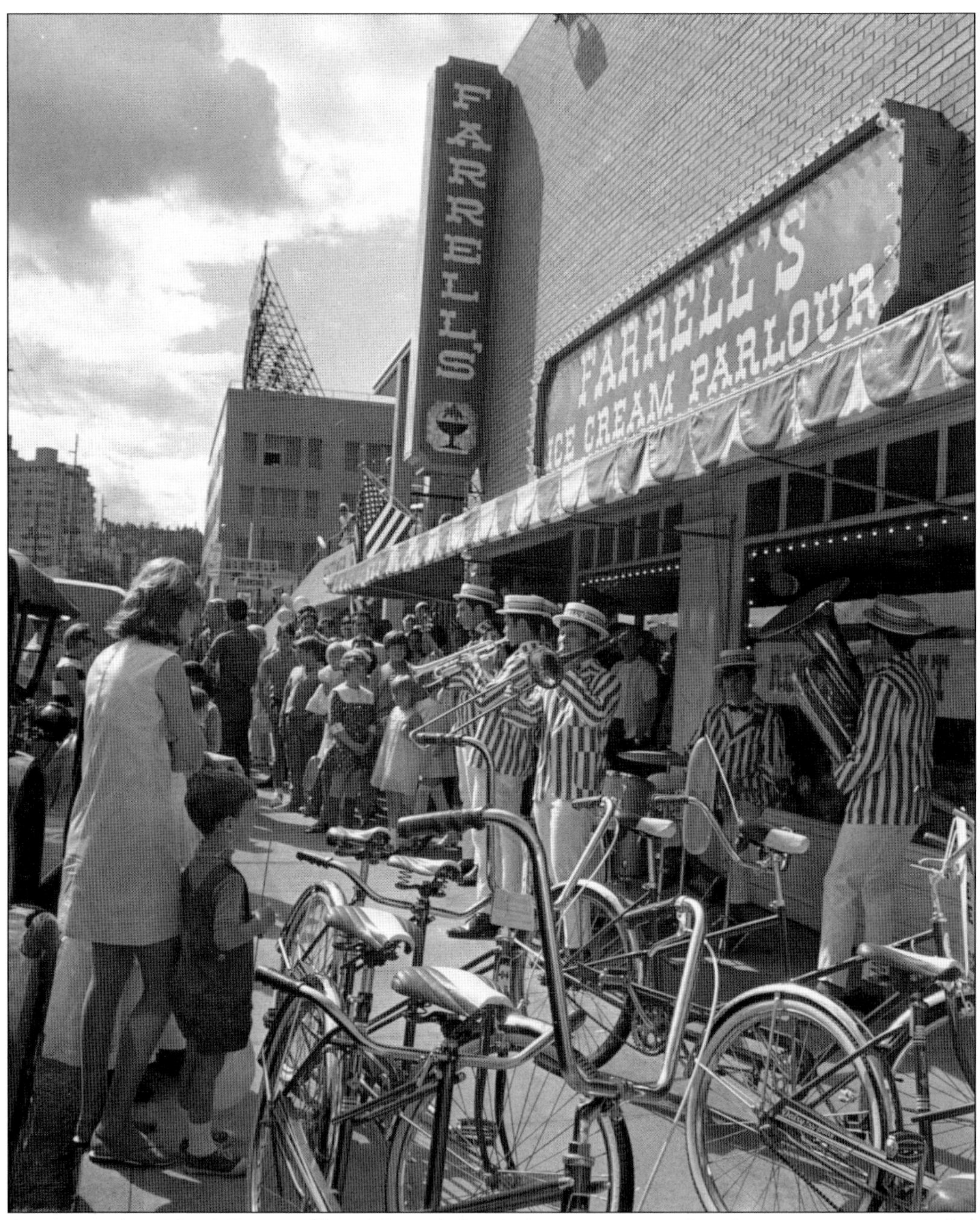

On September 13, 1969, Farrell's celebrated the sixth anniversary of its first store opening. It did so in a big way, starting at the original location at Twenty-first Avenue and Burnside Street.

The Rivergate Jazz Band is seen entertaining the customers with Dixieland music inside the Burnside Street location, along with a cowboy to entertain the guests.

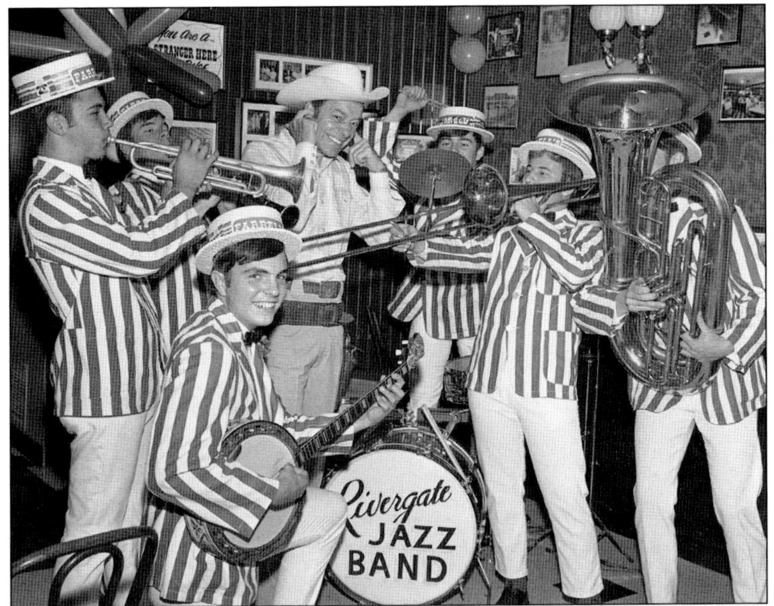

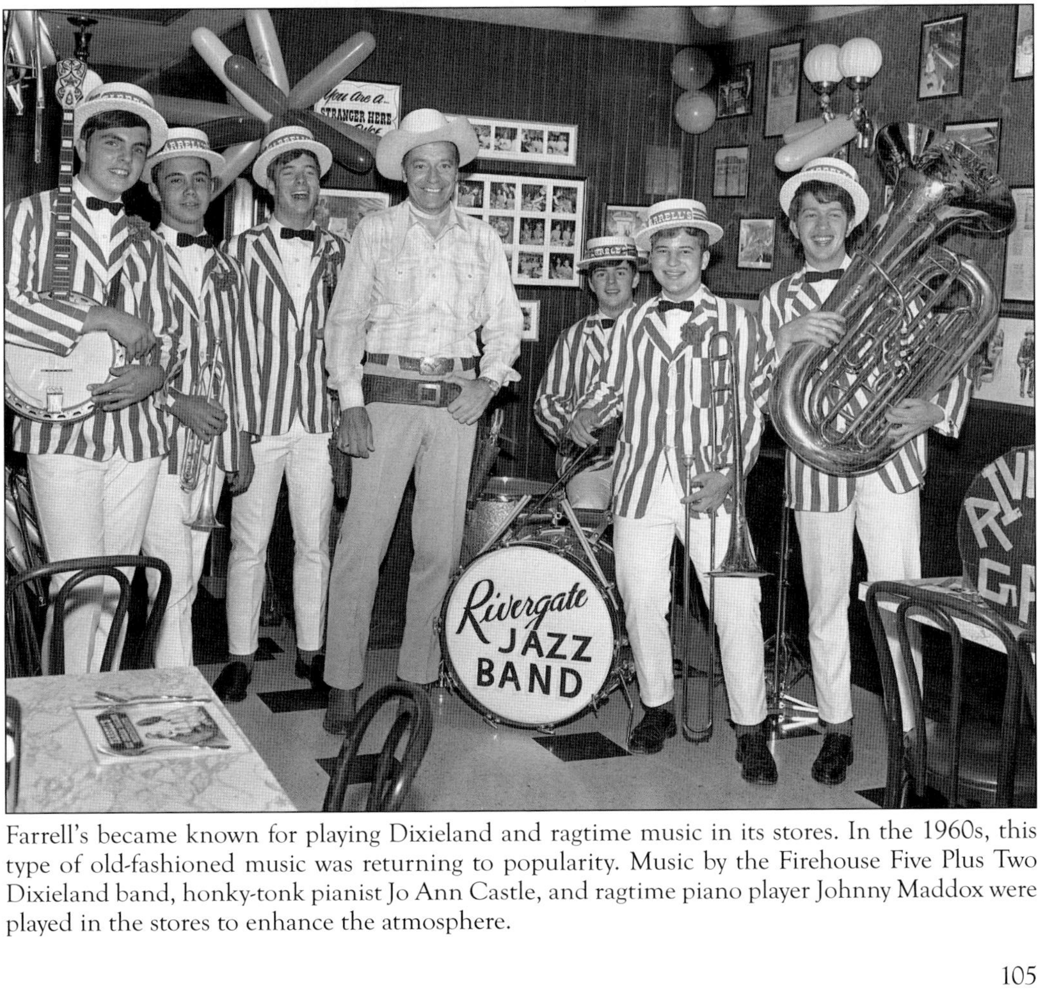

Farrell's became known for playing Dixieland and ragtime music in its stores. In the 1960s, this type of old-fashioned music was returning to popularity. Music by the Firehouse Five Plus Two Dixieland band, honky-tonk pianist Jo Ann Castle, and ragtime piano player Johnny Maddox were played in the stores to enhance the atmosphere.

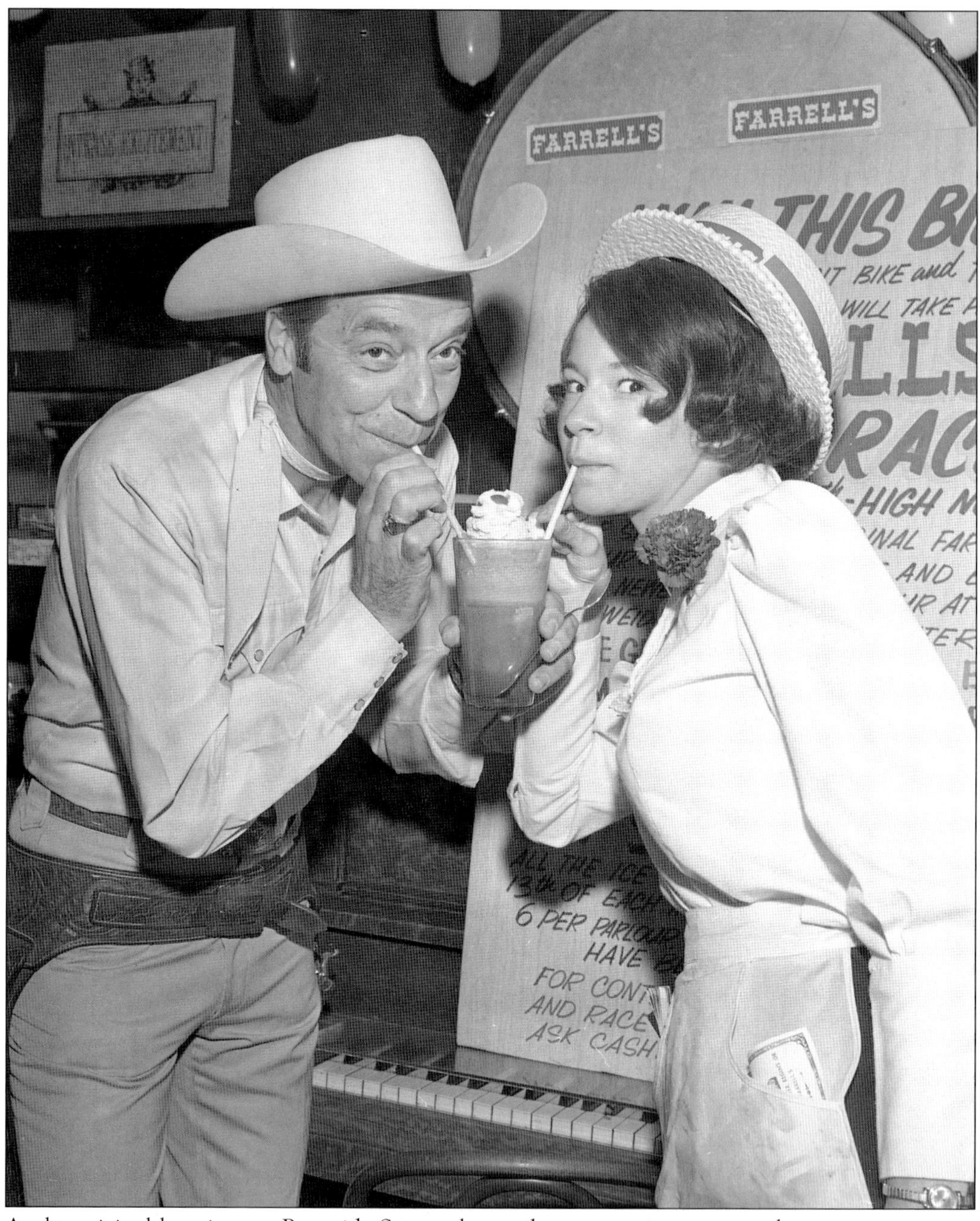

At the original location on Burnside Street, the cowboy entertainer is seen sharing an ice cream soda with a Farrell's waitress.

One of the events for the anniversary celebration was a three-mile tandem bicycle race from the original store on Burnside to the newest location near Lloyd Center. Bob Farrell is seen here corralling the riders and getting them ready to start the race.

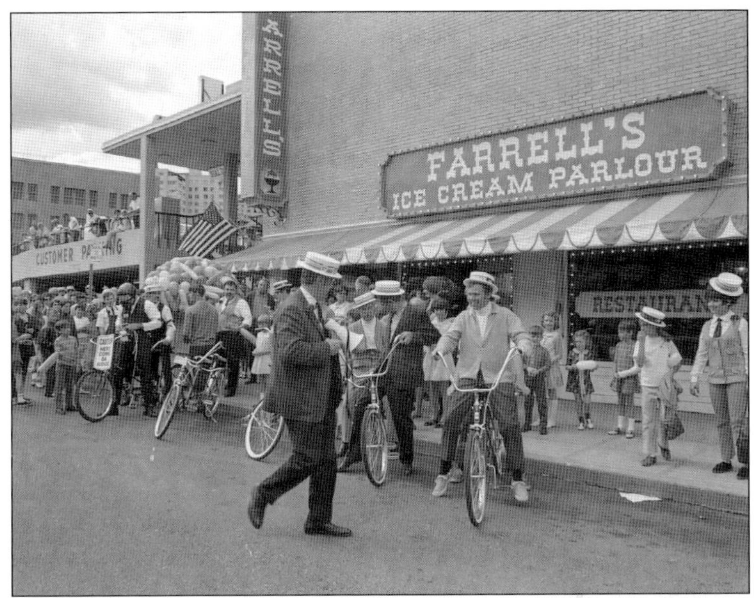

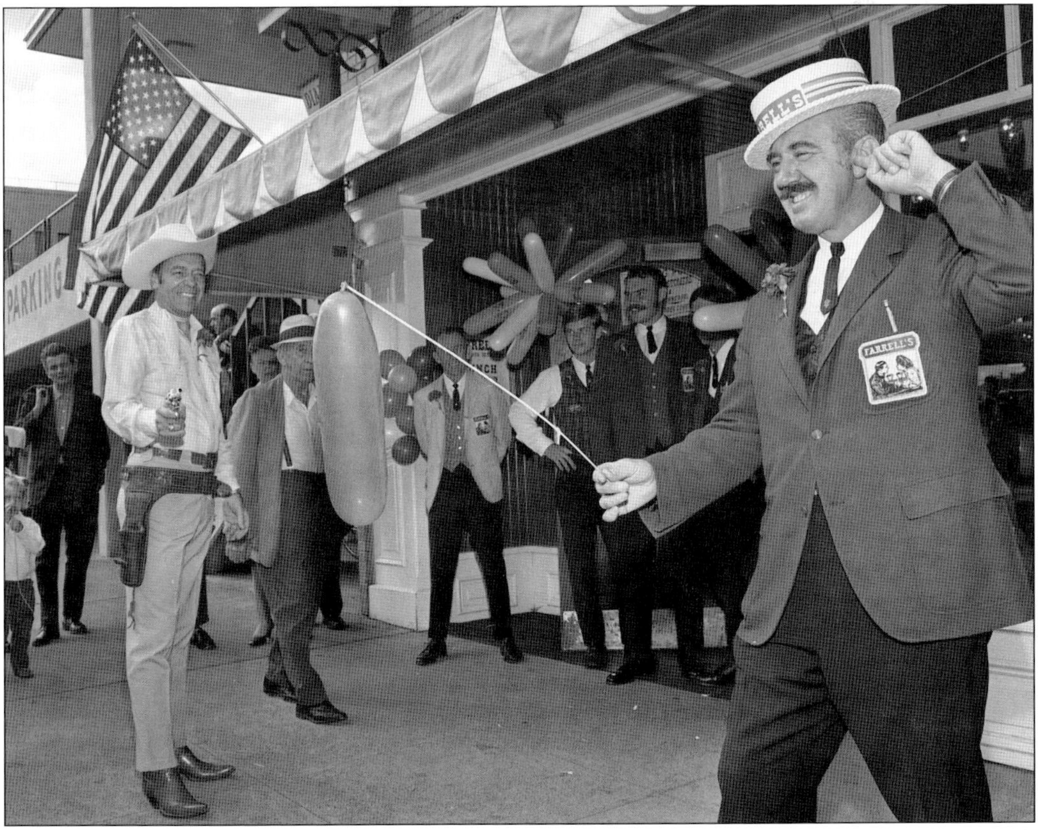

Outside the front door of the Burnside location, a cowboy prepares to shoot a balloon out of Bob Farrell's hand while Ken McCarthy watches. While Western television shows were declining in popularity by 1969, there was still enough interest to have a costumed cowboy participate in the anniversary celebration.

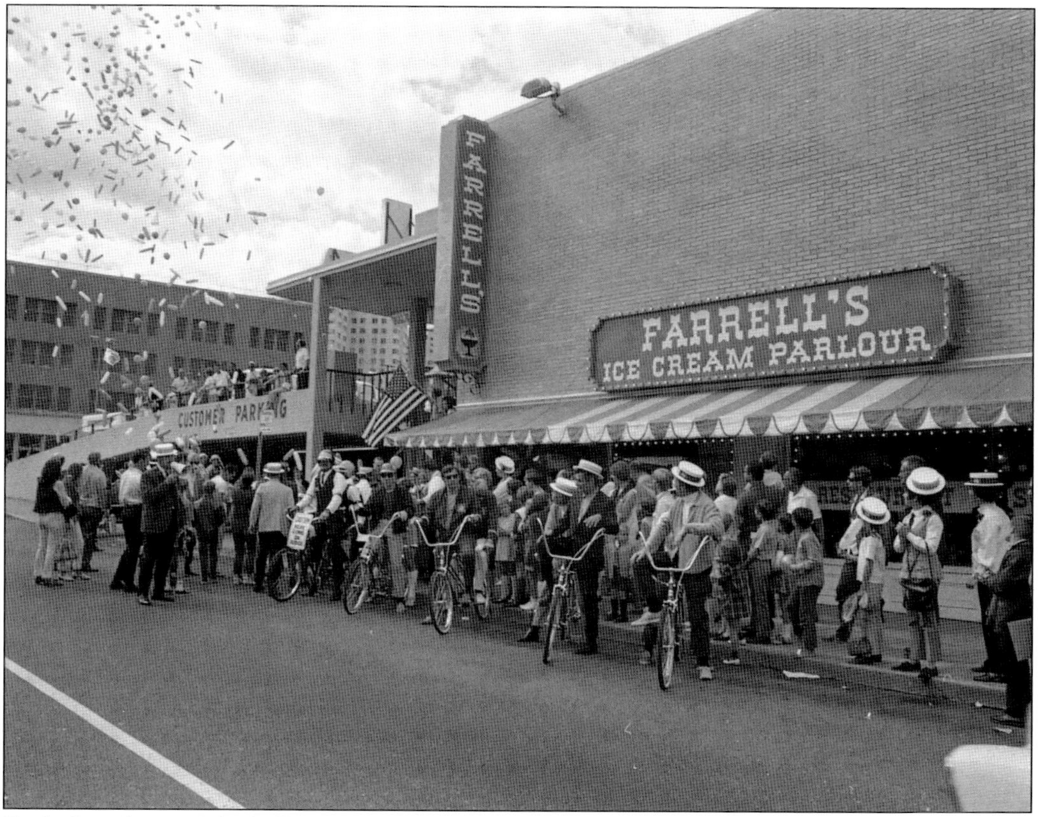

With the release of the balloons, Bob Farrell (at left with the megaphone) is seen announcing the start of the three-mile tandem bicycle race to the newest location near Lloyd Center.

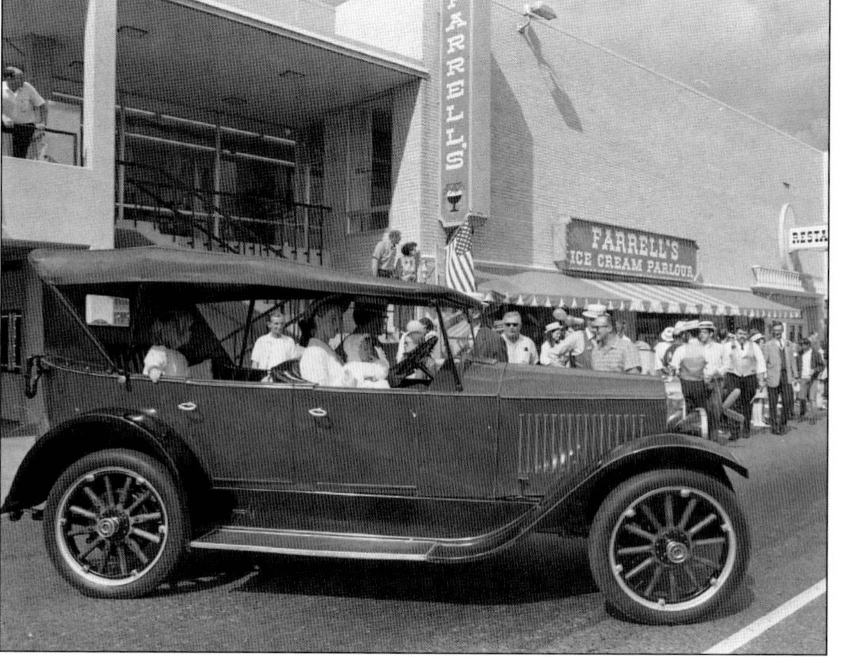

Farrell's arranged with owners of classic cars to parade their period-appropriate cars from the Burnside Street Farrell's to the location near Lloyd Center.

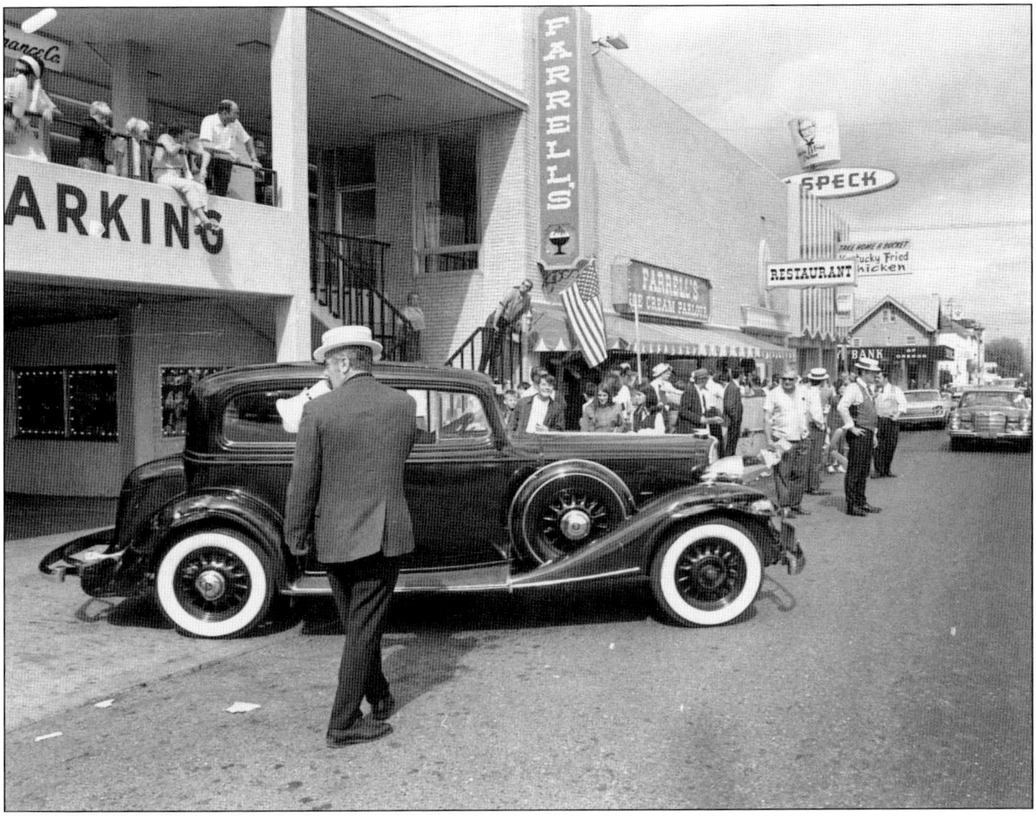

Bob Farrell directs the old-time automobiles out of the parking garage for the original Farrell's location on Burnside Street. The parade of cars would travel through Portland to the newest location near Lloyd Center.

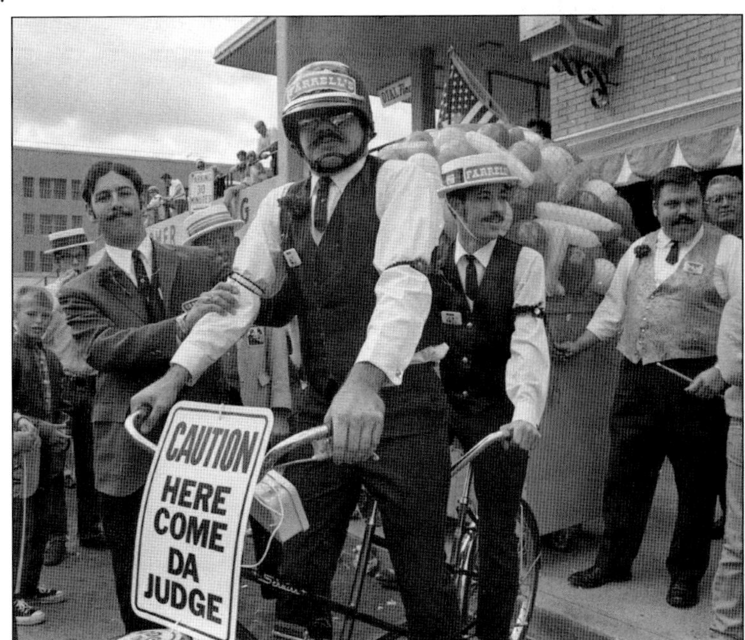

Even Farrell's employees are involved in the tandem bicycle race between the locations as a manager provides encouragement.

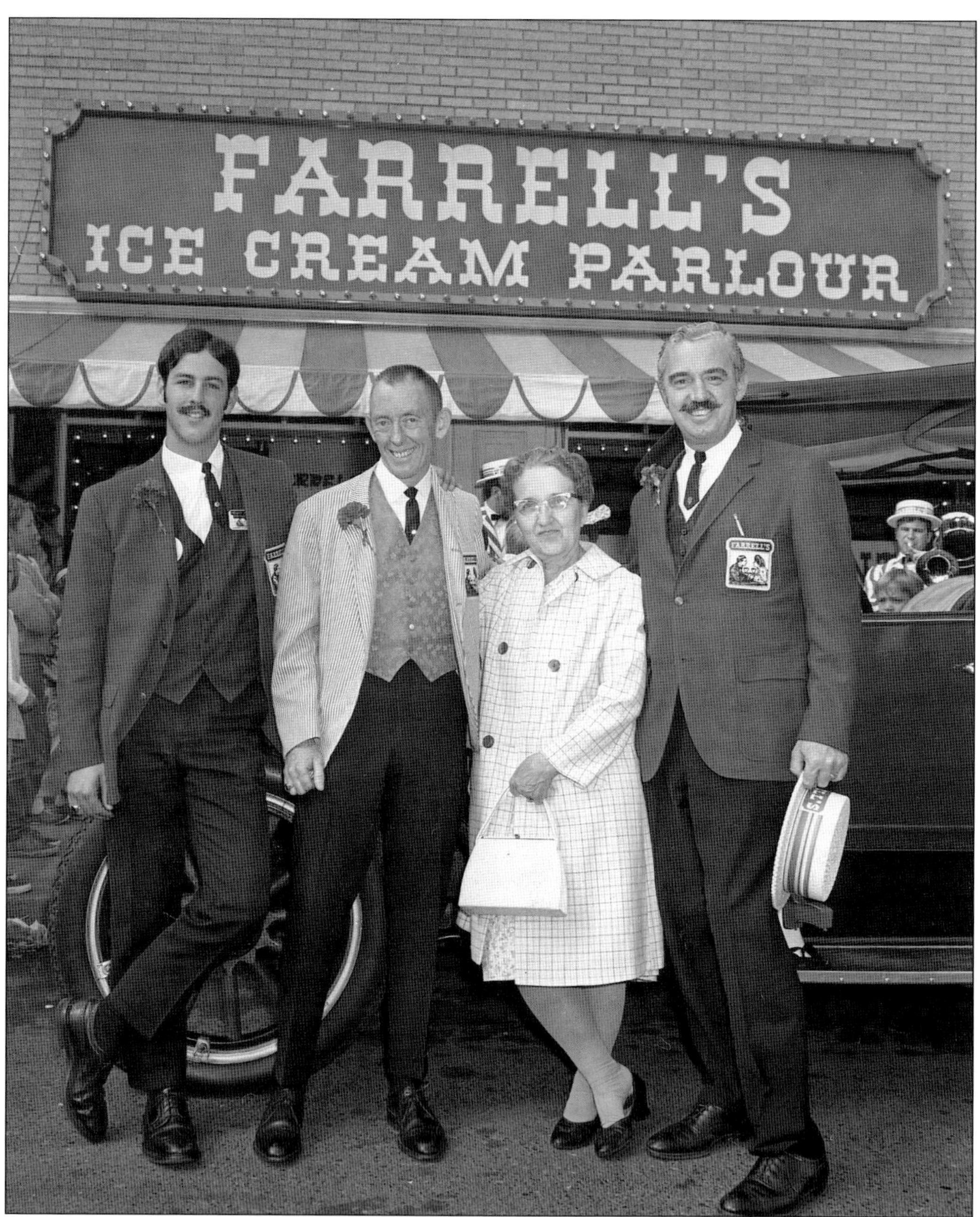

From left to right, manager Jay Mason, Ken McCarthy, Sophia Wirkkenen, and Bob Farrell pose in front of the original location in Portland, Oregon. Mason was an early Farrell's employee who worked himself up to become a manager. Wirkkenen was the first employee of Farrell's when it opened in 1963. Despite the smiles, the relationship between the two founding partners was beginning to strain.

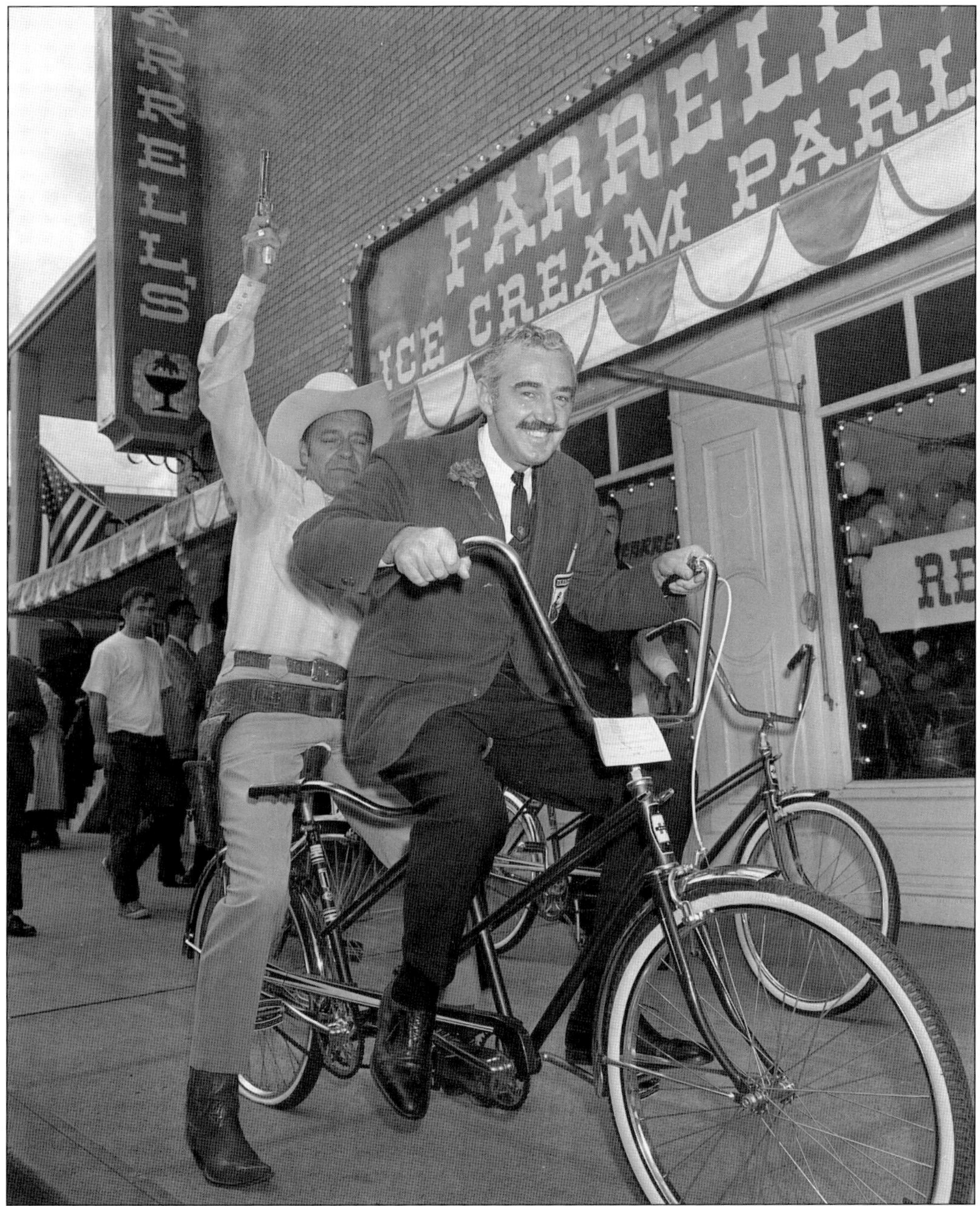

While Bob Farrell and the cowboy entertainer tried out the tandem bicycle, they did not participate in the race from the Burnside Street Farrell's to the Lloyd Center location.

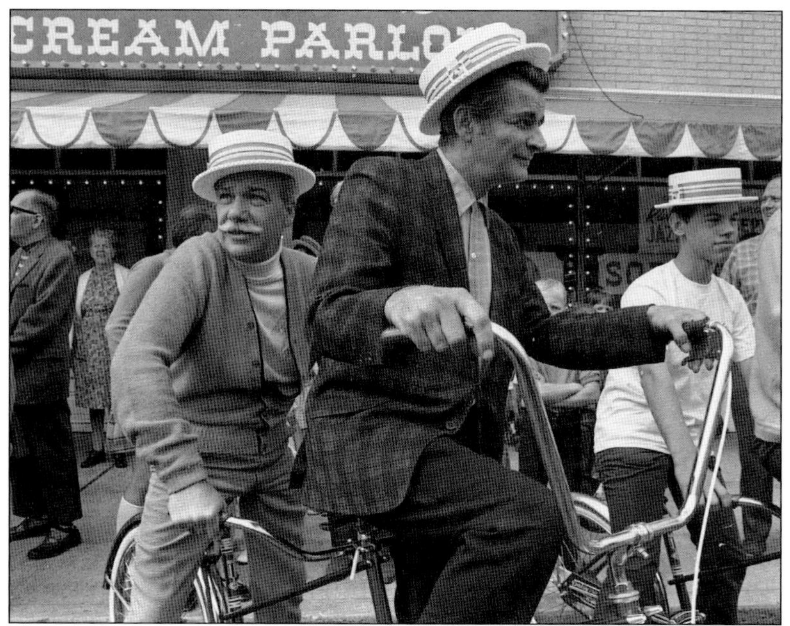

Despite the overcast day, these two gentlemen were willing to ride a tandem bicycle to the newest location.

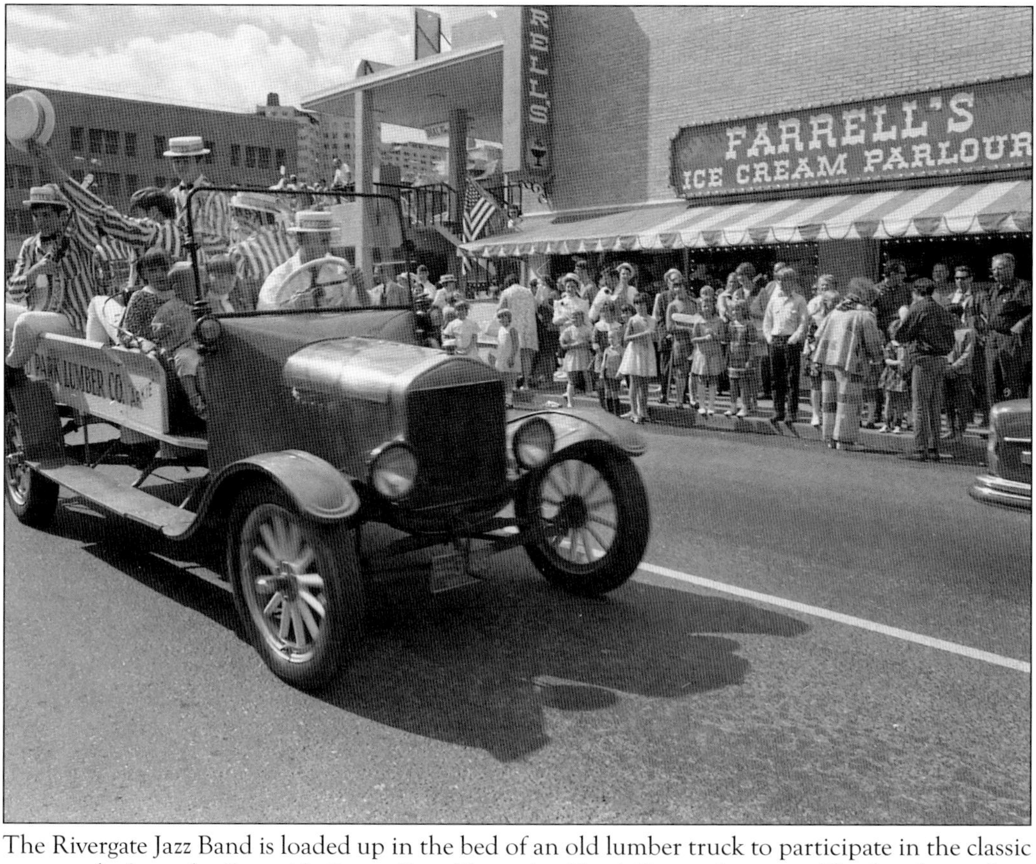

The Rivergate Jazz Band is loaded up in the bed of an old lumber truck to participate in the classic car parade from the Burnside Street Farrell's to the Lloyd Center location. The band members performed for onlookers along the parade route.

Ken McCarthy (left) and a store manager Bud Jacobsen (right) are riding a tandem bicycle in front of the Lloyd Center store as the anniversary celebration continues in the newest Portland location.

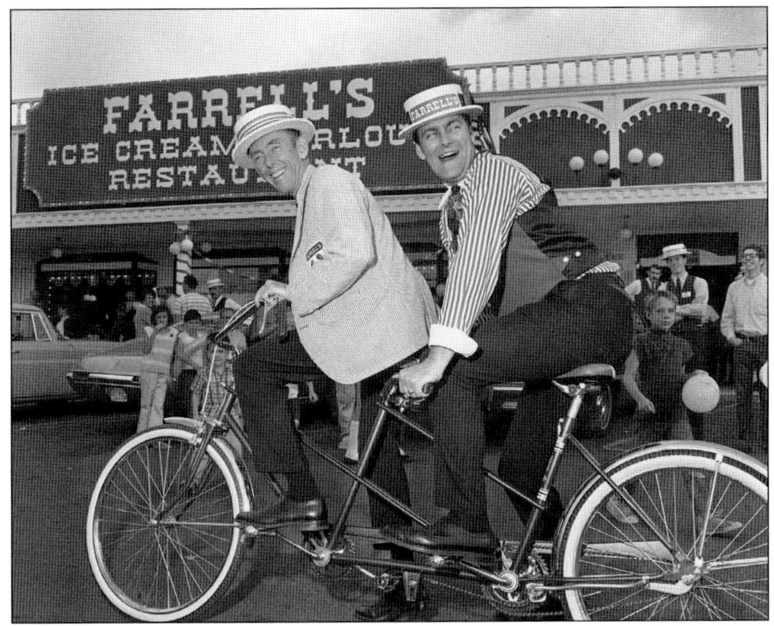

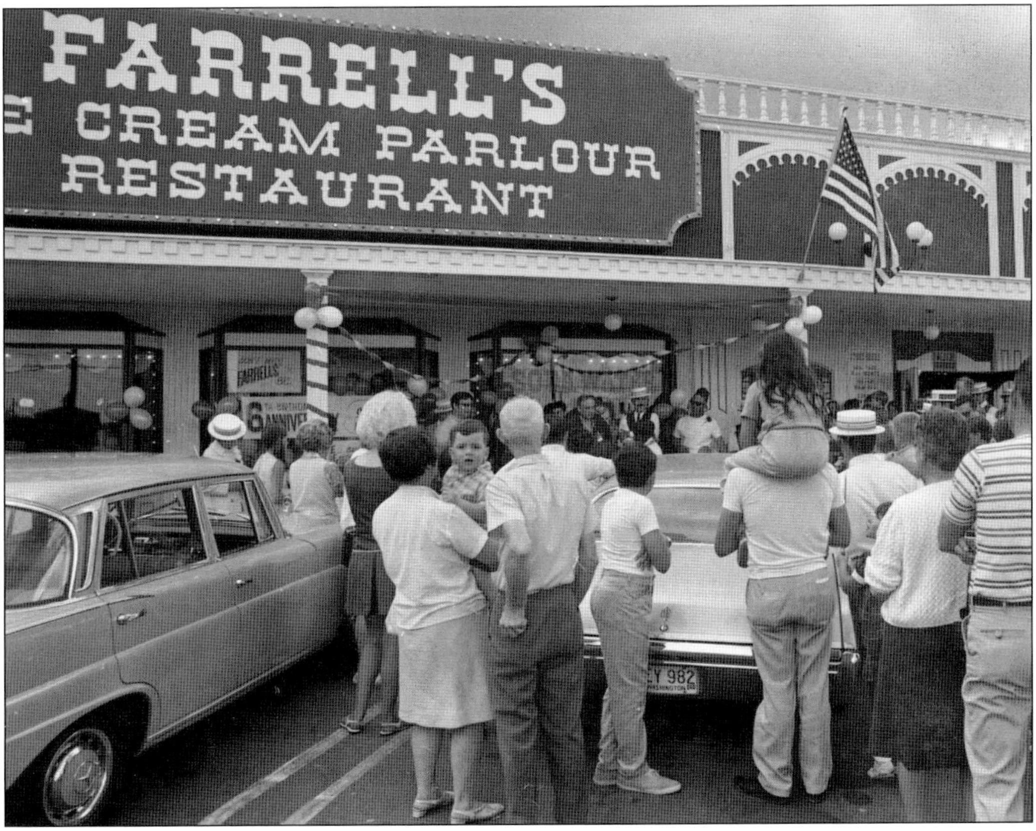

The crowd of guests and Farrell's employees are seen gathering outside of the Lloyd Center location in anticipation of Bob Farrell presenting the award for the winning riding duo of the tandem bicycle race.

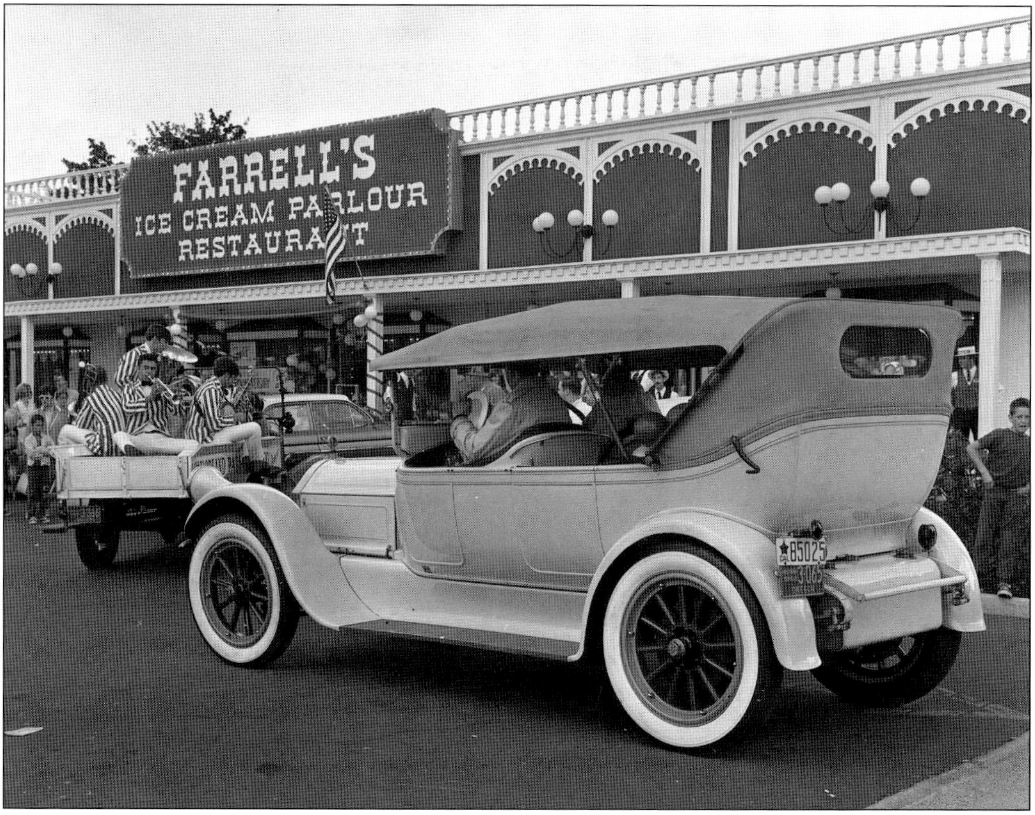

A classic car is shown arriving at the Lloyd Center location behind the old lumber truck carrying the Rivergate Jazz Band. After entertaining guests at the Burnside Street Farrell's and along the classic car parade route, the band performed for guests at the Lloyd Center location.

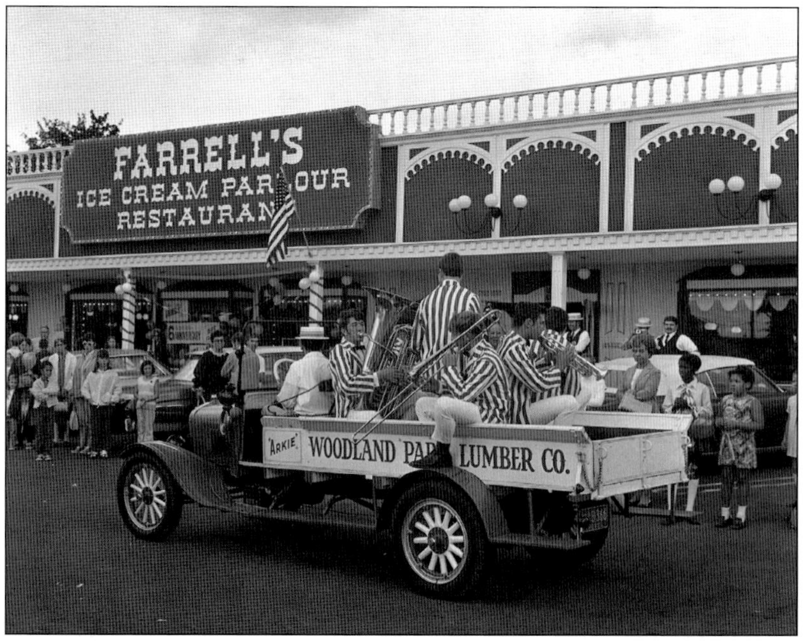

In the parking lot of the Lloyd Center location, the Rivergate Jazz Band entertains the Farrell's guests and employees with Dixieland music from the bed of a classic lumber truck.

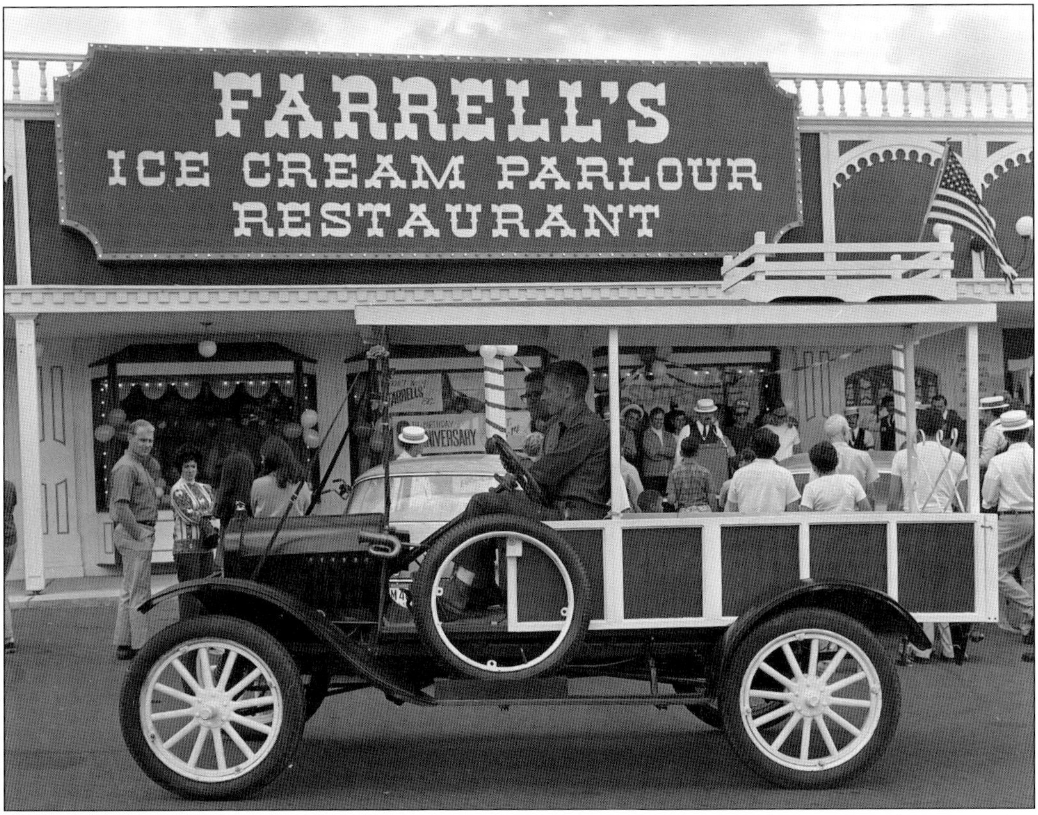

In this photograph, the owner of a classic truck pulls up in front of the Lloyd Center location after the parade of classic cars as part of the sixth-anniversary celebration.

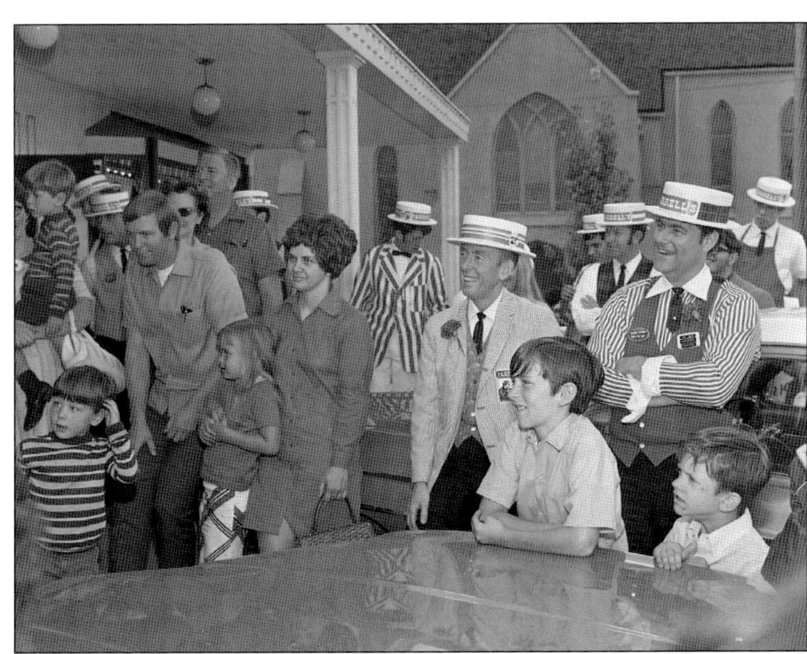

Ken McCarthy (wearing a carnation on his jacket) and store manager Bud Jacobsen (with arms crossed) join the guests and other Farrell's employees outside the Lloyd Center location to watch Bob Farrell award the trophy to the winning bicyclists.

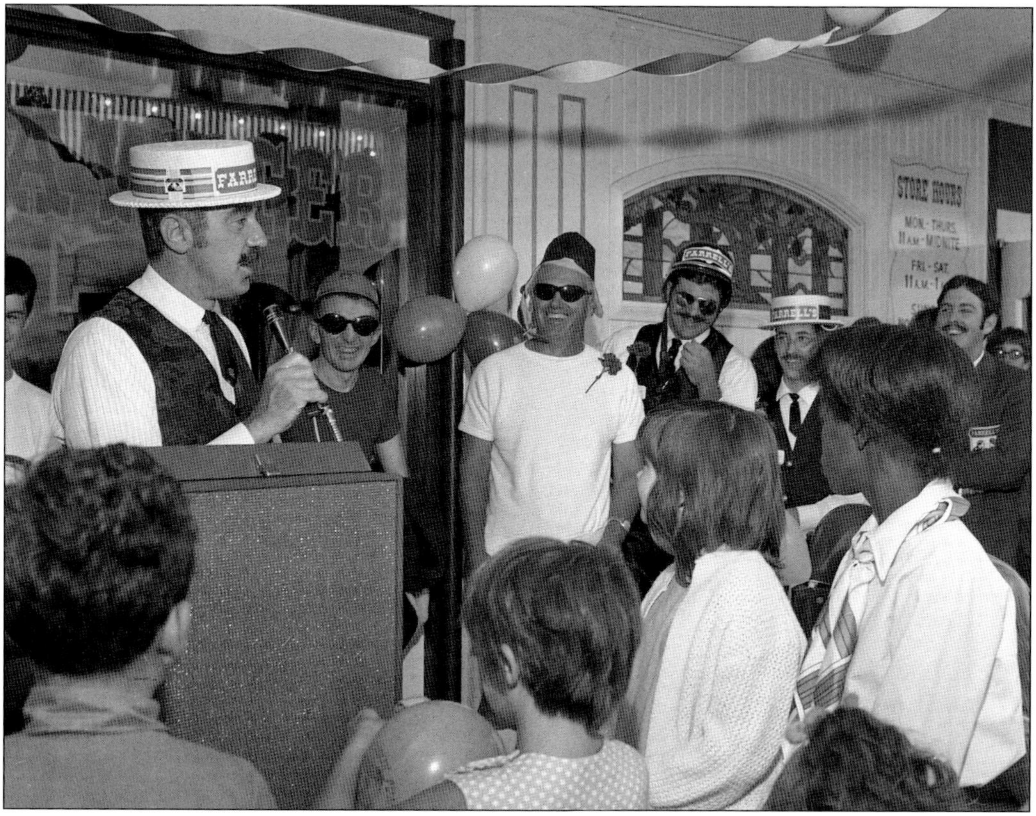

Bob Farrell is seen turning on his charm as he begins the award presentation. After retiring from the restaurant business, Farrell became a popular motivational speaker, telling stories about the growth of Farrell's and his other restaurant investments.

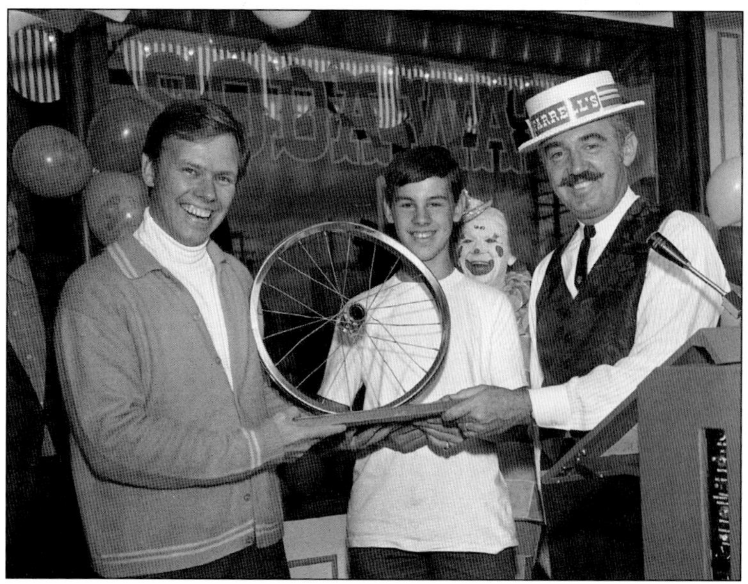

The winning bicyclists are shown receiving the spoked trophy from Bob Farrell. Many of the contestants were from local radio stations to better promote the anniversary celebration.

More balloons are released as Farrell's employees and customers gather in front of the Lloyd Center location for the sixth-anniversary celebration.

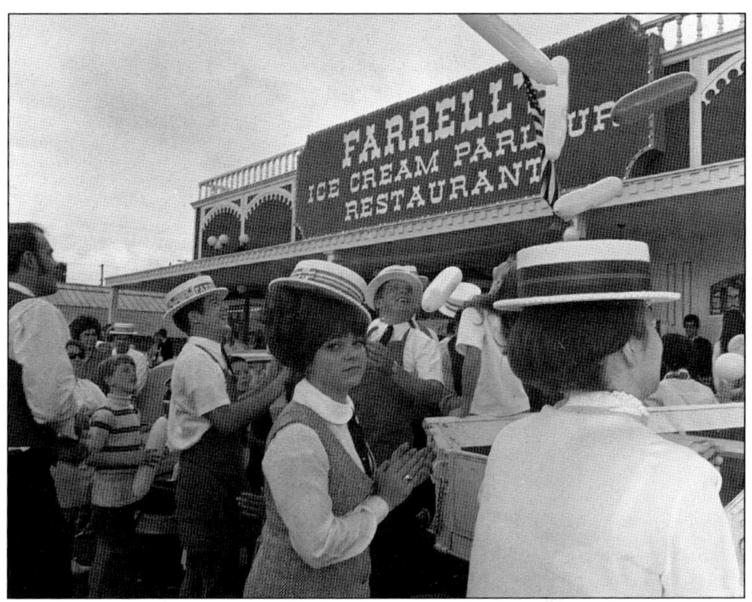

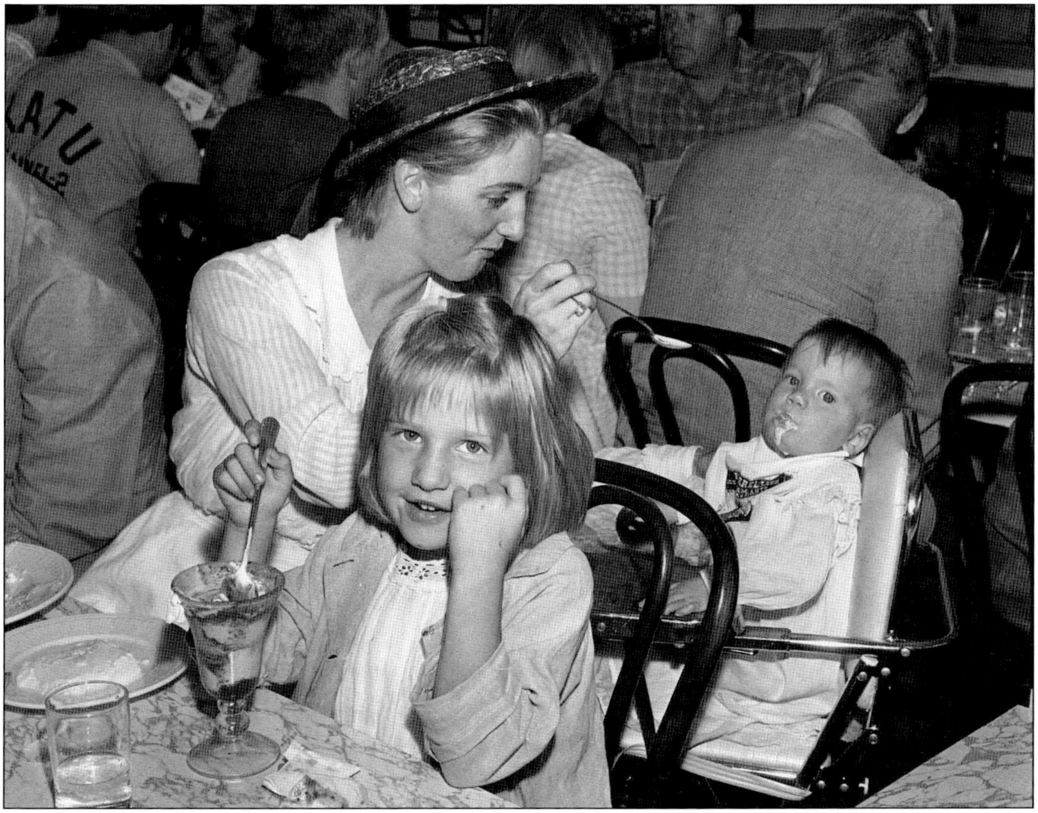

Guests dressed up in period costumes are seen enjoying ice cream sundaes inside the Lloyd Center location. Along with the classic cars, Farrell's invited guests to dress up in period-appropriate costumes to help celebrate the anniversary.

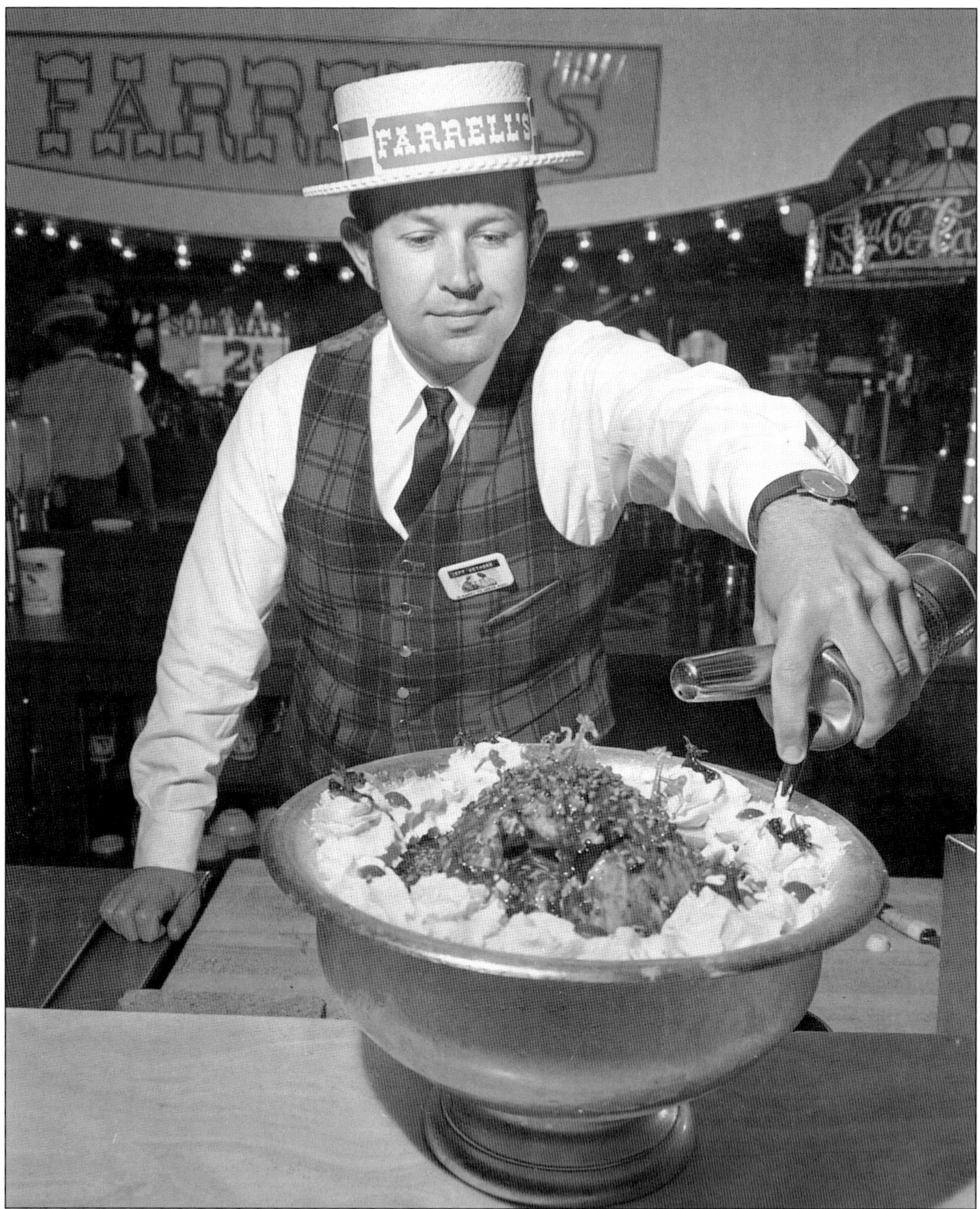

Jeff Wetmore, a Farrell's manager, is putting the finishing touches on a Portland Zoo sundae in the fountain. Until 1970, Farrell's used heavy cream from whipped cream dispensers. The canisters were stored unpressurized until needed. When a new canister was needed, a fountain man would call out, "Crack a whip," which meant inserting a canister of nitrous oxide to create the whipped cream.

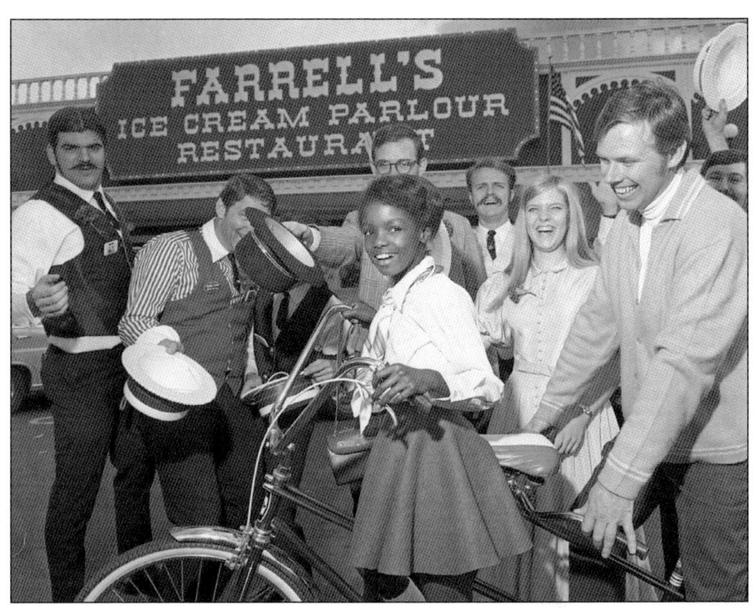

Surrounded by Farrell's managers and employees, this young guest is seen taking her turn riding a tandem bicycle as part of Farrell's sixth-anniversary celebration.

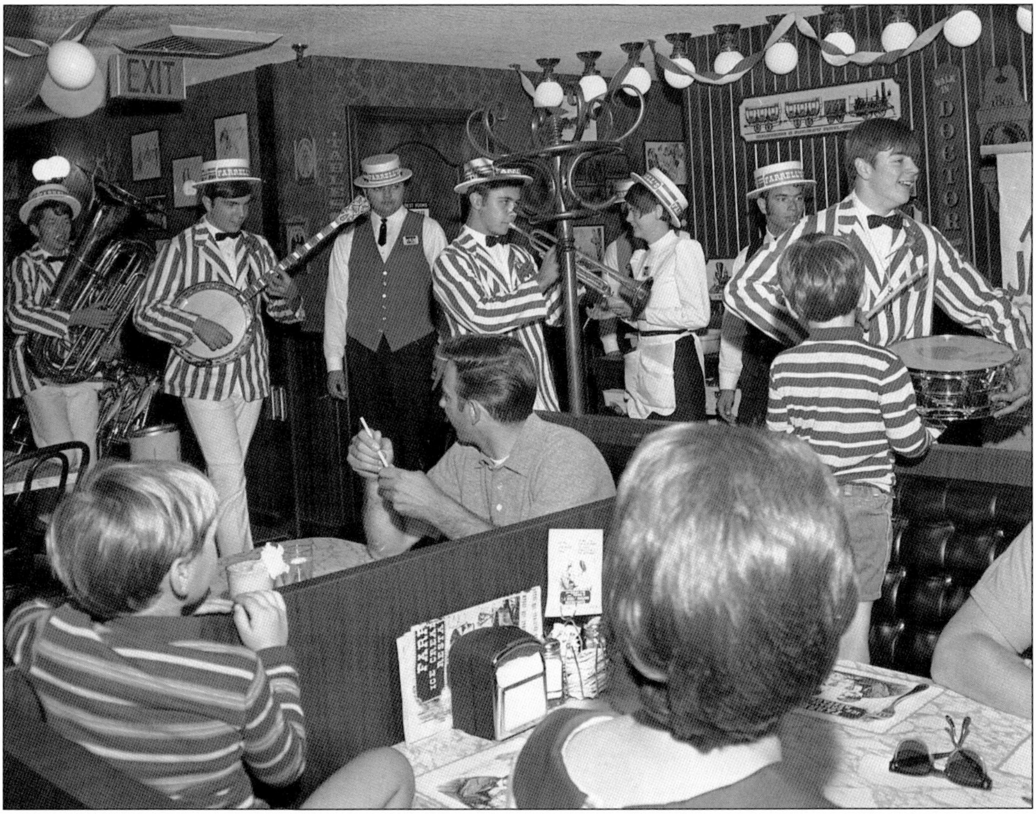

Once again, the Rivergate Jazz Band is seen entertaining the customers inside the Lloyd Center location. Bob Farrell said the anniversary celebration was a raucous affair and received a lot of attention from the Portland media.

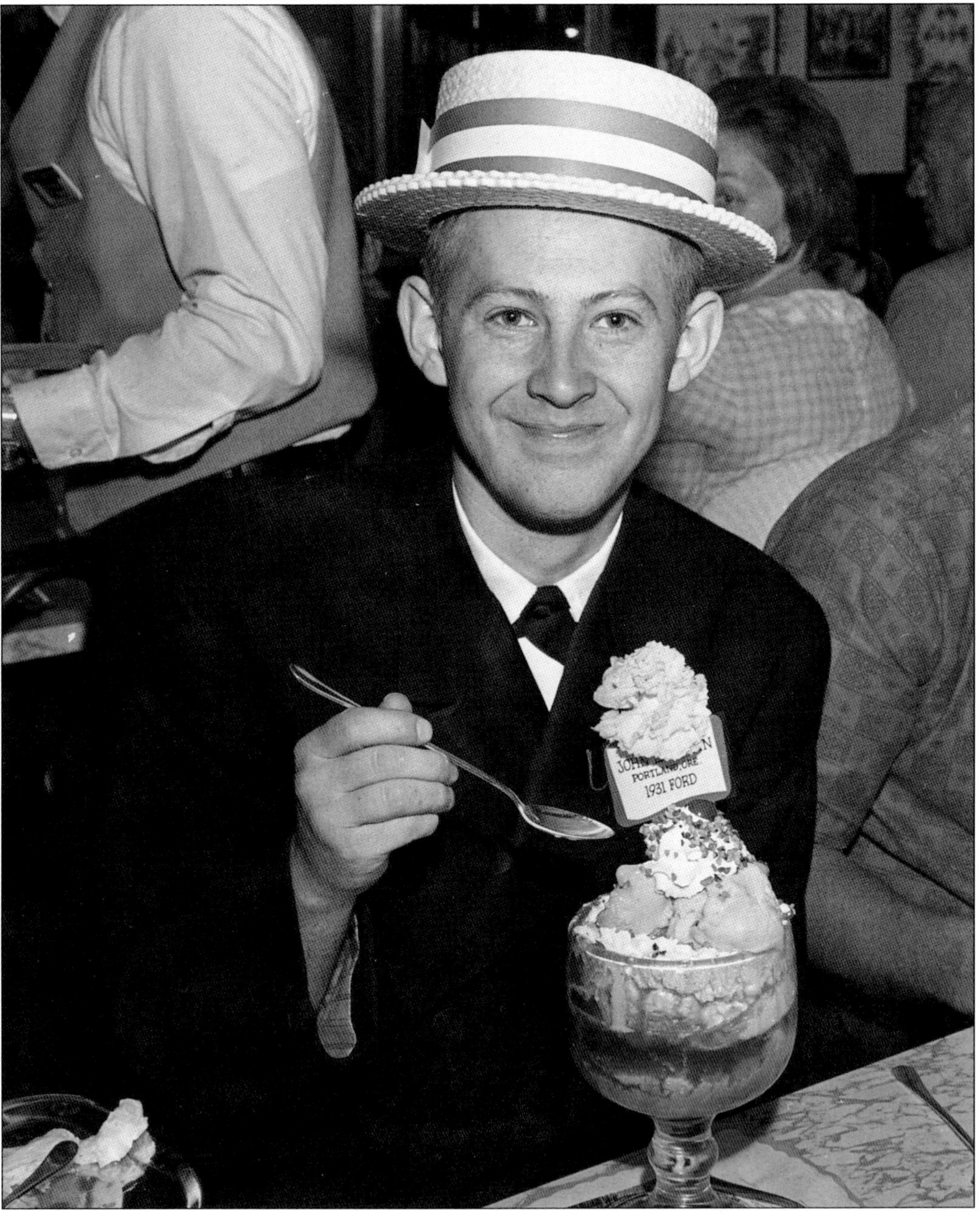

The driver of one of the classic cars enjoys a Gibson Girl sundae. Farrell's paid for the classic car parade with the promise of free food and sundaes for the car owners.

Ken McCarthy escorts two guests dressed in period-appropriate costumes at the Raleigh Hills location. For the anniversary celebration, Farrell's encouraged guests to wear costumes that would go along with the 1905 theme of the restaurant.

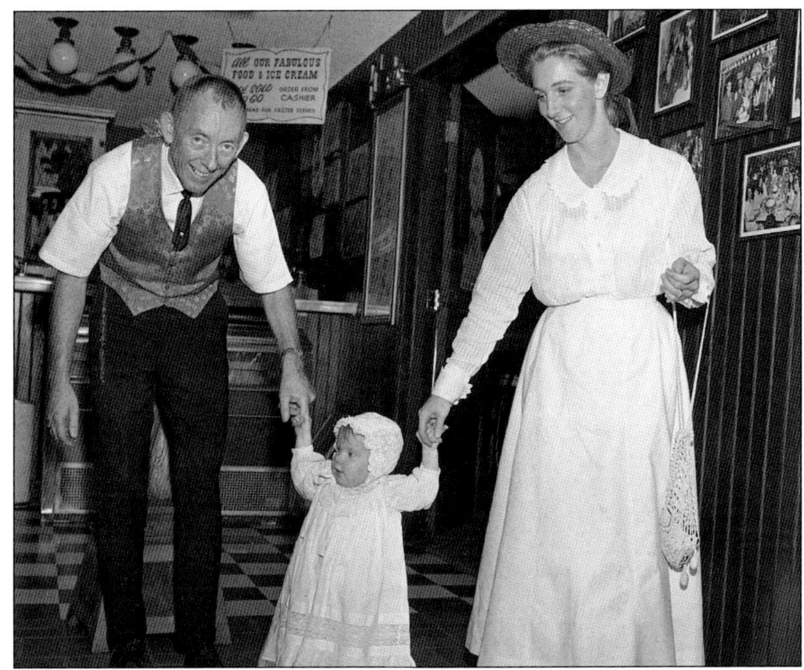

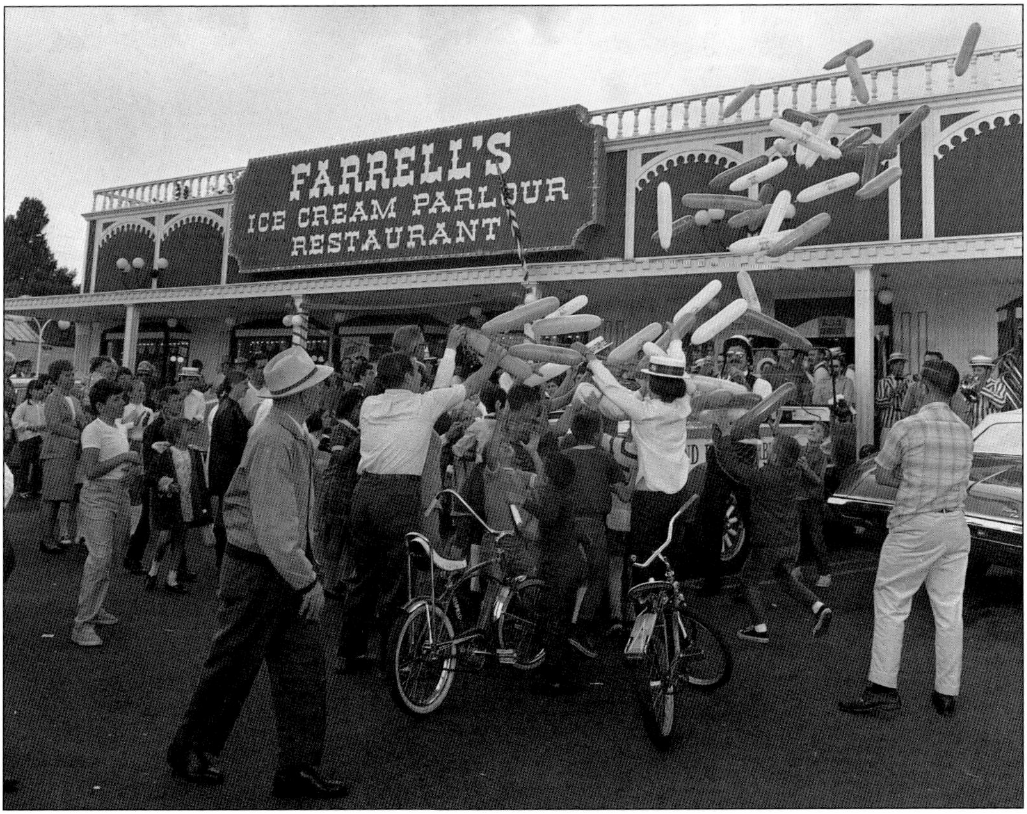

At the end of the tandem bike race and old car parade, Farrell's has another balloon release at the Lloyd Center location.

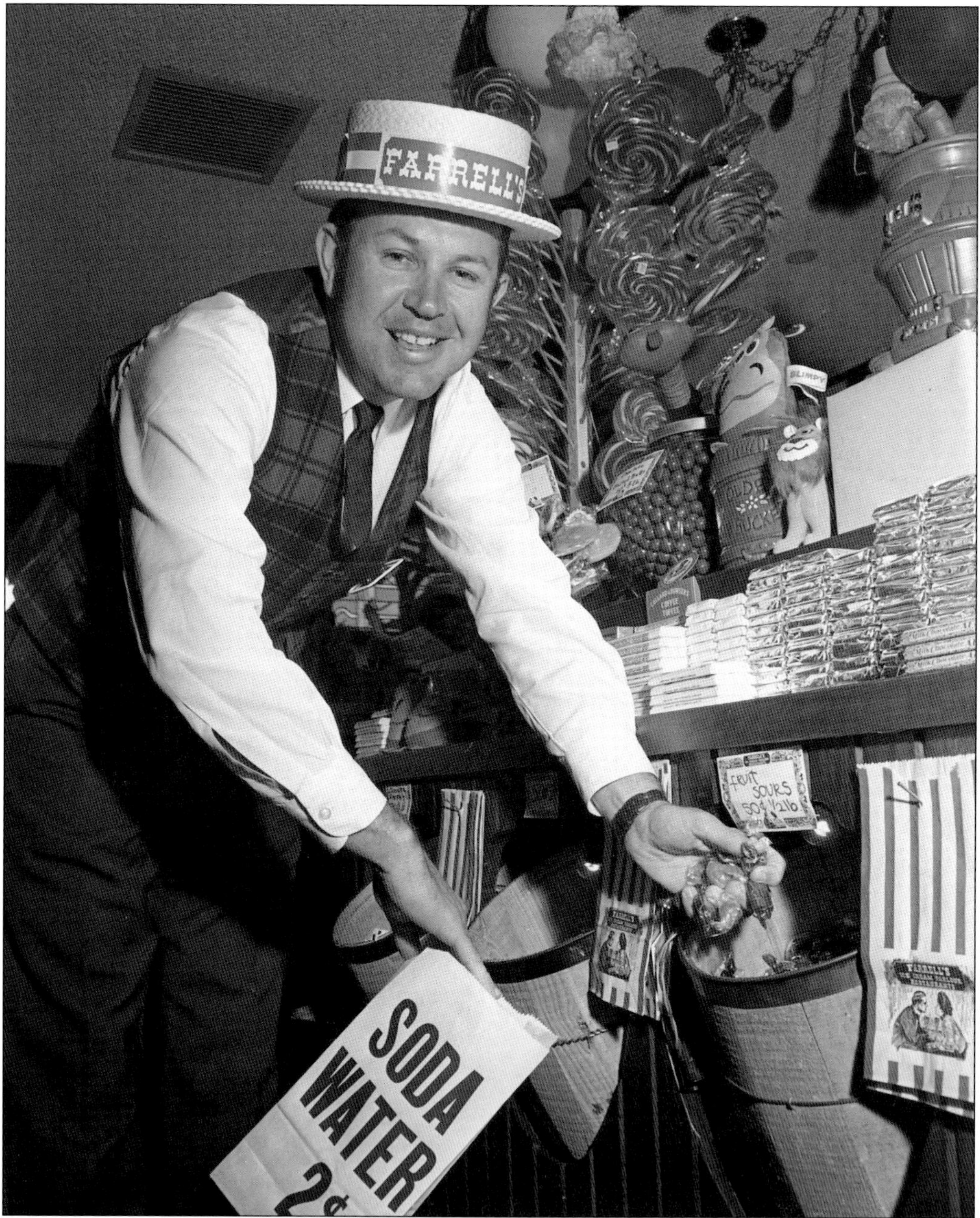

Jeff Wetmore is shown filling a bag with penny candy from the candy barrels. The barrels of candy were meant to harken back to a simpler time when children would get penny candy from an old-time candy store.

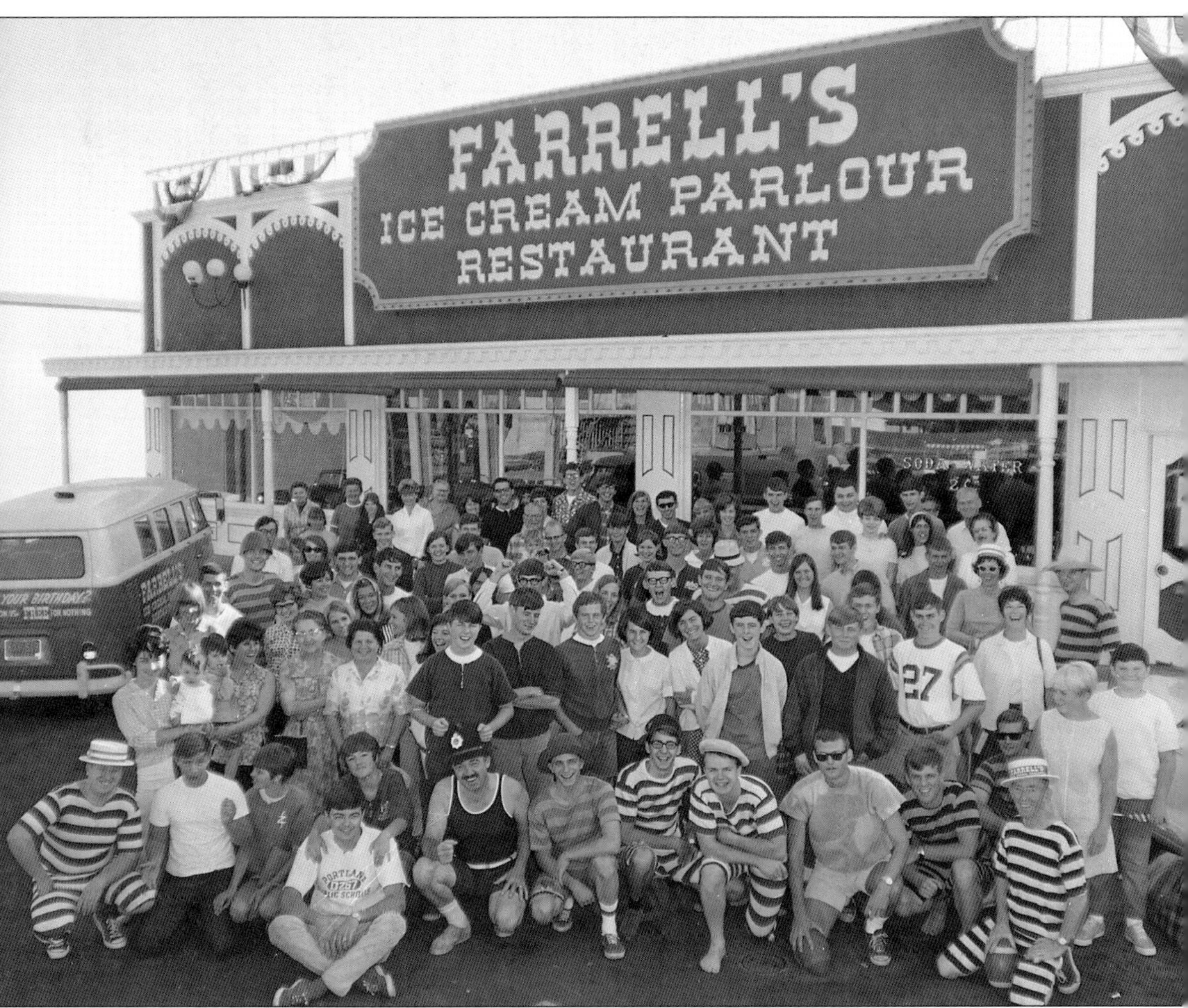

The Portland Farrell's employees gather in front of the Halsey location before heading off to the beach for the annual Labor Day picnic. During the first couple of years, the Portland Farrell's locations would close on Labor Day and hold a company-wide picnic.

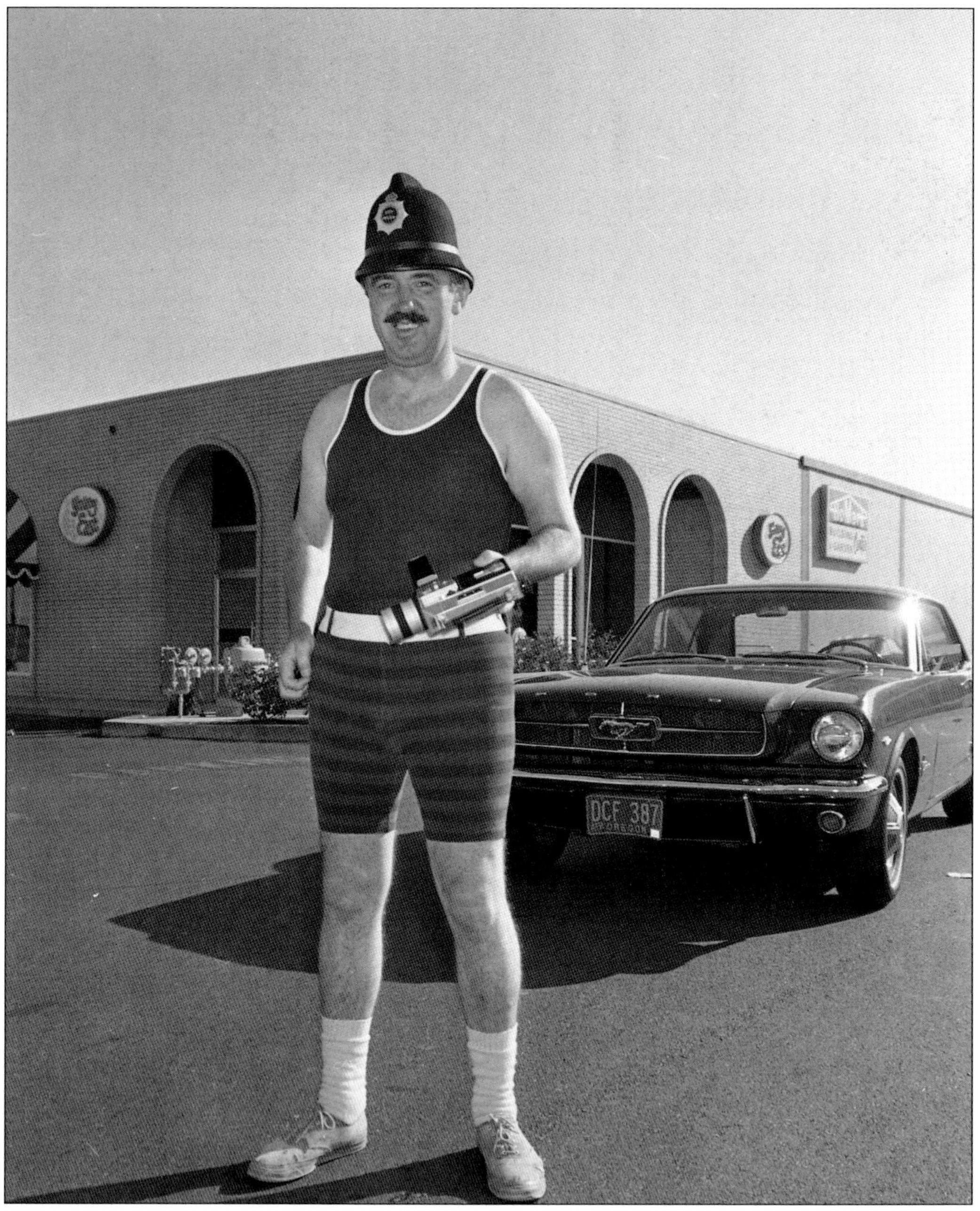

Bob Farrell appears ready for swimming dressed up in an old-time bathing suit and carrying a home movie camera for the Labor Day beach party.

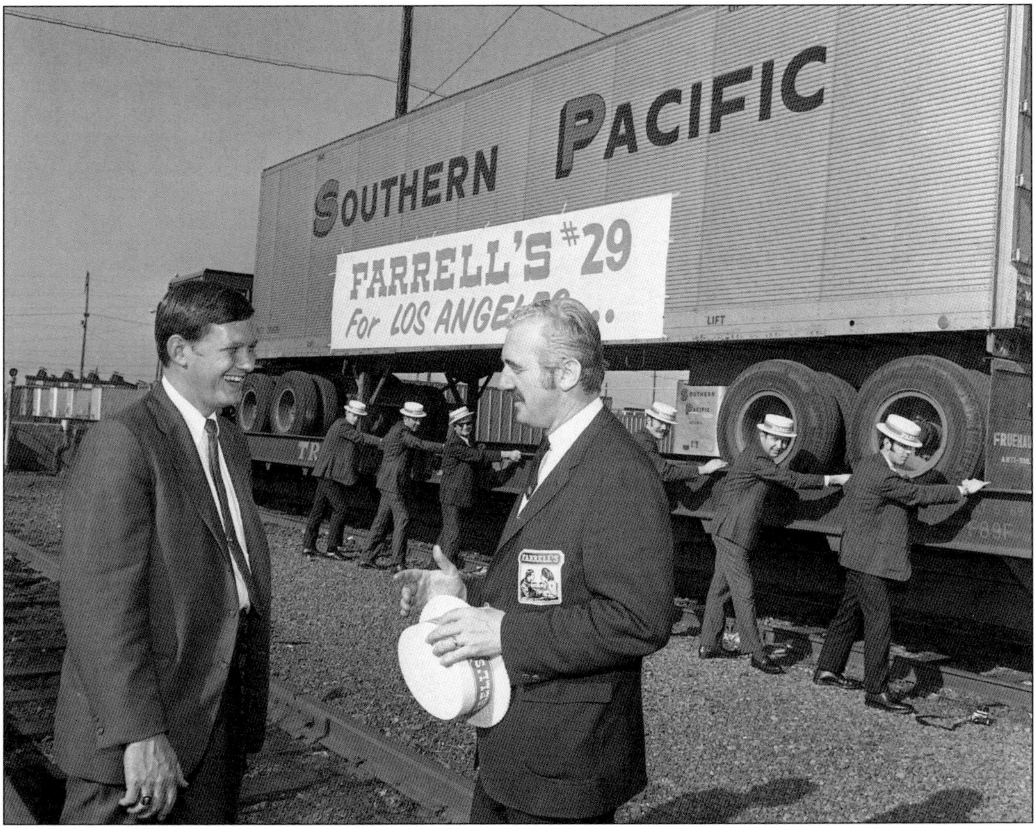

Bob Farrell is pictured with a representative from Arden-Mayfair as they prepare to send the store merchandise for the 29th location. Arden-Mayfair opened 12 Farrell's in the Los Angeles market before the sale of the chain to Marriott.

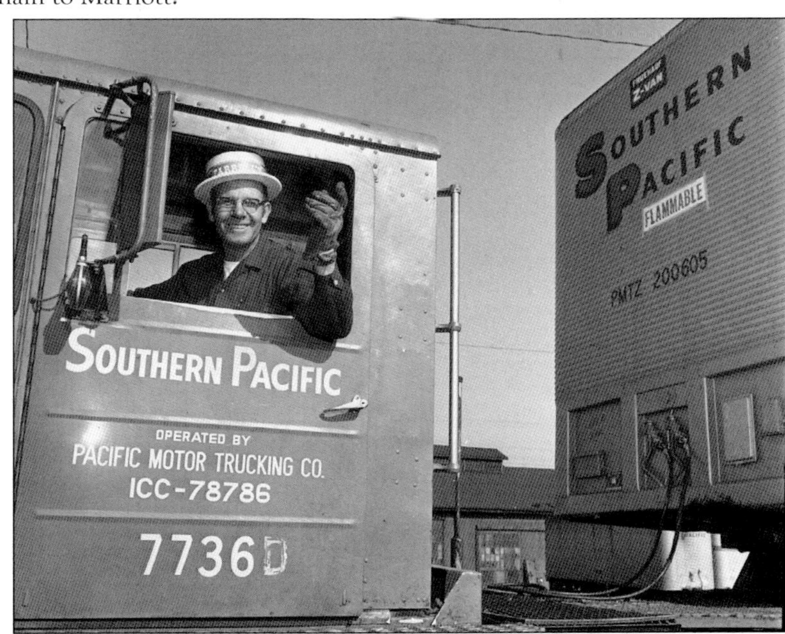

Even the truck driver wears a Farrell's skimmer hat. While made of Styrofoam, these hats became popular novelty items for customers to purchase.

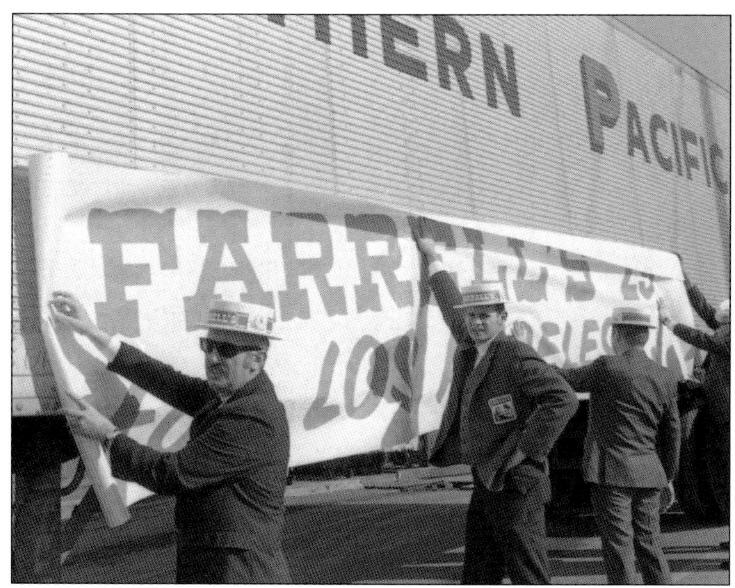

On April 3, 1970, Bob Farrell (left) and some of the store managers from Portland put a banner on a truck bound for Los Angeles. At this point, Ken McCarthy had retired from Farrell's and expansion was accelerating. While company-owned locations made up most of the Northern California operations, Los Angeles and San Diego were franchised. New franchises were opening in Michigan, Minnesota, and Texas.

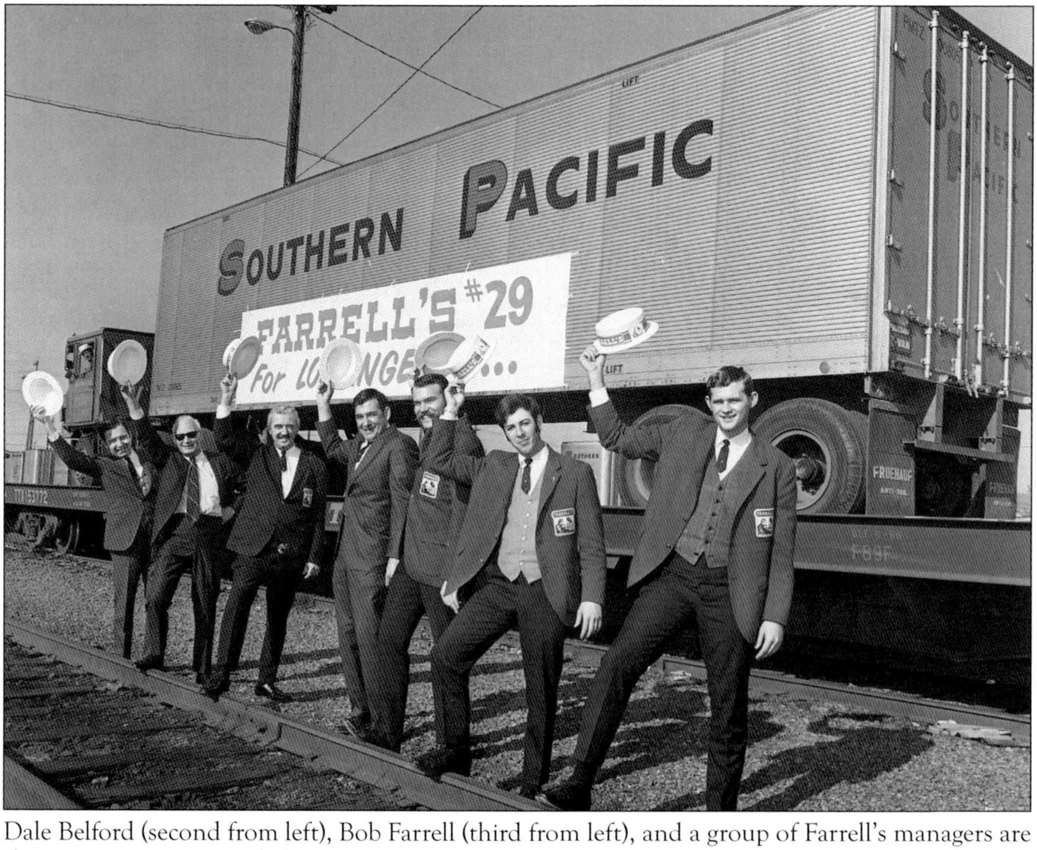

Dale Belford (second from left), Bob Farrell (third from left), and a group of Farrell's managers are shown preparing to send the store fixtures off to the newest location in California. Farrell's used Atlas Hotel Supply Company to build, equip, and furnish new locations.

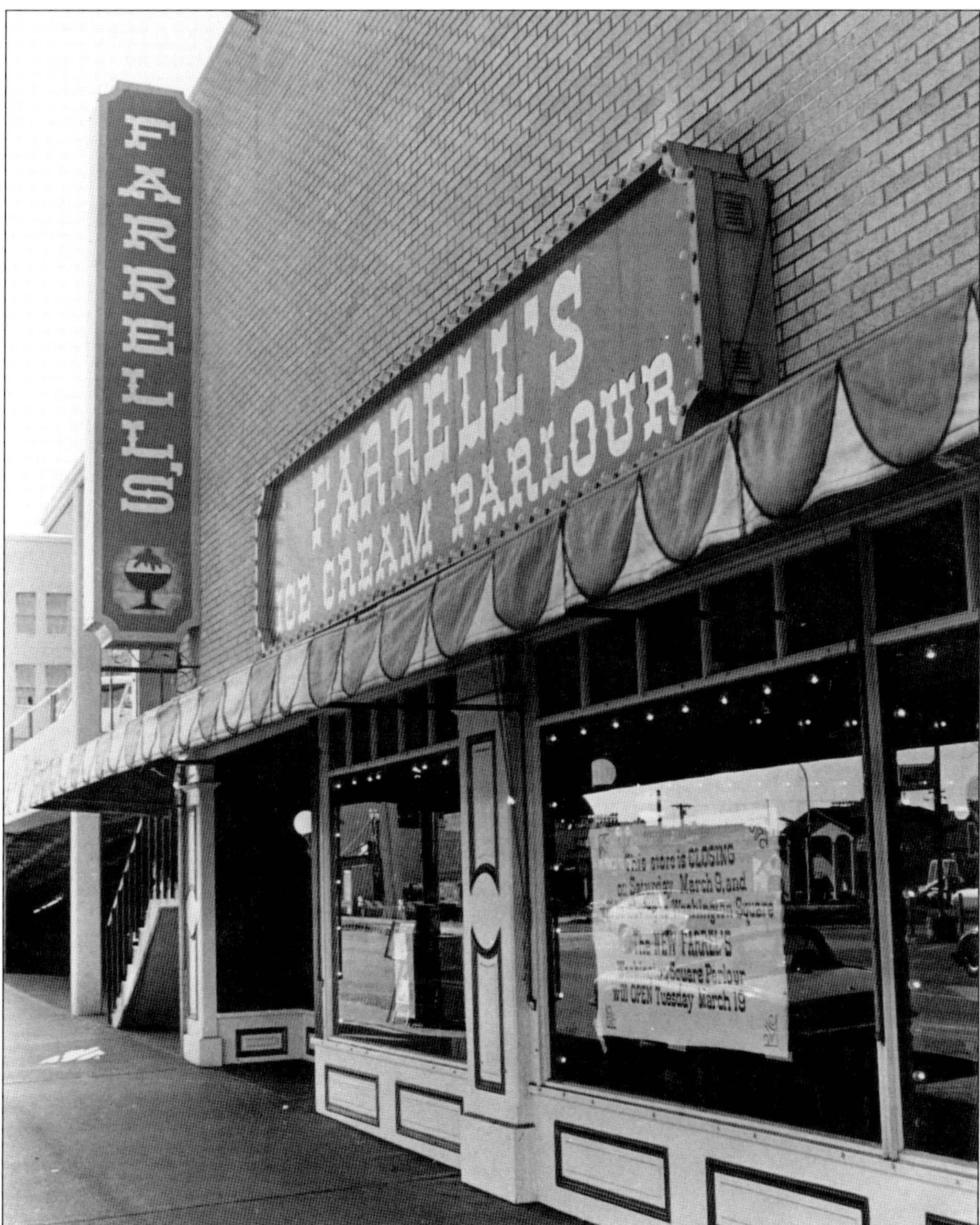

The original location closed on March 9, 1974, just a little more than 11 years after it opened. Now owned by Marriott Corporation, Farrell's was expanding as a result of the growth of shopping malls. But, by 1975, Farrell's was losing nearly $4 million a year. Operational changes returned Farrell's to limited profitability by the end of the 1970s. Changes in ownership over the succeeding years resulted in intermittent success. But the success of the chain would never match the success of the first nine years under Bob Farrell, Ken McCarthy, and Dale Belford.